THE **ABC** OF

BRITISH RAILWAYS LOCOMOTIVES

PART 1 - Nos. 1-9999

AND STANDARD LOCOMOTIVES

SUMMER
1954
EDITION

Ian Allan

PUBLISHING

NOTES ON THE USE OF THIS BOOK

1. This booklet lists British Railways locomotives numbered between 1 and 9999 in service at March 28th, 1954. This range of numbers covers Western Region (ex-G.W.R.) engines with the exception of diesel and gas turbine locomotives, which are dealt with in the ABC OF BRITISH RAILWAYS LOCOMOTIVES Part 2—Nos. 10000-39999.

2. For convenience, the full list of British Railways Standard classes and Class " WD " 2-8-0 locomotives in service are now included in this part of the ABC OF BRITISH RAILWAYS LOCOMOTIVES, as well as in Part 4.

3. With the exception of Diesel locomotives, Western Region locomotives retain their original Great Western numbers.

4. This book is divided into three parts :—

(a) An alphabetical list of ex-G.W. classes, with dimensions and sub-divisions, and summary of locomotives in the class.

(b) A numerical list of ex-G.W. locomotives showing the class of each, and the name, if any.

(c) A list of B.R. standard locomotives.

5. The following notes are a guide to the system of reference marks and other details given in the lists of dimensions shown for each class in the alphabetical list of classes.

(a) In the lists of dimensions " Su " indicates a superheated class, and " SS " indicates that some locomotives of the class are superheated.

(b) Locomotives are fitted with two inside cylinders, slide valves and Stephenson link motion, except where otherwise shown, e.g. (O) indicates outside cylinders and " P.V." piston valves.

(c) The date on which a design of locomotive first appeared is indicated by " Introduced."

6. All locomotives are of G.W.R. origin, except where other-wise shown.

7. The following is a list of abbreviations used to indicate the pre-grouping owners of certain Western Region locomotives :

AD	Alexandra (Newport and South Wales) Docks & Railway.	Car.R.	Cardiff Railway.
		P & M	Powlesland & Mason (Contractor).
BPGV	Burry Port & Gwendraeth Valley Railway.		
		RR	Rhymney Railway.
Cam.R.	Cambrian Railways.	SHT	Swansea Harbour Trust.

TV   Taff Vale Railway.
V of R Cambrian   Railways   (Vale   of
        Rheidol).

W & L Cambrian Railways (Welshpool
        and Llanfair).

WESTERN REGION LOCOMOTIVE RUNNING SHEDS AND SHED CODES

Code	Depot	Code	Depot	Code	Depot
81A	**Old Oak Common**	84A	**Wolverhampton** **(Stafford Rd.)**	87A	**Neath** Glyn Neath Neath (N. & B.)
81B	Slough Marlow Watlington	84B	Oxley		
		84C	Banbury	87B	Duffryn Yard
81C	Southall	84D	Leamington Spa	87C	Danygraig
81D	Reading Henley-on-T.	84E	Tyseley Stratford-on-Avon	87D	Swansea East Dock
		84F	Stourbridge	87E	Landore
81E	Didcot Newbury Wallingford	84G	Shrewsbury Clee Hill Knighton Builth Road	87F	Llanelly Burry Port Pantyfynnon
81F	Oxford Fairford			87G	Carmarthen
		84H	Wellington (Salop)	87H	Neyland Cardigan Milford Haven Pembroke Dock Whitland
82A	**Bristol (Bath Road)** Bath Wells Weston-super-Mare Yatton	84J	Croes Newydd Bala Trawsfynydd Penmaenpool		
				87J	Goodwick
		84K	Chester	87K	Swansea (Victoria) Upper Bank Gurnos Llandovery
82B	Bristol (S.P.M.)	85A	**Worcester** Evesham Kingham		
82C	Swindon Chippenham				
82D	Westbury Frome	85B	Gloucester Brimscombe Cheltenham Cirencester Lydney Tetbury	88A	**Cardiff (Cathays)** Radyr
82E	Yeovil			88B	Cardiff East Dock
82F	Weymouth Bridport			88C	Barry
		85C	Hereford Ledbury Leominster • Ross	88D	Merthyr Cae Harris Dowlais Central Rhymney
83A	**Newton Abbot** Ashburton Kingsbridge				
83B	Taunton Bridgwater Minehead	85D	Kidderminster	88E	Abercynon
		86A	**Newport** **(Ebbw Jc.)**	88F	Treherbert Ferndale
83C	Exeter Tiverton Junc.	86B	Newport (Pill)		
83D	Laira (Plymouth) Launceston Princetown	86C	Cardiff (Canton)	89A	**Oswestry** Llanidloes Moat Lane Welshpool (W & L)
		86D	Llantrisant		
		86E	Severn Tunnel Junc.		
83E	St. Blazey Bodmin Moorswater	86F	Tondu	89B	Brecon Builth Wells
		86G	Pontypool Road	89C	Machynlleth Aberayron Aberystwyth Aberystwyth (V. of R.) Portmadoc Pwllheli
83F	Truro	86H	Aberbeeg		
83G	Penzance Helston St. Ives	86J	Aberdare		
		86K	Abergavenny Tredegar		

SUMMARY OF WESTERN REGION STEAM LOCOMOTIVE CLASSES

WITH HISTORICAL NOTES AND DIMENSIONS

In this list the classes are arranged by wheel arrangement in the following order : 4-6-0, 4-4-0, 2-8-0, 2-6-0, 0-6-0, 2-8-2T, 2-8-0T, 2-6-2T, 0-6-2T, 0-6-0T, 0-4-2T, 0-4-0T. Codes in small bold type at the head of each class denote B.R. power classification.

4-6-0   6MT   1000 Class "County"

Introduced 1945: Hawksworth design.

Weights: Loco.   76 tons 17 cwt.
         Tender 49 tons 0 cwt.
Pressure: 280 lb. Su.
Cyls.: (O) 18½″ × 30″
Driving Wheels: 6′ 3″
T.E.: 32,580 lb.
P.V.

1000–29   **Total 30**

4-6-0   5P   4000 Class "Star"

Introduced 1907: Churchward design, developed from No. 4000 (originally No. 40, introduced 1906 as a 4-4-2), earlier locomotives subsequently fitted with new boilers and super-heaters, remainder built as such.

Weights: Loco.   75 tons 12 cwt.
         Tender 46 tons 14 cwt.
Pressure: 225 lb. Su.
Cyls.: (4) 15″ × 26″
Driving Wheels: 6′ 8½″
T.E.: 27,800 lb.
Inside Walschaerts gear and rocking shafts.   P.V.

4053/6/61/2

            Total 4

4-6-0   7P   4073 Class "Castle"

Introduced 1923: Collett design, developed from "Star" (4000/37, 5083-92 converted from "Star").

Weights: Loco.   79 tons 17 cwt.
         Tender 46 tons 14 cwt.
Pressure: 225 lb. Su.
Cyls.: (4) 16″ × 26″
Driving Wheels: 6′ 8½″
T.E.: 31,625 lb.
Inside Walschaerts gear and rocking shafts.   P.V.

4000/37/73–99,   5000–99,
   7000–37   **Total 167**

4-6-0   5MT   4900 Class "Hall"

*Introduced 1924: Collett rebuild with 6′ 0″ driving wheels of "Saint" (built 1907).

†Introduced 1928: Modified design for new construction, with higher-pitched boiler, modified footplating and detail differences.

Weights: Loco. { 72 tons 10 cwt.*
               { 75 tons 0 cwt.†
         Tender 46 tons 14 cwt.
Pressure: 225 lb. Su.
Cyls.: (O) 18½″ × 30″
Driving Wheels: 6′ 0″
T.E.: 27,275 lb.
*4900
†4901–10/2–99, 5900–99, 6900–58   **Total 258**

1000 Class 4-6-0 No. 1029, *County of Worcester*, passing Ruislip Gardens on the Sunday
4.10 p.m. Paddington–Birmingham express.   [*C. R. L. Coles*

Ex-W. & L. 0-6-0T No. 823.   [R. J. Buckley

V. of R. 2-6-2Ts Nos. 7 (left) and 9 (right).   [B. A. Butt

1101 Class 0-4-0T No. 1106.   [A. Delicata

Ex-S.H.T. 0-4-0ST No. 1143 (Peckett)   [*J. N. Westwood*

Ex-P. & M. 0-4-0ST No. 1151 (Peckett)   [*R. S. Potts*

Ex-P. & M. 0-4-0ST No. 1153 (Hawthorn Leslie)   [*R. J. Buckley*

Left: Ex - B.P.G.V.
0-6-0ST No. 2176
(Avonside).

[*R. Griffiths*

Above: Ex - A.D.
0-6-0T No. 666
(Kerr Stuart)

[*R. Griffiths*

Left: Ex - B.P.G.V.
0-6-0T No. 2198
(Hudswell Clarke).

C. S. Cann

Right: Ex - B.P.G.V. 0-6-0T No. 2168 (rebuilt by G.W.R.).
[R. Griffiths

Above: 1361 Class 0-6-0ST No. 1365.
[R. J. Buckley

Right : 1366 Class 0-6-0PT No. 1370.
[A. R. Carpenter

Ex-R.R. 0-6-0T No. 95 (rebuilt by G.W.R. ; since scrapped).   [*G. Wheeler*

1500 Class 0-6-0PT No. 1506.   [*J. N. Westwood*

9400 Class 0-6-0PT No. 8436 (saturated).   [*A. R. Carpenter*

Ex-R.R. 0-6-2T No. 59 (rebuilt by G.W.R.).

[C. G. Pearson

Ex-T.V. 0-6-2T No. 385.

[W. A. Richards

5600 Class 0-6-2T No. 5602.

[R. K. Evans

Ex-Cardiff Rly. 0-6-0PT No. 683 (rebuilt by G.W.R.). [*J. N. Westwood*

2021 Class 0-6-0PT No. 2134. [*A. Delicata*

5700 Class 0-6-0PT No. 6744. [*C. G. Pearson*

4-6-0   8P   6000 Class
" King "

*Introduced 1927: Collett design.
†Introduced 1947. Fitted with high superheat.
Weights: Loco.   89 tons 0 cwt.
        Tender 46 tons 14 cwt.
Pressure: 250 lb. Su.
Cyls.: (4) 16¼" × 28"
Driving Wheels: 6' 6"
T.E.: 40,285 lb.
Inside Walschaerts gear and rocking shafts.   P.V.

*6002/4/7-9/12/4/8/9/21/3/4/6/7/9
†6000/1/3/5/6/10/1/3/5-7/20/2/5/8
Total 30

4-6-0   5MT   6800 Class
" Grange "

Introduced 1936: Collett design, variation of " Hall " with smaller wheels, incorporating certain parts of withdrawn 4300 2-6-0 locos.
Weights: Loco.   74 tons 0 cwt.
        Tender 40 tons 0 cwt.
Pressure: 225 lb. Su.
Cyls.: (O) 18½" × 30"
Driving Wheels: 5' 8"
T.E.: 28,875 lb.
P.V.
6800-79   **Total 80**

4-6-0   5MT   6959 Class
" Modified Hall "

Introduced 1944: Hawksworth development of " Hall," with larger superheater, " one-piece " main frames and plate framed bogie.
Weights: Engine 75 tons 16 cwt.
        Tender 46 tons 14 cwt.
Pressure: 225 lb. Su.
Cyls.: (O) 18½" × 30"
Driving Wheels: 6' 0"
T.E.: 27,275 lb.
P.V.

6959-99, 7900-29
Total 71

4-6-0   5MT   7800 Class
" Manor "

Introduced 1938: Collett design for secondary lines, incorporating certain parts of withdrawn 4300 2-6-0 locos.
Weights: Loco.   68 tons 18 cwt.
        Tender 40 tons 0 cwt.
Pressure: 225 lb. Su.
Cyls.: (O) 18" × 30"
Driving Wheels: 5' 8"
T.E.: 27,340 lb.
P.V.
7800-29
Total 30

4-4-0   2P   9000 Class

Introduced 1936: Collett rebuild, incorporating " Duke " type boiler and " Bulldog " frames, for light lines.
Weights: Loco.   49 tons 0 cwt.
      Tender { 40 tons 0 cwt.
             36 tons 15 cwt.
Pressure: 180 lb. SS.
Cyls.: 18" × 26"
Driving Wheels: 5' 8"
T.E.: 18,955 lb.

9000/2-5/8-18/20-8   **Total 25**

2-8-0   8F   2800 Class

*Introduced 1903: Churchward design, earlier locos. subsequently fitted with new boilers and superheaters.
†Introduced 1938: Collett locos., with side window cabs and detail alterations.
Weights: Loco. { 75 tons 10 cwt.*
              76 tons 5 cwt.†
        Tender 40 tons 0 cwt.
Pressure: 225 lb. Su.
Cyls.: (O) 18½" × 30"
Driving Wheels: 4' 7½"
T.E.: 35,380 lb.
P.V.

*2800-2883
†2884-99, 3800-66   **Total 167**

2-8-0 7F R.O.D. Class

Introduced 1911: Robinson G. C. design (L.N.E.R. O4), built from 1917 for Railway Operating Division, R.E., taken into G.W. stock from 1919, and subsequently fitted with G.W. boiler mountings and details.

Weights: Loco. 73 tons 11 cwt.
    Tender 47 tons 16 cwt.

Pressure: 185 lb. Su.

Cyls.: (O) 21″ × 26″

Driving Wheels: 4′ 8″

T.E.: 32,200 lb.

P.V.

3010–2/4–8/20/2–6/8/9/31/2/6/8/
40–4/8   **Total 26**

2-8-0 7F 4700 Class

Introduced 1919: Churchward mixed traffic design (4700 built with smaller boiler and later rebuilt).

Weights: Loco. 82 tons 0 cwt.
    Tender 46 tons 14 cwt.

Pressure: 225 lb. Su.

Cyls.: (O) 19″ × 30″

Driving Wheels: 5′ 8″

T.E.: 30,460 lb.

P.V.

4700–8   **Total 9**

2-6-0 4MT 4300 Class

*Introduced 1911: Churchward design.
†Introduced 1925: Locos. with detail alterations affecting weight.
‡Introduced 1932: Locos. with side window cabs and detail alterations.

Weights: Loco. $\begin{cases} 62 \text{ tons } 0 \text{ cwt.*} \\ 64 \text{ tons } 0 \text{ cwt.†} \\ 65 \text{ tons } 6 \text{ cwt.‡} \end{cases}$
    Tender 40 tons 0 cwt.

Pressure: 200 lb. Su.

Cyls.: (O) 18½″ × 30″

Driving Wheels: 5′ 8″

T.E.: 25,670 lb.

P.V

*4326/58/75/7, 5306/7/10–9/
21–8/30–9/41/4/5/7/50/1/
3/5–8/60–2/7–72/5–82/4–6/8/
90–9, 6300–14/6–99, 7305–21
†7300–4   ‡9300–19
    Total 217

0-6-0 3MT 2251 Class

Introduced 1930: Collett design.

Weights:
 Loco. 43 tons 8 cwt.
 Tender $\begin{cases} 36 \text{ tons } 15 \text{ cwt.} \\ 47 \text{ tons } 6 \text{ cwt. (ex-R.O.D} \\ \text{tender from 3000 Class} \\ \text{2-8-0).} \end{cases}$

Pressure: 200 lb. Su.

Cyls.: 17½″ × 24″

Driving Wheels: 5′ 2″

T.E.: 20,155 lb.

2200–99, 3200–19 **Total 120**

0-6-0 2MT 2301 Class

Introduced 1883: Dean design, later fitted with superheaters.

Weights: Loco. 36 tons 16 cwt.
    Tender 34 tons 5 cwt.

Pressure: 180 lb. Su.

Cyls.: $\begin{cases} 17″ \times 24″ \\ 17½″ \times 24″ \end{cases}$

Driving Wheels : 5′ 2″

T.E.: $\begin{cases} 17,120 \text{ lb.} \\ 18,140 \text{ lb.} \end{cases}$

2340, 2458/74/84,
 2513/6/32/8/41

    Total 9

0-6-0 2MT Cam.

Introduced 1903: Jones Cambrian " 89 " class, reboilered by G.W. from 1924.

Weights: Loco. 38 tons 17 cwt.
    Tender 31 tons 13 cwt.

Pressure: 160 lb. SS.

Cyls.: 18″ × 26″

Driving Wheels: 5′ 1½″

T.E.: 18,625 lb.

844/9/55/95   **Total 4**

2-8-2T 8F 7200 Class

Introduced 1934: Collett rebuild with
extended bunker and trailing wheels
of Churchward 4200 class 2-8-0T.
Weight: 92 tons 2 cwt.
Pressure: 200 lb. Su.
Cyls.: (O) 19" × 30"
Driving Wheels: 4' 7½"
T.E.: 33,170 lb.
P.V.

7200–53

Total 54

2-8-0T {7F* 8F†} 4200 Class

*Introduced 1910: Churchward design.
†Introduced 1923: 5205 class, with
enlarged cyls. and detail alterations.
Weight {81 tons 12 cwt.*
{82 tons 2 cwt.†
Pressure: 200 lb. Su.
Cyls.: {(O) 18½" × 30"*
{(O) 19" × 30"†
Driving Wheels: 4' 7½"
T.E.: {31,450 lb.*
{33,170 lb.†
P.V.
*4200/1/3/6–8/11–5/7/8/21–33/5–
8/41–3/6–8/50–99, 5200–4
†5205–64   **Total 151**

2-6-2T 4MT 3100 Class

Introduced 1938: Collett rebuild with
higher pressure and smaller wheels of
Churchward 3150 class (introduced
1906).
Weight: 81 tons 9 cwt.
Pressure: 225 lb. Su.
Cyls.: (O) 18½" × 30"
Driving Wheels: 5' 3"
T.E.: 31,170 lb.
P.V.

3100–4   **Total 5**

2-6-2T 4MT 3150 Class

Introduced 1906: Churchward design,
developed from his original 3100
class of 1903, but with larger boiler,
subsequently fitted with superheaters.
Weight: 81 tons 12 cwt.
Pressure: 200 lb. Su.
Cyls.: (O) 18½" × 30"
Driving Wheels: 5' 8"
T.E.: 25,670 lb
P.V.
3150/63/4/70–2/4/6/7/80/3/5–7/
90   **Tota! 15**

2-6-2T 3MT 4400 Class

Introduced 1904: Churchward design
for light branches, subsequently fitted
with superheaters.
Weight: 56 tons 13 cwt.
Pressure: 180 lb. Su.
Cyls.: (O) 17" × 24"
Driving Wheels: 4' 1½"
T.E.: 21,440 lb.
P.V.

4401/5/6/10   **Total 4**

2-6-2T 4MT 4500 Class

*Introduced 1906: Churchward design
for light branches, developed from
4400 class with larger wheels, earlier
locos. subsequently fitted with superheaters.
†Introduced 1927: **4575 class** with detail
alterations and increased weight.
‡Introduced 1953. Push-and-pull fitted.
Weights {57 tons 0 cwt.*
{61 tons 0 cwt.†
Pressure: 200 lb. Su.
Cyls.: (O) 17" × 24"
Driving Wheels: 4' 7½"
T.E.: 21,250 lb.
P.V.
*4505–8/19/21–4/6/30/2–42/5–
74

†4575-7/9/80/2-8/90-9, 5500-10/2
-23/5-8/30-3/6-44/6-54/6-8/61-7/9
-71/3

‡4578/81/9, 5511/24/9/34/5/45/55
/9/60/8/72/4   **Total 152**

15

2-6-2T 4MT 5100 & 6100 Classes

*5100 class. Introduced 1928: Collett rebuild with detail alterations and increased weight o. Churchward 3100 class (introduced 1903 and subsequently fitted with superheaters).

†5101 class. Introduced 1929: Modified design for new construction.

‡6100 class. Introduced 1931: Locos. for London suburban area with increased boiler pressure.

Weights $\begin{cases} 75 \text{ tons } 10 \text{ cwt.*} \\ 78 \text{ tons } 9 \text{ cwt.†‡} \end{cases}$

Pressure $\begin{cases} 200 \text{ lb. Su.*†} \\ 225 \text{ lb. Su.‡} \end{cases}$

Cyls.: (O) 18″ × 30″

Driving Wheels: 5′ 8″

T.E. $\begin{cases} 24,300 \text{ lb.*†} \\ 27,340 \text{ lb.‡} \end{cases}$

P.V.

*5112/3/48
†4100–79, 5101–10/50–99
‡6100–69

Total 213

2-6-2T 4MT 8100 Class

Introduced 1938: Collett rebuild with higher pressure and smaller wheels of Churchward locos. in 5100 class.
Weight: 76 tons 11 cwt.
Pressure: 225 lb. Su.
Cyls.: (O) 18″ × 30″
Driving Wheels: 5′ 6″
T.E.: 28,165 lb.
P.V.

8100–9

Total 10

2-6-2T 4MT AD

Introduced 1920: Hawthorn Leslie design for A.D. Railway.
Weight: 65 tons 0 cwt.
Pressure: 160 lb.
Cyls.: (O) 19″ × 26″
Driving Wheels: 4′ 7″
T.E.: 23,210 lb.

1205

Total 1

2-6-2T unclass. V of R

*Introduced 1902: Davies and Metcalfe design for V. of R. 1′ 11½″ gauge. .
†Introduced 1923: G.W. development of V. of R. design.
Weight: 25 tons 0 cwt.
Pressure: 165 lb.

Cyls. (O) $\begin{cases} 11″ \times 17″* \\ 11½″ \times 17″† \end{cases}$

Driving Wheels: 2′ 6″

T.E. $\begin{cases} 9,615 \text{ lb.*} \\ 10,510 \text{ lb.†} \end{cases}$

*9
†7/8

Total 3

0-6-2T 5MT 5600 Class

*Introduced 1924: Collett design for service in Welsh valleys.
†Introduced 1927: Locos. with detail alterations.

Weights $\begin{cases} 68 \text{ tons } 12 \text{ cwt.*} \\ 69 \text{ tons } 7 \text{ cwt.†} \end{cases}$

Pressure: 200 lb. Su.
Cyls.: 18″ × 26″
Driving Wheels: 4′ 7½″
T.E.: 25,800 lb.
P.V.

*5600–99
†6600–99

Total 200

0-6-2T 4F Rhymney Rly.

*Introduced 1921: Hurry Riches Rhymney "R1" class, development of "R." (Introduced 1907.)
†Introduced 1926: Reboilered by G.W. with superheated taper boiler.

Weights $\begin{cases} 66 \text{ tons } 0 \text{ cwt.*} \\ 62 \text{ tons } 10 \text{ cwt.†} \end{cases}$

Pressure $\begin{cases} 175 \text{ lb.*} \\ 200 \text{ lb. Su.†} \end{cases}$

Cyls.: 18½″ × 26″
Driving Wheels: 4′ 6″

T.E. $\begin{cases} 24,520 \text{ lb.*} \\ 28,015 \text{ lb.†} \end{cases}$

*35–8, 41–3
†39, 44

Total 9

4F

*Introduced 1914 : Hurry Riches Rhymney Class "A1," built with Belpaire boiler.
†Introduced 1929: Reboilered by G.W. with superheated taper boiler.

Weights $\begin{cases} 64 \text{ tons } 3 \text{ cwt.*} \\ 63 \text{ tons } 0 \text{ cwt.†} \end{cases}$

Pressure $\begin{cases} 175 \text{ lb.*} \\ 175 \text{ lb. Su.†} \end{cases}$

Cyls.: $18'' \times 26''$*†
Driving Wheels: 4' 4½"
T.E.: 23,870 lb.*†

*68
†58/9/66/9, 70

Total 6

3P

*Introduced 1926: G.W. rebuild with superheated taper boiler of Hurry Riches Rhymney " P " class.
†Introduced 1928: Rebuild of Rhymney " AP " class (superheated development of " P," introduced 1921).

Weights $\begin{cases} 58 \text{ tons } 19 \text{ cwt.*} \\ 63 \text{ tons } 0 \text{ cwt.†} \end{cases}$

Pressure: 175 lb. Su.

Cyls.: $\begin{cases} 18'' \times 26''* \\ 18½'' \times 26''† \end{cases}$

Driving Wheels: 5' 0"

T.E.: $\begin{cases} 20,885 \text{ lb.*} \\ 21,700 \text{ lb.†} \end{cases}$

*82/3   †77/8/9/81   **Total 6**

0-6-2T   4F   TV

Introduced 1924: G.W. rebuild with superheated taper boiler of Hurry Riches T.V. ' O4 " class (introduced 1907).
Weight: 61 tons 0 cwt.
Pressure: 175 lb. Su.
Cyls.: 17½" × 26"
Driving Wheels: 4' 6½"
T.E.: 21,730 lb.

204/5/8/10/1/5/6/79/82/90

Total 10

For full details of
DIESEL & GAS TURBINE LOCOMOTIVES
running on the Western Region,
see the
A.B.C. OF B.R. LOCOMOTIVES
PT. 2. Nos. 10000-39999

4P

Introduced 19.4: G.W. rebuild with superheated taper boiler of Cameron T.V. " A " class (introduced 1914). Two sizes of cylinder.
Weight: 65 tons 14 cwt.

Pressure $\begin{cases} 175 \text{ lb. Su.*} \\ 200 \text{ lb. Su.†} \end{cases}$

Cyls. $\begin{cases} 18½'' \times 26''* \\ 17½'' \times 26''† \end{cases}$

Driving Wheels: 5' 3"

T.E.: $\begin{cases} 21,000 \text{ lb.*} \\ 21,480 \text{ lb.†} \end{cases}$

*307/8/22/49/52/60/1/6/70-2/80/ 7/8

†303-6/12/6/43/5-8/51/6/7/62/4/ 5/7/8/73-9/81-6/9-91/3/4/7-9

Total 54

0-6-0PT   2F   850 Class

Introduced 1910: Rebuilt with pannier tanks.
Weight: 36 tons 3 cwt.
Pressure: 165 lb.
Cyls.: 16" × 24"
Driving Wheels: 4' 1½"
T.E.: 17,410 lb.

2008/11/2

Total 3

0-6-0ST   0F   1361 Class

Introduced 1910: Churchward design for dock shunting.
Weight: 35 tons 4 cwt.
Pressure: 150 lb.
Cyls.: (O) 16" × 20"
Driving Wheels: 3' 8"
T.E.: 14,835 lb.

1361-5

Total 5

0-6-0PT   IF   1366 Class

Introduced 1934: Collett development of 1361 class, with pannier tanks.
Weight: 35 tons 15 cwt.
Pressure: 165 lb.
Cyls.: (O) 16" × 20"
Driving Wheels: 3' 8"
T.E.: 16,320 lb.

1366-71

Total 6

0-6-0PT 4F 1500 Class

Introduced 1949: Hawksworth short-wheelbase heavy shunting design.
Weight: 58 tons 4 cwt.
Pressure: 200 lb.
Cyls.: (O) 17½″ × 24″
Driving Wheels: 4′ 7½″
T.E.: 22,515 lb.
Walschaerts gear, P.V.

1500–9   **Total 10**

0-6-0PT 2F 1600 Class

Introduced 1949: Hawksworth light branch line and shunting design.
Weight: 41 tons 12 cwt.
Pressure: 165 lb.
Cyls.: 16½″ × 24″
Driving Wheels: 4′ 1½″
T.E.: 18,515 lb.

1600–59

N.B.—Locomotives of this class are still being delivered.

0-6-0PT 2F 2021 & 2181 Classes

2021 class. Introduced 1897: Dean saddletank, subsequently rebuilt with pannier tanks. Nos. 2101 onwards built with domeless Belpaire boilers, interchanged later throughout the class.
†2181 class. Introduced 1939: 2021 class modified with increased brake power for heavy gradients.
Weight: 39 tons 15 cwt.
Pressure: 165 lb.
Cyls.: 16½″ × 24″
Driving Wheels: 4′ 1½″
T.E.: 18,515 lb.

*2027/34/5/40/3/60/1/9/70/2/81/
  2/8/90/2/7/9, 2101/7/8/12/34/
  6/8/44/60
†2182/3/6

**Totals : 2021 Class 26
            2181 Class 3**

0-6-0PT IP 5400 Class

Introduced 1931: Collett design for light passenger work, push-and-pull fitted.
Weight: 46 tons 12 cwt.
Pressure: 165 lb.
Cyls.: 16½″ × 24″
Driving Wheels: 5′ 2″
T.E.: 14,780 lb.

5400–24

                                Total 25

0-6-0PT 3F 5700 Class

*Introduced 1929: Collett design for shunting and light goods work, developed from 2021 class.
†Introduced 1930: Locos. with steam brake and no A.T.C. fittings, for shunting only.
‡Introduced 1933: Locos. with condensing gear for working over L.T. Metropolitan line.
§Introduced 1933: Locos. with detail alterations, modified cab (except 8700) and increased weight.
**Introduced 1948: Steam brake locos. with increased weight.
Weights { 47 tons 10 cwt.*†
         { 50 tons 15 cwt.‡
         { 49 tons 0 cwt.§**
Pressure: 200 lb.
Cyls.: 17½″ × 24″
Driving Wheels: 4′ 7½″
T.E.: 22,515 lb.

*5700–99, 7700–99, 8701–49
†6700–49
‡9700–10
§3600–3799, 4600–99, 8700/50–99,
  9600–92, 9711–99
6750–79   **Total 863

0-6-0PT 2P* 2F† 6400 & 7400 Classes

*6400 class. Introduced 1932: Collett design for light passenger work, variation of 5400 class with smaller wheels, push-and-pull fitted.

18

†7400 class. Introduced 1936: Non-push-and-pull fitted locos.

Weights $\begin{cases} 45 \text{ tons } 12 \text{ cwt.*} \\ 45 \text{ tons } 9 \text{ cwt.†} \end{cases}$

Pressure: 180 lb.

Cyls.: $16\frac{1}{2}'' \times 24''$

Driving Wheels: 4' 7½"

T.E.: 18,010 lb.

*6400–39
†7400–49

Totals : 6400 Class 40
7400 Class 50

0-6-0PT 4F 9400 Class

*Introduced 1947: Hawksworth taper-boiler design for heavy shunting.

†Introduced 1949: Locos. with non-superheated boilers.

Weight: 55 tons 7 cwt.

Pressure: 200 lb. SS.

Cyls.: $17\frac{1}{2}'' \times 24''$

Driving Wheels: 4' 7½"

T.E.: 22,515 lb.

*9400–9
†3400–9, 8400–99, 9410–99

N.B.—Locomotives of this class are still being delivered.

0-6-0T 3F AD

Introduced 1917: Kerr Stuart design for Railway Operating Division, R.E., purchased by A.D. Railway 1919.

Weight: 50 tons 0 cwt.

Pressure: 160 lb.

Cyls.: (O) $17'' \times 24''$

Driving Wheels: 4' 0"

T.E.: 19,650 lb.

666/7   **Total 2**

0-6-0T IF BPGV

Introduced 1910 : Hudswell Clarke design for B.P.G.V. rebuilt by G.W.R.

Weight : 37 tons 15 cwt.

Pressure: 165 lb.

Cyls: (O) $15'' \times 22''$

Driving wheels : 3' 9"

T.E.: 15,430 lb.

2198   **Total I**

2F

*Introduced 1912: Hudswell Clarke design for B.P.G.V.

†Rebuilt by G.W.R.

Weight: 37 tons 15 cwt.

Pressure: 160 lb.

Cyls.: (O) $16'' \times 24''$

Driving Wheels: 3' 9"

T.E.: 18,570 lb.

*2166
†2162/5/8   **Total 4**

0-6-0ST IF BPGV

Introduced 1907: Avonside design for B.P.G.V., rebuilt by G.W.R.

Weight: 38 tons 5 cwt.

Pressure: 165 lb.

Cyls.: (O) $15'' \times 22''$

Driving Wheels: 3' 6"

T.E.: 16,530 lb.

2176   **Total I**

IF

Introduced 1906: Avonside design for B.P.G.V.

Weight: 38 tons 0 cwt.

Pressure: 170 lb.

Cyls.: (O) $15'' \times 22''$

Driving Wheels: 3' 6"

T.E.: 17,030 lb.

2196   **Total I**

0-6-0PT 4F Cardiff Rly.

Introduced 1920: Hope and Hudswell Clarke design for Cardiff Railway, rebuilered by G.W. and fitted with pannier tanks.

Weight: 45 tons 6 cwt.
Pressure: 165 lb.
Cyls.: 18″ × 24″
Driving Wheels: 4′ 1½″
T.E.: 22,030 lb.

681/3/4   **Total 3**

0-6-0T 4F Rhymney Rly.

Introduced 1930: Hurry Riches Rhymney " S " class (introduced 1908), rebuilt by G.W. with taper boiler.

Weight: 54 tons 8 cwt.
Pressure: 175 lb.
Cyls.: 18″ × 26″
Driving Wheels: 4′ 4½″
T.E.: 23,870 lb.

93/4   **Total 2**

4F

Introduced 1920: Hurry Riches Rhymney " S1 " class.

Weight: 56 tons 8 cwt.
Pressure: 175 lb.
Cyls. 18″ × 26″
Driving Wheels: 4′ 4½″
T.E. 23,870 lb.

91/2   **Total 2**

0-6-0T Unclass. W & L

Introduced 1902: Beyer Peacock design for 2′ 6½″ gauge W. & L. Section, Cam. Railways.

Weight: 19 tons 18 cwt.
Gauge: 2′ 6½″
Pressure: 150 lb.
Cyls.: (O) 11½″ × 16″
Driving Wheels: 2′ 9″
T.E.: 8,175 lb.

822/3   **Total 2**

0-4-2T 1P
1400 & 5800 Classes

*1400 class introduced 1932: Collett design for light branch work (originally designated 4800 class). Push-and-pull fitted.

†5800 class introduced 1933: Non push-and-pull fitted locos.

Weight: 41 tons 6 cwt.
Pressure: 165 lb.
Cyls. 16″ × 24″
Driving Wheels: 5′ 2″
T.E.: 13,900 lb.

*1400–74 †5800–19 **Total 95**

0-4-0T 3F 1101 Class

Introduced 1926: Avonside Engine Co., design to G.W requirements for dock shunting.

Weight: 38 tons 4 cwt.
Pressure: 170 lb.
Cyls.: (O) 16″ × 24″
Driving Wheels: 3′ 9½″
T.E.: 19,510 lb.
Walschaerts gear.

1101–6   **Total 6**

0-4-0ST 0F Car.R

Introduced 1898: Kitson design for Cardiff Railway.

Weight: 25 tons 10 cwt.
Pressure: 160 lb.
Cyls.: (O) 14″ × 21″
Driving Wheels: 3′ 2½″
T.E.: 14,540 lb.
Hawthorn Kitson valve gear.

1338   **Total 1**

0-4-0ST 0F P & M

Introduced 1907: Peckett design for P. & M.

Weight: 33 tons 10 cwt.
Pressure: 150 lb.
Cyls.: (O) 15″ × 21″
Driving Wheels: 3′ 7″ T.E.: 14,010 lb.

1151/2   **Total 2**

Introduced 1903: Hawthorn Leslie design
for P. & M., reboilered by G.W.R.
Weight: 26 tons 13 cwt.
Pressure: 120 lb
Cyls.: (O) 14″ × 20″
Driving Wheels: 3′ 6″   T.E.. 9,520 lb.

1153   **Total 1**

0-4-0ST   0F   SHT

Introduced 1905: Barclay design for
S.H.T
Weight: 28 tons 0 cwt.
Pressure: 160 lb.
Cyls.: (O) 14″ × 22″
Driving Wheels: 3′ 5″   T.E.: 14,305 lb.

1140   **Total 1**

Introduced 1906: Peckett design for
S.H.T. (similar to 1151/2).
Weight: 33 tons 10 cwt.
Pressure: 150 lb.

Cyls.: (O) 15″ × 21″
Driving Wheels: 3′ 7″
T.E.: 14,010 lb.

1143/5   **Total 2**

Introduced 1909: Hawthorn Leslie de-
sign for S.H.T.
Weight: 26 tons 17 cwt.
Pressure: 150 lb.
Cyls.: (O) 14″ × 22″
Driving Wheels: 3′ 6″
T.E.: 13,090 lb.

1144   **Total 1**

Introduced 1911: Hudswell Clarke
design for S.H.T.
Weight: 28 tons 15 cwt.
Pressure: 160 lb.
Cyls.: (O) 15″ × 22″
Driving Wheels: 3′ 4″
T.E.: 16,830 lb.

1142   **Total 1**

LOCOMOTIVE SUPERINTENDENTS AND CHIEF MECHANICAL ENGINEERS OF THE G.W.R. & W.R.

Sir Daniel Gooch	1837—1864
Joseph Armstrong	{ 1854—1864*
	{ 1864—1877
George Armstrong	{ 1864—
(*Bro. of J. Armstrong*)	{ 1877—1892*
William Dean	{ —1877*
	{ 1877—1902
G. J. Churchward	1902—1921
Charles B. Collett	1922—1941
F. W. Hawksworth	1941—1949

* In charge of standard gauge locomotives at Stafford Road
Works, Wolverhampton, with wide powers in design and construction. The exact dates of Geo. Armstrong's and Dean's
terms of service there cannot be definitely ascertained from
existing records.

NUMERICAL LIST OF WESTERN REGION
STEAM LOCOMOTIVES

Locomotives are of G.W. origin except where
indicated by initials

2-6-2T			V of R
7	8	9	

0-6-2T			RR
35	41	59	78
36	42	66	79
37	43	68	81
38	44	69	82
39	58	70	83

0-6-0T		RR
91	93	
92	94	

0-6-2T			TV
204	282	308	347
205	290	312	348
208	303	316	349
210	304	322	351
211	305	343	352
215	306	345	356
216	307	346	357
279			

0-6-2T			TV
360	371	380	389
361	372	381	390
362	373	382	391
364	374	383	393
365	375	384	394
366	376	385	397
367	377	386	398
368	378	387	399
370	379	388	

0-6-0T		AD
666	667	

0-6-0PT			Car.R.
681	683	684	

0-6-0T		W & L.
822	823	

0-6-0			Cam.R.
844	849	855	895

4-6-0   1000 Class
" County "

1000 County of Middlesex
1001 County of Bucks
1002 County of Berks
1003 County of Wilts
1004 County of Somerset
1005 County of Devon
1006 County of Cornwall
1007 County of Brecknock
1008 County of Cardigan
1009 County of Carmarthen
1010 County of Caernarvon
1011 County of Chester
1012 County of Denbigh
1013 County of Dorset
1014 County of Glamorgan
1015 County of Gloucester
1016 County of Hants
1017 County of Hereford
1018 County of Leicester
1019 County of Merioneth
1020 County of Monmouth
1021 County of Montgomery
1022 County of Northampton
1023 County of Oxford
1024 County of Pembroke
1025 County of Radnor
1026 County of Salop
1027 County of Stafford
1028 County of Warwick
1029 County of Worcester

0-4-0T   1101 Class

1101	1103	1105
1102	1104	1106

0-4-0T   SHT

1140	1143	1145
1142	1144	

0-4-0T   PM

1151	1152	1153

2-6-2T   AD

1205

0-4-0ST   Car.R.

1338

0-6-0ST   1361 Class

1361	1363	1365
1362	1364	

0-6-0PT   1366 Class

1366	1368	1370
1367	1369	1371

0-4-2T   1400 Class

1400	1415	1430	1445
1401	1416	1431	1446
1402	1417	1432	1447
1403	1418	1433	1448
1404	1419	1434	1449
1405	1420	1435	1450
1406	1421	1436	1451
1407	1422	1437	1452
1408	1423	1438	1453
1409	1424	1439	1454
1410	1425	1440	1455
1411	1426	1441	1456
1412	1427	1442	1457
1413	1428	1443	1458
1414	1429	1444	1459

1460	1464	1468	1472
1461	1465	1469	1473
1462	1466	1470	1474
1463	1467	1471	

0-6-0PT   1500 Class

1500	1503	1506	1509
1501	1504	1507	
1502	1505	1508	

0-6-0PT   1600 Class

1600	1615	1630	1645
1601	1616	1631	1646
1602	1617	1632	1647
1603	1618	1633	1648
1604	1619	1634	1649
1605	1620	1635	1650
1606	1621	1636	1651
1607	1622	1637	1652
1608	1623	1638	1653
1609	1624	1639	1654
1610	1625	1640	1655
1611	1626	1641	1656
1612	1627	1642	1657
1613	1628	1643	1658
1614	1629	1644	1659

0-6-0PT   850 Class

2008	2011	2012

0-6-0PT   2021 Class

2027	2069	2092	2134
2034	2070	2097	2136
2035	2072	2099	2138
2040	2081	2101	2144
2043	2082	2107	2160
2060	2088	2108	
2061	2090	2112	

0-6-0T   BPGV Rly.

2162	2165	2166	2168

23

0-6-0ST　　　BPGV Rly.
2176

0-6-0PT　　　2181 Class
2182 | 2183 | 2186

0-6-0ST　　　BPGV Rly.
2196 Gwendraeth

0-6-0T　　　BPGV Rly.
2198

0-6-0　　　2251 Class

2200	2225	2250	2275
2201	2226	2251	2276
2202	2227	2252	2277
2203	2228	2253	2278
2204	2229	2254	2279
2205	2230	2255	2280
2206	2231	2256	2281
2207	2232	2257	2282
2208	2233	2258	2283
2209	2234	2259	2284
2210	2235	2260	2285
2211	2236	2261	2286
2212	2237	2262	2287
2213	2238	2263	2288
2214	2239	2264	2289
2215	2240	2265	2290
2216	2241	2266	2291
2217	2242	2267	2292
2218	2243	2268	2293
2219	2244	2269	2294
2220	2245	2270	2295
2221	2246	2271	2296
2222	2247	2272	2297
2223	2248	2273	2298
2224	2249	2274	2299

0-6-0　　　2301 Class

2340	2484	2516	2538
2458	2513	2532	2541
2474			

2-8-0　　　2800 Class

2800	2825	2850	2875
2801	2826	2851	2876
2802	2827	2852	2877
2803	2828	2853	2878
2804	2829	2854	2879
2805	2830	2855	2880
2806	2831	2856	2881
2807	2832	2857	2882
2808	2833	2858	2883
2809	2834	2859	2884
2810	2835	2860	2885
2811	2836	2861	2886
2812	2837	2862	2887
2813	2838	2863	2888
2814	2839	2864	2889
2815	2840	2865	2890
2816	2841	2866	2891
2817	2842	2867	2892
2818	2843	2868	2893
2819	2844	2869	2894
2820	2845	2870	2895
2821	2846	2871	2896
2822	2847	2872	2897
2823	2848	2873	2898
2824	2849	2874	2899

2-8-0　　　R.O.D. Class

3010	3018	3028	3041
3011	3020	3029	3042
3012	3022	3031	3043
3014	3023	3032	3044
3015	3024	3036	3048
3016	3025	3038	
3017	3026	3040	

2-6-2T   3100 Class

| 3100 | 3102 | 3103 | 3104 |
| 3101 | | | |

2-6-2T   3150 Class

3150	3171	3177	3186
3163	3172	3180	3187
3164	3174	3183	3190
3170	3176	3185	

0-6-0   2251 Class

3200	3205	3210	3215
3201	3206	3211	3216
3202	3207	3212	3217
3203	3208	3213	3218
3204	3209	3214	3219

0-6-0PT   9400 Class

3400	3403	3406	3408
3401	3404	3407	3409
3402	3405		

0-6-0PT   5700 Class

3600	3617	3634	3651
3601	3618	3635	3652
3602	3619	3636	3653
3603	3620	3637	3654
3604	3621	3638	3655
3605	3622	3639	3656
3606	3623	3640	3657
3607	3624	3641	3658
3608	3625	3642	3659
3609	3626	3643	3660
3610	3627	3644	3661
3611	3628	3645	3662
3612	3629	3646	3663
3613	3630	3647	3664
3614	3631	3648	3665
3615	3632	3649	3666
3616	3633	3650	3667

3668	3701	3734	3767
3669	3702	3735	3768
3670	3703	3736	3769
3671	3704	3737	3770
3672	3705	3738	3771
3673	3706	3739	3772
3674	3707	3740	3773
3675	3708	3741	3774
3676	3709	3742	3775
3677	3710	3743	3776
3678	3711	3744	3777
3679	3712	3745	3778
3680	3713	3746	3779
3681	3714	3747	3780
3682	3715	3748	3781
3683	3716	3749	3782
3684	3717	3750	3783
3685	3718	3751	3784
3686	3719	3752	3785
3687	3720	3753	3786
3688	3721	3754	3787
3689	3722	3755	3788
3690	3723	3756	3789
3691	3724	3757	3790
3692	3725	3758	3791
3693	3726	3759	3792
3694	3727	3760	3793
3695	3728	3761	3794
3696	3729	3762	3795
3697	3730	3763	3796
3698	3731	3764	3797
3699	3732	3765	3798
3700	3733	3766	3799

2-8-0   2800 Class

3800	3811	3822	3833
3801	3812	3823	3834
3802	3813	3824	3835
3803	3814	3825	3836
3804	3815	3826	3837
3805	3816	3827	3838
3806	3817	3828	3839
3807	3818	3829	3840
3808	3819	3830	3841
3809	3820	3831	3842
3810	3821	3832	3843

3844	3850	3856	3862
3845	3851	3857	3863
3846	3852	3858	3864
3847	3853	3859	3865
3848	3854	3860	3866
3849	3855	3861	

4096 Highclere Castle
4097 Kenilworth Castle
4098 Kidwelly Castle
4099 Kilgerran Castle

4-6-0   4073 Class
" Castle "

4000 North Star
4037 The South Wales Borderers

4-6-0   4000 Class
" Star "

4053 Princess Alexandra
4056 Princess Margaret
4061 Glastonbury Abbey
4062 Malmesbury Abbey

4-6-0   4073 Class
" Castle "

4073 Caerphilly Castle
4074 Caldicot Castle
4075 Cardiff Castle
4076 Carmarthen Castle
4077 Chepstow Castle
4078 Pembroke Castle
4079 Pendennis Castle
4080 Powderham Castle
4081 Warwick Castle
4082 Windsor Castle
4083 Abbotsbury Castle
4084 Aberystwyth Castle
4085 Berkeley Castle
4086 Builth Castle
4087 Cardigan Castle
4088 Dartmouth Castle
4089 Donnington Castle
4090 Dorchester Castle
4091 Dudley Castle
4092 Dunraven Castle
4093 Dunster Castle
4094 Dynevor Castle
4095 Harlech Castle

2-6-2T   5100 Class

4100	4120	4140	4160
4101	4121	4141	4161
4102	4122	4142	4162
4103	4123	4143	4163
4104	4124	4144	4164
4105	4125	4145	4165
4106	4126	4146	4166
4107	4127	4147	4167
4108	4128	4148	4168
4109	4129	4149	4169
4110	4130	4150	4170
4111	4131	4151	4171
4112	4132	4152	4172
4113	4133	4153	4173
4114	4134	4154	4174
4115	4135	4155	4175
4116	4136	4156	4176
4117	4137	4157	4177
4118	4138	4158	4178
4119	4139	4159	4179

2-8-0T   4200 Class

4200	4226	4250	4268
4201	4227	4251	4269
4203	4228	4252	4270
4206	4229	4253	4271
4207	4230	4254	4272
4208	4231	4255	4273
4211	4232	4256	4274
4212	4233	4257	4275
4213	4235	4258	4276
4214	4236	4259	4277
4215	4237	4260	4278
4217	4238	4261	4279
4218	4241	4262	4280
4221	4242	4263	4281
4222	4243	4264	4282
4223	4246	4265	4283
4224	4247	4266	4284
4225	4248	4267	4285

4286	4290	4294	4293
4287	4291	4295	4299
4288	4292	4296	
4289	4293	4297	

2-6-0   4300 Class

4326	4358	4375	4377

2-6-2T   4400 Class

4401	4405	4406	4410

2-6-2T   4500 Class

4505	4541	4563	4583
4506	4542	4564	4584
4507	4545	4565	4585
4508	4546	4566	4586
4519	4547	4567	4587
4521	4548	4568	4588
4522	4549	4569	4589
4523	4550	4570	4590
4524	4551	4571	4591
4526	4552	4572	4592
4530	4553	4573	4593
4532	4554	4574	4594
4533	4555	4575	4595
4534	4556	4576	4596
4535	4557	4577	4597
4536	4558	4578	4598
4537	4559	4579	4599
4538	4560	4580	
4539	4561	4581	
4540	4562	4582	

0-6-0PT   5700 Class

4600	4607	4614	4621
4601	4608	4615	4622
4602	4609	4616	4623
4603	4610	4617	4624
4604	4611	4618	4625
4605	4612	4619	4626
4606	4613	4620	4627

4628	4646	4664	4682
4629	4647	4665	4683
4630	4643	4666	4684
4631	4649	4667	4685
4632	4650	4668	4686
4633	4651	4669	4687
4634	4652	4670	4688
4635	4653	4671	4689
4636	4654	4672	4690
4637	4655	4673	4691
4638	4656	4674	4692
4639	4657	4675	4693
4640	4658	4676	4694
4641	4659	4677	4695
4642	4660	4678	4696
4643	4661	4679	4697
4644	4662	4680	4698
4645	4663	4681	4699

2-8-0   4700 Class

4700	4703	4705	4707
4701	4704	4706	4708
4702			

4-6-0 "Hall" 4900 Classs

4900 Saint Martin
4901 Adderley Hall
4902 Aldenham Hall
4903 Astley Hall
4904 Binnegar Hall
4905 Barton Hall
4906 Bradfield Hall
4907 Broughton Hall
4908 Broome Hall
4909 Blakesley Hall
4910 Blaisdon Hall
4912 Berrington Hall
4913 Baglan Hall
4914 Cranmore Hall
4915 Condover Hall
4916 Crumlin Hall
4917 Crosswood Hall
4918 Dartington Hall
4919 Donnington Hall
4920 Dumbleton Hall
4921 Eaton Hall

4922 Enville Hall
4923 Evenley Hall
4924 Eydon Hall
4925 Eynsham Hall
4926 Fairleigh Hall
4927 Farnborough Hall
4928 Gatacre Hall
4929 Goytrey Hall
4930 Hagley Hall
4931 Hanbury Hall
4932 Hatherton Hall
4933 Himley Hall
4934 Hindlip Hall
4935 Ketley Hall
4936 Kinlet Hall
4937 Lanelay Hall
4938 Liddington Hall
4939 Littleton Hall
4940 Ludford Hall
4941 Llangedwyn Hall
4942 Maindy Hall
4943 Marrington Hall
4944 Middleton Hall
4945 Milligan Hall
4946 Moseley Hall
4947 Nanhoran Hall
4948 Northwick Hall
4949 Packwood Hall
4950 Patshull Hall
4951 Pendeford Hall
4952 Peplow Hall
4953 Pitchford Hall
4954 Plaish Hall
4955 Plaspower Hall
4956 Plowden Hall
4957 Postlip Hall
4958 Priory Hall
4959 Purley Hall
4960 Pyle Hall
4961 Pyrland Hall
4962 Ragley Hall
4963 Rignall Hall
4964 Rodwell Hall
4965 Rood Ashton Hall
4966 Shakenhurst Hall
4967 Shirenewton Hall
4968 Shotton Hall

4969 Shrugborough Hall
4970 Sketty Hall
4971 Stanway Hall
4972 Saint Brides Hall
4973 Sweeney Hall
4974 Talgarth Hall
4975 Umberslade Hall
4976 Warfield Hall
4977 Watcombe Hall
4978 Westwood Hall
4979 Wootton Hall
4980 Wrottesley Hall
4981 Abberley Hall
4982 Acton Hall
4983 Albert Hall
4984 Albrighton Hall
4985 Allesley Hall
4986 Aston Hall
4987 Brockley Hall
4988 Bulwell Hall
4989 Cherwell Hall
4990 Clifton Hall
4991 Cobham Hall
4992 Crosby Hall
4993 Dalton Hall
4994 Downton Hall
4995 Easton Hall
4996 Eden Hall
4997 Elton Hall
4998 Eyton Hall
4999 Gopsal Hall

4-6-0 "Castle" 4073 Class

5000 Launceston Castle
5001 Llandovery Castle
5002 Ludlow Castle
5003 Lulworth Castle
5004 Llanstephan Castle
5005 Manorbier Castle
5006 Tregenna Castle
5007 Rougemont Castle
5008 Raglan Castle
5009 Shrewsbury Castle
5010 Restormel Castle
5011 Tintagel Castle
5012 Berry Pomeroy Castle

5700 Class 0-6-0PT No. 9726 (with later design of cab). [A. R. Carpenter

5400 Class 0-6-0PT No. 5405. [R. K. Evans

6400 Class 0-6-0PT No. 6403. [G. Wheeler

6000 Class 4-6-0 No. 6026 *King John*.   [*G. Wheeler*

4073 Class 4-6-0 No. 4086 *Builth Castle*.   [*G. Wheeler*

4073 Class 4-6-0 No. 5097 *Sarum Castle* (with flush-sided tender).   [*H. A. Chalkley*

1000 Class 4-6-0 No. 1001 *County of Bucks.*   [*G. Wheeler*

4900 Class 4-6-0 No. 4960 *Pyle Hall.*   [*G. Wheeler*

6959 Class 4-6-0 No. 6995 *Benthall Hall.*   [*G. Wheeler*

4000 Class 4-6-0 No. 4056 *Princess Margaret*.　　　　　　　　　　　　　[G. Wheeler

6800 Class 4-6-0 No. 6844 *Penhydd Grange*.　　　　　　　　　　　　　[R. S. Potts

7800 Class 4-6-0 No. 7807 *Compton Manor*.　　　　　　　　　　　　　[G. Wheeler

5013 Abergavenny Castle
5014 Goodrich Castle
5015 Kingswear Castle
5016 Montgomery Castle
5017 The Gloucestershire
     Regiment 28th, 61st
5018 St. Mawes Castle
5019 Treago Castle
5020 Trematon Castle
5021 Whittington Castle
5022 Wigmore Castle
5023 Brecon Castle
5024 Carew Castle
5025 Chirk Castle
5026 Criccieth Castle
5027 Farleigh Castle
5028 Llantilio Castle
5029 Nunney Castle
5030 Shirburn Castle
5031 Totnes Castle
5032 Usk Castle
5033 Broughton Castle
5034 Corfe Castle
5035 Coity Castle
5036 Lyonshall Castle
5037 Monmouth Castle
5038 Morlais Castle
5039 Rhuddlan Castle
5040 Stokesay Castle
5041 Tiverton Castle
5042 Winchester Castle
5043 Earl of Mount Edgcumbe
5044 Earl of Dunraven
5045 Earl of Dudley
5046 Earl Cawdor
5047 Earl of Dartmouth
5048 Earl of Devon
5049 Earl of Plymouth
5050 Earl of St. Germans
5051 Earl Bathurst
5052 Earl of Radnor
5053 Earl Cairns
5054 Earl of Ducie
5055 Earl of Eldon
5056 Earl of Powis
5057 Earl Waldegrave
5058 Earl of Clancarty

5059 Earl St. Aldwyn
5060 Earl of Berkeley
5061 Earl of Birkenhead
5062 Earl of Shaftesbury
5063 Earl Baldwin
5064 Bishop's Castle
5065 Newport Castle
5066 Wardour Castle
5067 St. Fagans Castle
5068 Beverston Castle
5069 Isambard Kingdom Brunel
5070 Sir Daniel Gooch
5071 Spitfire
5072 Hurricane
5073 Blenheim
5074 Hampden
5075 Wellington
5076 Gladiator
5077 Fairey Battle
5078 Beaufort
5079 Lysander
5080 Defiant
5081 Lockheed Hudson
5082 Swordfish
5083 Bath Abbey
5084 Reading Abbey
5085 Evesham Abbey
5086 Viscount Horne
5087 Tintern Abbey
5088 Llanthony Abbey
5089 Westminster Abbey
5090 Neath Abbey
5091 Cleeve Abbey
5092 Tresco Abbey
5093 Upton Castle
5094 Tretower Castle
5095 Barbury Castle
5096 Bridgwater Castle
5097 Sarum Castle
5098 Clifford Castle
5099 Compton Castle

2-6-2T 5100 Class

| 5101 | 5103 | 5105 | 5107 |
| 5102 | 5104 | 5106 | 5108 |

5109-5607

5109	5159	5173	5187
5110	5160	5174	5188
5112	5161	5175	5189
5113	5162	5176	5190
5148	5163	5177	5191
5150	5164	5178	5192
5151	5165	5179	5193
5152	5166	5180	5194
5153	5167	5181	5195
5154	5168	5182	5196
5155	5169	5183	5197
5156	5170	5184	5198
5157	5171	5185	5199
5158	5172	5186	

5367	5376	5384	5393
5368	5377	5385	5394
5369	5378	5386	5395
5370	5379	5388	5396
5371	5380	5390	5397
5372	5381	5391	5398
5375	5382	5392	5399

0-6-0PT   5400 Class

5400	5407	5414	5421
5401	5408	5415	5422
5402	5409	5416	5423
5403	5410	5417	5424
5404	5411	5418	
5405	5412	5419	
5406	5413	5420	

2-8-0T   4200 Class

5200	5217	5234	5251
5201	5218	5235	5252
5202	5219	5236	5253
5203	5220	5237	5254
5204	5221	5238	5255
5205	5222	5239	5256
5206	5223	5240	5257
5207	5224	5241	5258
5208	5225	5242	5259
5209	5226	5243	5260
5210	5227	5244	5261
5211	5228	5245	5262
5212	5229	5246	5263
5213	5230	5247	5264
5214	5231	5248	
5215	5232	5249	
5216	5233	5250	

2-6-2T   4500 Class

5500	5519	5538	5557
5501	5520	5539	5558
5502	5521	5540	5559
5503	5522	5541	5560
5504	5523	5542	5561
5505	5524	5543	5562
5506	5525	5544	5563
5507	5526	5545	5564
5508	5527	5546	5565
5509	5528	5547	5566
5510	5529	5548	5567
5511	5530	5549	5568
5512	5531	5550	5569
5513	5532	5551	5570
5514	5533	5552	5571
5515	5534	5553	5572
5516	5535	5554	5573
5517	5536	5555	5574
5518	5537	5556	

2-6-0   4300 Class

5306	5319	5332	5347
5307	5321	5333	5350
5310	5322	5334	5351
5311	5323	5335	5353
5312	5324	5336	5355
5313	5325	5337	5356
5314	5326	5338	5357
5315	5327	5339	5358
5316	5328	5341	5360
5317	5330	5344	5361
5318	5331	5345	5362

0-6-2T   5600 Class

5600	5602	5604	5606
5601	5603	5605	5607

5608	5631	5654	5677	5784	5788	5792	5796
5609	5632	5655	5678	5785	5789	5793	5797
5610	5633	5656	5679	5786	5790	5794	5798
5611	5634	5657	5680	5787	5791	5795	5799
5612	5635	5658	5681				

0-4-2T   **1400 Class**

5613	5636	5659	5682
5614	5637	5660	5683

5800	5805	5810	5815
5801	5806	5811	5816
5802	5807	5812	5817
5803	5808	5813	5818
5804	5809	5814	5819

5608	5631	5654	5677
5609	5632	5655	5678
5610	5633	5656	5679
5611	5634	5657	5680
5612	5635	5658	5681
5613	5636	5659	5682
5614	5637	5660	5683
5615	5638	5661	5684
5616	5639	5662	5685
5617	5640	5663	5686
5618	5641	5664	5687
5619	5642	5665	5688
5620	5643	5666	5689
5621	5644	5667	5690
5622	5645	5668	5691
5623	5646	5669	5692
5624	5647	5670	5693
5625	5648	5671	5694
5626	5649	5672	5695
5627	5650	5673	5696
5628	5651	5674	5697
5629	5652	5675	5698
5630	5653	5676	5699

4-6-0   **4900 Class**
" Hall "

5900 Hinderton Hall
5901 Hazel Hall
5902 Howick Hall
5903 Keele Hall
5904 Kelham Hall
5905 Knowsley Hall
5906 Lawton Hall
5907 Marble Hall
5908 Moreton Hall
5909 Newton Hall
5910 Park Hall
5911 Preston Hall
5912 Queen's Hall
5913 Rushton Hall
5914 Ripon Hall
5915 Trentham Hall
5916 Trinity Hall
5917 Westminster Hall
5918 Walton Hall
5919 Worsley Hall
5920 Wycliffe Hall
5921 Bingley Hall
5922 Caxton Hall
5923 Colston Hall
5924 Dinton Hall
5925 Eastcote Hall
5926 Grotrian Hall
5927 Guild Hall
5928 Haddon Hall
5929 Hanham Hall
5930 Hannington Hall
5931 Hatherley Hall

0-6-0PT   **5700 Class**

5700	5721	5742	5763
5701	5722	5743	5764
5702	5723	5744	5765
5703	5724	5745	5766
5704	5725	5746	5767
5705	5726	5747	5768
5706	5727	5748	5769
5707	5728	5749	5770
5708	5729	5750	5771
5709	5730	5751	5772
5710	5731	5752	5773
5711	5732	5753	5774
5712	5733	5754	5775
5713	5734	5755	5776
5714	5735	5756	5777
5715	5736	5757	5778
5716	5737	5758	5779
5717	5738	5759	5780
5718	5739	5760	5781
5719	5740	5761	5782
5720	5741	5762	5783

35

5932 Haydon Hall	5979 Cruckton Hall
5933 Kingsway Hall	5980 Dingley Hall
5934 Kneller Hall	5981 Frensham Hall
5935 Norton Hall	5982 Harrington Hall
5936 Oakley Hall	5983 Henley Hall
5937 Stanford Hall	5984 Linden Hall
5938 Stanley Hall	5985 Mostyn Hall
5939 Tangley Hall	5986 Arbury Hall
5940 Whitbourne Hall	5987 Brocket Hall
5941 Campion Hall	5988 Bostock Hall
5942 Doldowlod Hall	5989 Cransley Hall
5943 Elmdon Hall	5990 Dorford Hall
5944 Ickenham Hall	5991 Gresham Hall
5945 Leckhampton Hall	5992 Horton Hall
5946 Marwell Hall	5993 Kirby Hall
5947 Saint Benet's Hall	5994 Roydon Hall
5948 Siddington Hall	5995 Wick Hall
5949 Trematon Hall	5996 Mytton Hall
5950 Wardley Hall	5997 Sparkford Hall
5951 Clyffe Hall	5998 Trevor Hall
5952 Cogan Hall	5999 Wollaton Hall
5953 Dunley Hall	
5954 Faendre Hall	
5955 Garth Hall	
5956 Horsley Hall	**4-6-0 6000 Class**
5957 Hutton Hall	**" King "**
5958 Knolton Hall	6000 King George V
5959 Mawley Hall	6001 King Edward VII
5960 Saint Edmund Hall	6002 King William IV
5961 Toynbee Hall	6003 King George IV
5962 Wantage Hall	6004 King George III
5963 Wimpole Hall	6005 King George II
5964 Wolseley Hall	6006 King George I
5965 Woollas Hall	6007 King William III
5966 Ashford Hall	6008 King James II
5967 Bickmarsh Hall	6009 King Charles II
5968 Cory Hall	6010 King Charles I
5969 Honington Hall	6011 King James I
5970 Hengrave Hall	6012 King Edward VI
5971 Merevale Hall	6013 King Henry VIII
5972 Olton Hall	6014 King Henry VII
5973 Rolleston Hall	6015 King Richard III
5974 Wallsworth Hall	6016 King Edward V
5975 Winslow Hall	6017 King Edward IV
5976 Ashwicke Hall	6018 King Henry VI
5977 Beckford Hall	6019 King Henry V
5978 Bodinnick Hall	6020 King Henry IV

6021 King Richard II
6022 King Edward III
6023 King Edward II
6024 King Edward I
6025 King Henry III
6026 King John
6027 King Richard I
6028 King George VI
6029 King Edward VIII

2-6-2T   6100 Class

6100	6118	6136	6153
6101	6119	6137	6154
6102	6120	6138	6155
6103	6121	6139	6156
6104	6122	6140	6157
6105	6123	6141	6158
6106	6124	6142	6159
6107	6125	6143	6160
6108	6126	6144	6161
6109	6127	6145	6162
6110	6128	6146	6163
6111	6129	6147	6164
6112	6130	6148	6165
6113	6131	6149	6166
6114	6132	6150	6167
6115	6133	6151	6168
6116	6134	6152	6169
6117	6135		

2-6-0   4300 Class

6300	6313	6327	6340
6301	6314	6328	6341
6302	6316	6329	6342
6303	6317	6330	6343
6304	6318	6331	6344
6305	6319	6332	6345
6306	6320	6333	6346
6307	6321	6334	6347
6308	6322	6335	6348
6309	6323	6336	6349
6310	6324	6337	6350
6311	6325	6338	6351
6312	6326	6339	6352

6353	6365	6377	6389
6354	6366	6378	6390
6355	6367	6379	6391
6356	6368	6380	6392
6357	6369	6381	6393
6358	6370	6382	6394
6359	6371	6383	6395
6360	6372	6384	6396
6361	6373	6385	6397
6362	6374	6386	6398
6363	6375	6387	6399
6364	6376	6388	

0-6-0PT   6400 Class

6400	6410	6420	6430
6401	6411	6421	6431
6402	6412	6422	6432
6403	6413	6423	6433
6404	6414	6424	6434
6405	6415	6425	6435
6406	6416	6426	6436
6407	6417	6427	6437
6408	6418	6428	6438
6409	6419	6429	6439

0-6-2T   5600 Class

6600	6620	6640	6660
6601	6621	6641	6661
6602	6622	6642	6662
6603	6623	6643	6663
6604	6624	6644	6664
6605	6625	6645	6665
6606	6626	6646	6666
6607	6627	6647	6667
6608	6628	6648	6668
6609	6629	6649	6669
6610	6630	6650	6670
6611	6631	6651	6671
6612	6632	6652	6672
6613	6633	6653	6673
6614	6634	6654	6674
6615	6635	6655	6675
6616	6636	6656	6676
6617	6637	6657	6677
6618	6638	6658	6678
6619	6639	6659	6679

6680	6685	6690	6695
6681	6686	6691	6696
6682	6687	6692	6697
6683	6688	6693	6698
6684	6689	6694	6699

0-6-0PT 5700 Class

6700	6720	6740	6760
6701	6721	6741	6761
6702	6722	6742	6762
6703	6723	6743	6763
6704	6724	6744	6764
6705	6725	6745	6765
6706	6726	6746	6766
6707	6727	6747	6767
6708	6728	6748	6768
6709	6729	6749	6769
6710	6730	6750	6770
6711	6731	6751	6771
6712	6732	6752	6772
6713	6733	6753	6773
6714	6734	6754	6774
6715	6735	6755	6775
6716	6736	6756	6776
6717	6737	6757	6777
6718	6738	6758	6778
6719	6739	6759	6779

4-6-0 6800 Class
" Grange "

6800 Arlington Grange
6801 Aylburton Grange
6802 Bampton Grange
6803 Bucklebury Grange
6804 Brockington Grange
6805 Broughton Grange
6806 Blackwell Grange
6807 Birchwood Grange
6808 Beenham Grange
6809 Burghclere Grange
6810 Blakemere Grange
6811 Cranbourne Grange
6812 Chesford Grange
6813 Eastbury Grange
6814 Enborne Grange

6815 Frilford Grange
6816 Frankton Grange
6817 Gwenddwr Grange
6818 Hardwick Grange
6819 Highnam Grange
6820 Kingstone Grange
6821 Leaton Grange
6822 Manton Grange
6823 Oakley Grange
6824 Ashley Grange
6825 Llanvair Grange
6826 Nannerth Grange
6827 Llanfrechfa Grange
6828 Trellech Grange
6829 Burmington Grange
6830 Buckenhill Grange
6831 Bearley Grange
6832 Brockton Grange
6833 Calcot Grange
6834 Dummer Grange
6835 Eastham Grange
6836 Estevarney Grange
6837 Forthampton Grange
6838 Goodmoor Grange
6839 Hewell Grange
6840 Hazeley Grange
6841 Marlas Grange
6842 Nunhold Grange
6843 Poulton Grange
6844 Penhydd Grange
6845 Paviland Grange
6846 Ruckley Grange
6847 Tidmarsh Grange
6848 Toddington Grange
6849 Walton Grange
6850 Cleeve Grange
6851 Hurst Grange
6852 Headbourne Grange
6853 Morehampton Grange
6854 Roundhill Grange
6855 Saighton Grange
6856 Stowe Grange
6857 Tudor Grange
6858 Woolston Grange
6859 Yiewsley Grange
6860 Aberporth Grange

6861 Crynant Grange
6862 Derwent Grange
6863 Dolhywel Grange
6864 Dymock Grange
6865 Hopton Grange
6866 Morfa Grange
6867 Peterston Grange
6868 Penrhos Grange
6869 Resolven Grange
6870 Bodicote Grange
6871 Bourton Grange
6872 Crawley Grange
6873 Caradoc Grange
6874 Haughton Grange
6875 Hindford Grange
6876 Kingsland Grange
6877 Llanfair Grange
6878 Longford Grange
6879 Overton Grange

4-6-0   4900 Class
" Hall "

6900 Abney Hall
6901 Arley Hall
6902 Butlers Hall
6903 Belmont Hall
6904 Charfield Hall
6905 Claughton Hall
6906 Chicheley Hall
6907 Davenham Hall
6908 Downham Hall
6909 Frewin Hall
6910 Gossington Hall
6911 Holker Hall
6912 Helmster Hall
6913 Levens Hall
6914 Langton Hall
6915 Mursley Hall
6916 Misterton Hall
6917 Oldlands Hall
6918 Sandon Hall
6919 Tylney Hall
6920 Barningham Hall
6921 Borwick Hall
6922 Burton Hall
6923 Croxteth Hall

6924 Grantley Hall
6925 Hackness Hall
6926 Holkham Hall
6927 Lilford Hall
6928 Underley Hall
6929 Whorlton Hall
6930 Aldersey Hall
6931 Aldborough Hall
6932 Burwarton Hall
6933 Birtles Hall
6934 Beachamwell Hall
6935 Browsholme Hall
6936 Breccles Hall
6937 Conyngham Hall
6938 Corndean Hall
6939 Calveley Hall
6940 Didlington Hall
6941 Fillongley Hall
6942 Eshton Hall
6943 Farnley Hall
6944 Fledborough Hall
6945 Glasfryn Hall
6946 Heatherden Hall
6947 Helmingham Hall
6948 Holbrooke Hall
6949 Haberfield Hall
6950 Kingsthorpe Hall
6951 Impney Hall
6952 Kimberley Hall
6953 Leighton Hall
6954 Lotherton Hall
6955 Lydcott Hall
6956 Mottram Hall
6957 Norcliffe Hall
6958 Oxburgh Hall

4-6-0   6959 Class
" Modified Hall "

6959 Peatling Hall
6960 Raveningham Hall
6961 Stedham Hall
6962 Soughton Hall
6963 Throwley Hall
6964 Thornbridge Hall
6965 Thirlestaine Hall
6966 Witchingham Hall

6967 Willesley Hall
6968 Woodcock Hall
6969 Wraysbury Hall
6970 Whaddon Hall
6971 Athelhampton Hall
6972 Beningbrough Hall
6973 Bricklehampton Hall
6974 Bryngwyn Hall
6975 Capesthorne Hall
6976 Graythwaite Hall
6977 Grundisburgh Hall
6978 Haroldstone Hall
6979 Helperly Hall
6980 Llanrumney Hall
6981 Marbury Hall
6982 Melmerby Hall
6983 Otterington Hall
6984 Owsden Hall
6985 Parwick Hall
6986 Rydal Hall
6987 Shervington Hall
6988 Swithland Hall
6989 Wightwick Hall
6990 Witherslack Hall
6991 Acton Burnell Hall
6992 Arborfield Hall
6993 Arthog Hall
6994 Baggrave Hall
6995 Benthall Hall
6996 Blackwell Hall
6997 Bryn-Ivor Hall
6998 Burton Agnes Hall
6999 Capel Dewi Hall

4-6-0   4073 Class
" Castle "

7000 Viscount Portal
7001 Sir James Milne
7002 Devizes Castle
7003 Elmley Castle
7004 Eastnor Castle
7005 Lamphey Castle
7006 Lydford Castle
7007 Great Western
7008 Swansea Castle

7009 Athelney Castle
7010 Avondale Castle
7011 Banbury Castle
7012 Barry Castle
7013 Bristol Castle
7014 Caerhays Castle
7015 Carn Brea Castle
7016 Chester Castle
7017 G. J. Churchward
7018 Drysllwyn Castle
7019 Fowey Castle
7020 Gloucester Castle
7021 Haverfordwest Castle
7022 Hereford Castle
7023 Penrice Castle
7024 Powis Castle
7025 Sudeley Castle
7026 Tenby Castle
7027 Thornbury Castle
7028 Cadbury Castle
7029 Clun Castle
7030 Cranbrook Castle
7031 Cromwell's Castle
7032 Denbigh Castle
7033 Hartlebury Castle
7034 Ince Castle
7035 Ogmore Castle
7036 Taunton Castle
7037 Swindon

2-8-2T   7200 Class

7200	7214	7228	7242
7201	7215	7229	7243
7202	7216	7230	7244
7203	7217	7231	7245
7204	7218	7232	7246
7205	7219	7233	7247
7206	7220	7234	7248
7207	7221	7235	7249
7208	7222	7236	7250
7209	7223	7237	7251
7210	7224	7238	7252
7211	7225	7239	7253
7212	7226	7240	
7213	7227	7241	

2-6-0   4300 Class

7300	7306	7312	7318
7301	7307	7313	7319
7302	7308	7314	7320
7303	7309	7315	7321
7304	7310	7316	
7305	7311	7317	

0-6-0PT   7400 Class

7400	7413	7426	7438
7401	7414	7427	7439
7402	7415	7428	7440
7403	7416	7429	7441
7404	7417	7430	7442
7405	7418	7431	7443
7406	7419	7432	7444
7407	7420	7433	7445
7408	7421	7434	7446
7409	7422	7435	7447
7410	7423	7436	7448
7411	7424	7437	7449
7412	7425		

0-6-0PT   5700 Class

7700	7721	7742	7763
7701	7722	7743	7764
7702	7723	7744	7765
7703	7724	7745	7766
7704	7725	7746	7767
7705	7726	7747	7768
7706	7727	7748	7769
7707	7728	7749	7770
7708	7729	7750	7771
7709	7730	7751	7772
7710	7731	7752	7773
7711	7732	7753	7774
7712	7733	7754	7775
7713	7734	7755	7776
7714	7735	7756	7777
7715	7736	7757	7778
7716	7737	7758	7779
7717	7738	7759	7780
7718	7739	7760	7781
7719	7740	7761	7782
7720	7741	7762	7783

7784	7788	7792	7796
7785	7789	7793	7797
7786	7790	7794	7798
7787	7791	7795	7799

4-6-0   7800 Class
" Manor "

7800 Torquay Manor
7801 Anthony Manor
7802 Bradley Manor
7803 Barcote Manor
7804 Baydon Manor
7805 Broome Manor
7806 Cockington Manor
7807 Compton Manor
7808 Cookham Manor
7809 Childrey Manor
7810 Draycott Manor
7811 Dunley Manor
7812 Erlestoke Manor
7813 Freshford Manor
7814 Fringford Manor
7815 Fritwell Manor
7816 Frilsham Manor
7817 Garsington Manor
7818 Granville Manor
7819 Hinton Manor
7820 Dinmore Manor
7821 Ditcheat Manor
7822 Foxcote Manor
7823 Hook Norton Manor
7824 Iford Manor
7825 Lechlade Manor
7826 Longworth Manor
7827 Lydham Manor
7828 Odney Manor
7829 Ramsbury Manor

4-6-0   6959 Class
" Modified Hall "

7900 Saint Peter's Hall
7901 Dodington Hall
7902 Eaton Mascot Hall
7903 Foremarke Hall
7904 Fountains Hall

7905 Fowey Hall
7906 Fron Hall
7907 Hart Hall
7908 Henshall Hall
7909 Heveningham Hall
7910 Hown Hall
7911 Lady Margaret Hall
7912 Little Linford Hall
7913 Little Wyrley Hall
7914 Lleweni Hall
7915 Mere Hall
7916 Mobberley Hall
7917 North Aston Hall
7918 Rhose Wood Hall
7919 Runter Hall
7920 Coney Hall
7921 Edstone Hall
7922 Salford Hall
7923 Speke Hall
7924 Thornycroft Hall
7925 Westol Hall
7926 Willey Hall
7927 Willington Hall
7928 Wolf Hall
7929 Wyke Hall

2-6-2T   8100 Class

8100	8103	8106	8108
8101	8104	8107	8109
8102	8105		

0-6-0PT   9400 Class

8400	8414	8428	8442
8401	8415	8429	8443
8402	8416	8430	8444
8403	8417	8431	8445
8404	8418	8432	8446
8405	8419	8433	8447
8406	8420	8434	8448
8407	8421	8435	8449
8408	8422	8436	8450
8409	8423	8437	8451
8410	8424	8438	8452
8411	8425	8439	8453
8412	8426	8440	8454
8413	8427	8441	8455

8456	8467	8478	8489
8457	8468	8479	8490
8458	8469	8480	8491
8459	8470	8481	8492
8460	8471	8482	8493
8461	8472	8483	8494
8462	8473	8484	8495
8463	8474	8485	8496
8464	8475	8486	8497
8465	8476	8487	8498
8466	8477	8488	8499

0-6-0PT   5700 Class

8700	8725	8750	8775
8701	8726	8751	8776
8702	8727	8752	8777
8703	8728	8753	8778
8704	8729	8754	8779
8705	8730	8755	8780
8706	8731	8756	8781
8707	8732	8757	8782
8708	8733	8758	8783
8709	8734	8759	8784
8710	8735	8760	8785
8711	8736	8761	8786
8712	8737	8762	8787
8713	8738	8763	8788
8714	8739	8764	8789
8715	8740	8765	8790
8716	8741	8766	8791
8717	8742	8767	8792
8718	8743	8768	8793
8719	8744	8769	8794
8720	8745	8770	8795
8721	8746	8771	8796
8722	8747	8772	8797
8723	8748	8773	8798
8724	8749	8774	8799

4-4-0   9000 Class

9000	9010	9016	9023
9002	9011	9017	9024
9003	9012	9018	9025
9004	9013	9020	9026
9005	9014	9021	9027
9008	9015	9022	9028
9009			

2-6-0   4300 Class

9300	9305	9310	9315
9301	9306	9311	9316
9302	9307	9312	9317
9303	9308	9313	9318
9304	9309	9314	9319

0-6-0PT   9400 Class

9400	9425	9450	9475
9401	9426	9451	9476
9402	9427	9452	9477
9403	9428	9453	9478
9404	9429	9454	9479
9405	9430	9455	9480
9406	9431	9456	9481
9407	9432	9457	9482
9408	9433	9458	9483
9409	9434	9459	9484
9410	9435	9460	9485
9411	9436	9461	9486
9412	9437	9462	9487
9413	9438	9463	9483
9414	9439	9464	9489
9415	9440	9465	9490
9416	9441	9466	9491
9417	9442	9467	9492
9418	9443	9468	9493
9419	9444	9469	9494
9420	9445	9470	9495
9421	9446	9471	9496
9422	9447	9472	9497
9423	9448	9473	9498
9424	9449	9474	9499

0-6-0PT   5700 Class

9600	9611	9622	9633
9601	9612	9623	9634
9602	9613	9624	9635
9603	9614	9625	9636
9604	9615	9626	9637
9605	9616	9627	9638
9606	9617	9628	9639
9607	9618	9629	9640
9608	9619	9630	9641
9609	9620	9631	9642
9610	9621	9632	9643

9644	9679	9731	9766
9645	9680	9732	9767
9646	9681	9733	9768
9647	9682	9734	9769
9648	9700	9735	9770
9649	9701	9736	9771
9650	9702	9737	9772
9651	9703	9738	9773
9652	9704	9739	9774
9653	9705	9740	9775
9654	9706	9741	9776
9655	9707	9742	9777
9656	9708	9743	9778
9657	9709	9744	9779
9658	9710	9745	9780
9659	9711	9746	9781
9660	9712	9747	9782
9661	9713	9748	9783
9662	9714	9749	9784
9663	9715	9750	9785
9664	9716	9751	9786
9665	9717	9752	9787
9666	9718	9753	9788
9667	9719	9754	9789
9668	9720	9755	9790
9669	9721	9756	9791
9670	9722	9757	9792
9671	9723	9758	9793
9672	9724	9759	9794
9673	9725	9760	9795
9674	9726	9761	9796
9675	9727	9762	9797
9676	9728	9763	9798
9677	9729	9764	9799
9678	9730	9765	

SERVICE LOCOMOTIVES

Petrol

22, 23, 24, 26 and 27

Total 5

43

STREAM-LINED DIESEL RAIL-CARS

Car No.	Date	Engines	Total b.h.p.	Seats	Car No.	Date	Engines	Total b.h.p.	Seats
1	1934	1	121	69	18§	1937	2	242	70
3/4*	1934	2	242	44	19-21/3-32	1940	2	210	48
5-7	1935	2	242	70	33	1941	2	210	48
8	1936	2	242	70	34‡	1941	2	210	—
10-12†	1936	2	242	63	35, 36‖	1941	4	420	104
13-16	1936	2	242	70	22, 38‖	1942	4	420	104
17‡	1936	2	242	—					

* Buffet and lavatory facilities.
† Lavatory facilities
‡ Parcels cars.
§ Experimentally geared to haul trailer car, became prototype of subsequent designs.

‖ Twin-coach units with buffet and lavatory facilities. Adjoining statistics apply per 2-car unit. When new, some of these units worked as 3-car rakes by the addition of an ordinary 70 ft. corridor coach.

1	6	11	15	19	23	27	31	35
3	7	12	16	20	24	28	32	36
4	8	13	17	21	25	29	33	38
5	10	14	18	22	26	30	34	

BRITISH RAILWAYS STANDARD LOCOMOTIVES

Chief Officer (Mechanical Engineering) :

R. C. BOND.

4-6-2 Class 7MT

Introduced 1951. Designed at Derby.
Weights : Loco. 94 tons 0 cwt.
          Tender 47 tons 4 cwt.
Pressure : 250 lb. Su.
Cyls. : (O) 20″ × 28″.
Driving Wheels : 6′ 2″. T.E. : 32,150 lb.
Walschaerts gear. P.V.

70000	Britannia
70001	Lord Hurcomb
70002	Geoffrey Chaucer
70003	John Bunyan
70004	William Shakespeare
70005	John Milton
70006	Robert Burns
70007	Coeur-de-Lion
70008	Black Prince
70009	Alfred the Great
70010	Owen Glendower
70011	Hotspur
70012	John of Gaunt
70013	Oliver Cromwell
70014	Iron Duke
70015	Apollo
70016	Ariel
70017	Arrow
70018	Flying Dutchman
70019	Lightning
70020	Mercury
70021	Morning Star
70022	Tornado
70023	Venus
70024	Vulcan
70025	Western Star
70026	Polar Star
70027	Rising Star
70028	Royal Star
70029	Shooting Star
70030	William Wordsworth
70031	Byron
70032	Tennyson
70033	Charles Dickens
70034	Thomas Hardy

70035	Rudyard Kipling
70036	Boadicea
70037	Hereward the Wake
70038	Robin Hood
70039	Sir Christopher Wren
70040	Clive of India
70041	Sir John Moore
70042	Lord Roberts
70043	Earl Kitchener
70044	Earl Haig
70045	
70046	
70047	
70048	
70049	
70050	
70051	
70052	
70053	
70054	

Engines of this class are still being delivered. The names of Nos. 70043/4 are temporarily not affixed.

4-6-2   Class 8P

Introduced 1954. Designed at Derby.
Weights : Loco. 101 tons 5 cwt.
            Tender 55 tons 10 cwt.
Pressure : 250 lb. Su.
Cyls. : (3) 18″ × 28″.
Driving Wheels : 6′ 2″. T.E. : 39,080 lb.
Caprotti valve gear.

71000 Duke of Gloucester

4-6-2   Class 6MT

Introduced 1952. Designed at Derby.
Weights : Loco. 86 tons 19 cwt.
            Tender 47 tons 4 cwt.
Pressure : 225 lb. Su.
Cyls. : (O) 19½″ × 28″.
Driving Wheels : 6′ 2″. T.E. : 27,520 lb.
Walschaerts gear. P.V.

72000	Clan Buchanan
72001	Clan Cameron
72002	Clan Campbell
72003	Clan Fraser
72004	Clan Macdonald

72005	Clan Macgregor
72006	Clan Mackenzie
72007	Clan Mackintosh
72008	Clan Macleod
72009	Clan Stewart

Total 10

4-6-0   Class 5MT

Introduced 1951. Designed at Doncaster.
Weights : Loco. 76 tons 4 cwt.
            Tender 47 tons 4 cwt.
Pressure : 225 lb. Su.
Cyls. : (O) 19″ × 28″.
Driving Wheels : 6′ 2″. T.E. : 26,120 lb.
Walschaerts gear. P.V.

73000	73019	73038	73057
73001	73020	73039	73058
73002	73021	73040	73059
73003	73022	73041	73060
73004	73023	73042	73061
73005	73024	73043	73062
73006	73025	73044	73063
73007	73026	73045	73064
73008	73027	73046	73065
73009	73028	73047	73066
73010	73029	73048	73067
73011	73030	73049	73068
73012	73031	73050	73069
73013	73032	73051	73070
73014	73033	73052	73071
73015	73034	73053	73072
73016	73035	73054	73073
73017	73036	73055	73074
73018	73037	73056	

Engines of this class are still being delivered.

4-6-0   Class 4MT

Introduced 1951. Designed at Brighton.
Weights : Loco. 69 tons 0 cwt.
            Tender 43 tons 3 cwt.
Pressure : 225 lb. Su.
Cyls. : (O) 18″ × 28″.
Driving Wheels : 5′ 8″. T.E. : 25,100 lb.
Walschaerts gear. P.V.

75000	75005	75010	75015
75001	75006	75011	75016
75002	75007	75012	75017
75003	75008	75013	75018
75004	75009	75014	75019

75020	75035	75050	75065
75021	75036	75051	75066
75022	75037	75052	75067
75023	75038	75053	75068
75024	75039	75054	75069
75025	75040	75055	75070
75026	75041	75056	75071
75027	75042	75057	75072
75028	75043	75058	75073
75029	75044	75059	75074
75030	75045	75060	75075
75031	75046	75061	75076
75032	75047	75062	75077
75033	75048	75063	75078
75034	75049	75064	75079

Engines of this class are still being delivered.

2-6-0　　　　　Class 4MT

Introduced 1953. Designed at Doncaster.
Weights : Loco.　59 tons 2 cwt.
　　　　　Tender 42 tons 3 cwt.
Pressure : 225 lb. Su.
Cyls. : (O) 17½″ × 26″.
Driving Wheels : 5′ 3″. T.E. : 24,170 lb.
Walschaerts gear. P.V.

76000	76012	76024	76036
76001	76013	76025	76037
76002	76014	76026	76038
76003	76015	76027	76039
76004	76016	76028	76040
76005	76017	76029	76041
76006	76018	76030	76042
76007	76019	76031	76043
76008	76020	76032	76044
76009	76021	76033	
76010	76022	76034	
76011	76023	76035	

Engines of this class are still being delivered.

2-6-0　　　　　Class 3MT

Introduced 1954.
Weights : Loco. 57 tons 9 cwt.
　　　　　Tender 42 tons 3 cwt.
Pressure : 200 lb. Su.
Cyls. : (O) 17½″ × 26″.
Driving Wheels : 5′ 3″. T.E. : 21,490 lb.
Walschaerts gear. P.V.

77000	77003	77006	77009
77001	77004	77007	77010
77002	77005	77008	77011
77012	77014	77016	77018
77013	77015	77017	77019

2-6-0　　　　　Class 2MT

Introduced 1953. Designed at Derby.
Weights : Loco.　49 tons 5 cwt.
　　　　　Tender 36 tons 17 cwt.
Pressure : 200 lb. Su.
Cyls. : (O) 16½″ × 24″.
Driving Wheels : 5′ 0″. T.E. : 15,515 lb.
Walschaerts gear. P.V.

78000	78012	78024	78036
78001	78013	78025	78037
78002	78014	78026	78038
78003	78015	78027	78039
78004	78016	78028	78040
78005	78017	78029	78041
78006	78018	78030	78042
78007	78019	78031	78043
78008	78020	78032	78044
78009	78021	78033	
78010	78022	78034	
78011	78023	78035	

Engines of this class are still being delivered.

2-6-4T　　　　Class 4MT

Introduced 1951. Designed at Brighton.
Weight : 88 tons 10 cwt.
Pressure : 225 lb.
Cyls. : (O) 18″ × 28″.
Driving Wheels : 5′ 8″. T.E. : 25,100 lb.
Walschaerts gear. P.V.

80000	80019	80038	80057
80001	80020	80039	80058
80002	80021	80040	80059
80003	80022	80041	80060
80004	80023	80042	80061
80005	80024	80043	80062
80006	80025	80044	80063
80007	80026	80045	80064
80008	80027	80046	80065
80009	80028	80047	80066
80010	80029	80048	80067
80011	80030	80049	80068
80012	80031	80050	80069
80013	80032	80051	80070
80014	80033	80052	80071
80015	80034	80053	80072
80016	80035	80054	80073
80017	80036	80055	80074
80018	80037	80056	80075

80076	80086	80096	80106
80077	80087	80097	80107
80078	80088	80098	80108
80079	80089	80099	80109
80080	80090	80100	80110
80081	80091	80101	80111
80082	80092	80102	80112
80083	80093	80103	80113
80084	80094	80104	80114
80085	80095	80105	80115

Engines of this class are still being delivered.

2-6-2T   Class 3MT

Introduced 1952. Designed at Swindon.
Weight : 73 tons 10 cwt.
Pressure : 200 lb. Su.
Cyls. : (O) 17½″ × 26″.
Driving Wheels : 5′ 3″. T.E. : 21,490 lb.
Walschaerts gear. P.V.

82000	82012	82024	82036
82001	82013	82025	82037
82002	82014	82026	82038
82003	82015	82027	82039
82004	82016	82028	82040
82005	82017	82029	82041
82006	82018	82030	82042
82007	82019	82031	82043
82008	82020	82032	82044
82009	82021	82033	
82010	82022	82034	
82011	82023	82035	

Engines of this class are still being delivered.

2-6-2T   Class 2MT

Introduced 1953. Designed at Derby.
Weight : 63 tons 5 cwt.
Pressure : 200 lb. Su.
Cyls. : (O) 16½″ × 24″.
Driving Wheels : 5′ 0″. T.E. : 18,515 lb.
Walschaerts gear. P.V.

84000	84008	84016	84024
84001	84009	84017	84025
84002	84010	84018	84026
84003	84011	84019	84027
84004	84012	84020	84028
84005	84013	84021	84029
84006	84014	84022	
84007	84015	84023	

2-8-0   BF   Class WD

Ministry of Supply " Austerity " 2-8-0
   locomotives purchased by British
   Railways, 1948.
Introduced 1943. Riddles M.o.S. design.
Weights : Loco.   70 tons 5 cwt.
               Tender 55 tons 10 cwt.
Pressure : 225 lb. Cyls. : (O) 19″ × 28″.
Driving Wheels : 4′ 8½″. T.E. : 34,215 lb
Walschaerts gear. P.V.

90000	90039	90078	90117
90001	90040	90079	90118
90002	90041	90080	90119
90003	90042	90081	90120
90004	90043	90082	90121
90005	90044	90083	90122
90006	90045	90084	90123
90007	90046	90085	90124
90008	90047	90086	90125
90009	90048	90087	90126
90010	90049	90088	90127
90011	90050	90089	90128
90012	90051	90090	90129
90013	90052	90091	90130
90014	90053	90092	90131
90015	90054	90093	90132
90016	90055	90094	90133
90017	90056	90095	90134
90018	90057	90096	90135
90019	90058	90097	90136
90020	90059	90098	90137
90021	90060	90099	90138
90022	90061	90100	90139
90023	90062	90101	90140
90024	90063	90102	90141
90025	90064	90103	90142
90026	90065	90104	90143
90027	90066	90105	90144
90028	90067	90106	90145
90029	90068	90107	90146
90030	90069	90108	90147
90031	90070	90109	90148
90032	90071	90110	90149
90033	90072	90111	90150
90034	90073	90112	90151
90035	90074	90113	90152
90036	90075	90114	90153
90037	90076	90115	90154
90038	90077	90116	90155

90156	90204	90252	90300	90348	90396	90444	90492
90157	90205	90253	90301	90349	90397	90445	90493
90158	90206	90254	90302	90350	90398	90446	90494
90159	90207	90255	90303	90351	90399	90447	90495
90160	90208	90256	90304	90352	90400	90448	90496
90161	90209	90257	90305	90353	90401	90449	90497
90162	90210	90258	90306	90354	90402	90450	90498
90163	90211	90259	90307	90355	90403	90451	90499
90164	90212	90260	90308	90356	90404	90452	90500
90165	90213	90261	90309	90357	90405	90453	90501
90166	90214	90262	90310	90358	90406	90454	90502
90167	90215	90263	90311	90359	90407	90455	90503
90168	90216	90264	90312	90360	90408	90456	90504
90169	90217	90265	90313	90361	90409	90457	90505
90170	90218	90266	90314	90362	90410	90458	90506
90171	90219	90267	90315	90363	90411	90459	90507
90172	90220	90268	90316	90364	90412	90460	90508
90173	90221	90269	90317	90365	90413	90461	90509
90174	90222	90270	90318	90366	90414	90462	90510
90175	90223	90271	90319	90367	90415	90463	90511
90176	90224	90272	90320	90368	90416	90464	90512
90177	90225	90273	90321	90369	90417	90465	90513
90178	90226	90274	90322	90370	90418	90466	90514
90179	90227	90275	90323	90371	90419	90467	90515
90180	90228	90276	90324	90372	90420	90468	90516
90181	90229	90277	90325	90373	90421	90469	90517
90182	90230	90278	90326	90374	90422	90470	90518
90183	90231	90279	90327	90375	90423	90471	90519
90184	90232	90280	90328	90376	90424	90472	90520
90185	90233	90281	90329	90377	90425	90473	90521
90186	90234	90282	90330	90378	90426	90474	90522
90187	90235	90283	90331	90379	90427	90475	90523
90188	90236	90284	90332	90380	90428	90476	90524
90189	90237	90285	90333	90381	90429	90477	90525
90190	90238	90286	90334	90382	90430	90478	90526
90191	90239	90287	90335	90383	90431	90479	90527
90192	90240	90288	90336	90384	90432	90480	90528
90193	90241	90289	90337	90385	90433	90481	90529
90194	90242	90290	90338	90386	90434	90482	90530
90195	90243	90291	90339	90387	90435	90483	90531
90196	90244	90292	90340	90388	90436	90484	90532
90197	90245	90293	90341	90389	90437	90485	90533
90198	90246	90294	90342	90390	90438	90486	90534
90199	90247	90295	90343	90391	90439	90487	90535
90200	90248	90296	90344	90392	90440	90488	90536
90201	90249	90297	90345	90393	90441	90489	90537
90202	90250	90298	90346	90394	90442	90490	90538
90203	90251	90299	90347	90395	90443	90491	90539

4300 Class 2-6-0 No. 6322. [G. Wheeler

6300 Class 2-6-0 No. 9303 (with side-window cab). [A. R. Carpenter

R.O.D. Class 2-8-0 No. 3012. [R. K. Evans

4700 Class 2-9-0 No. 4705.   [A. R. Carpenter

2800 Class 2-8-0 No. 2883.   [R. K. Evans

2800 Class 2-8-0 No. 3840 (with side-window cab).   [R. H. G. Simpson

2301 Class 0-6-0 No. 2532.　　　　　　　　　　　　　　[P. J. Lynch

Ex-Cambrian 0-6-0 No. 849 (rebuilt by G.W.R.).　　　　[T. J. Saunders

2251 Class 0-6-0 No. 2250　　　　　　　　　　　　　[R. H. G. Simpson

9000 Class 4-4-0 No. 9005.   [*F. W. Day*

4200 Class 2-8-0T No. 4284.   [*R. K. Evans*

5205 Class 2-8-0T No. 5260.   [*G. Wheeler*

7200 Class 2-8-2T No. 7222. [A. R. Carpenter

7200 Class 2-8-2T No. 7212 (with running plate raised over cylinders) [R. K. Evans

Ex-M.S.W.J. 2-4-0 No. 1336 (now scrapped). [A. R. Carpenter

Left: Ex-A.D. 2-6-2T No. 1205.   [*R. K. Evans*

Centre: 3100 Class 2-6-2T No. 3100.   [*G. Wheeler*

Bottom: 6100 Class 2-6-2T No. 6152.   [*R. K. Evans*

Right: 4575 Class 2-6-2T
No. 5500.   [G. Wheeler

Centre: 4400 Class 2-6-2T
No. 4401.   [G. Wheeler

Bottom: 5800 Class 0-4-2T
No. 5800.   [L. Elsey

Diesel Railcar No. 1.   [A. R. Carpenter

Diesel Railcar No. 20.   [P. J. Lynch

Gas Turbine-Electric A-1-A-A-1-A No. 18000 (Brown-Boveri).   [R. H. G. Simpson

90540	90587	90634	90681
90541	90588	90635	90682
90542	90589	90636	90683
90543	90590	90637	90684
90544	90591	90638	90685
90545	90592	90639	90686
90546	90593	90640	90687
90547	90594	90641	90688
90548	90595	90642	90689
90549	90596	90643	90690
90550	90597	90644	90691
90551	90598	90645	90692
90552	90599	90646	90693
90553	90600	90647	90694
90554	90601	90648	90695
90555	90602	90649	90696
90556	90603	90650	90697
90557	90604	90651	90698
90558	90605	90652	90699
90559	90606	90653	90700
90560	90607	90654	90701
90561	90608	90655	90702
90562	90609	90656	90703
90563	90610	90657	90704
90564	90611	90658	90705
90565	90612	90659	90706
90566	90613	90660	90707
90567	90614	90661	90708
90568	90615	90662	90709
90569	90616	90663	90710
90570	90617	90664	90711
90571	90618	90665	90712
90572	90619	90666	90713
90573	90620	90667	90714
90574	90621	90668	90715
90575	90622	90669	90716
90576	90623	90670	90717
90577	90624	90671	90718
90578	90625	90672	90719
90579	90626	90673	90720
90580	90627	90674	90721
90581	90628	90675	90722
90582	90629	90676	90723
90583	90630	90677	90724
90584	90631	90678	90725
90585	90632	90679	90726
90586	90633	90680	90727

90728	90730	90732
90729	90731	Vulcan

Total 733

2-10-0 8F Class WD

Ministry of Supply " Austerity " 2-10-0 locomotives purchased by British Railways, 1948.

Introduced 1943. Riddles M.o.S. design.
Weights : Loco. 78 tons 6 cwt.
Tender 55 tons 10 cwt.
Pressure : 225 lb. Cyls. : (O) 19″ × 28″.
Driving Wheels : 4′ 8½″. T.E. : 34,215 lb
Walschaerts gear. P.V.

90750	90757	90764	90771
90751	90758	90765	90772
90752	90759	90766	90773
90753	90760	90767	90774
90754	90761	90768	
90755	90762	90769	
90756	90763	90770	

Total 25

2-10-0 Class 9F

Introduced 1954. Designed at Crewe.
Weights : Loco. 86 tons 14 cwt.
Tender 52 tons 10 cwt.
Pressure : 250 lb.
Cyls. : (O) 20″ × 28″.
Driving Wheels : 5′ 0″. T.E. : 39,670 lb.
Walschaerts gear. P.V.

92000	92010	92020	92030
92001	92011	92021	92031
92002	92012	92022	92032
92003	92013	92023	92033
92004	92014	92024	92034
92005	92015	92025	92035
92006	92016	92026	92036
92007	92017	92027	92037
92008	92018	92028	92038
92009	92019	92029	92039

Engines of this class are still being delivered.

POWER AND WEIGHT CLASSIFICATION

Since 1920 Western Region locomotives have been classified for power and weight by a letter on a coloured disc on the cab side. The letter represents the power of the locomotive, and is approximately proportional to the tractive effort as under

Power class	Tractive effort lb.	Power class	Tractive effort lb.
Special	Over 38,000	B	18,501–20,500
E	33,001–38,000	A	16,500–18,500
D	25,001–33,000	Un-grouped	
C	20,501–25,000		Below 16,500

The colour of the circle represents the routes over which the engine may work. Red engines are limited to the main lines and lines capable of carrying the heaviest locomotives ; blue engines are allowed over additional routes, yellow engines over nearly the whole system and uncoloured engines are more or less unrestricted. The double red circles on the "King" class represent special restrictions for these engines.

Class	Power Class	Route Restriction Colour
4-6-0		
1000	D	Red
4000	D	Red
4073	D	Red
4900	D	Red
6000	Special	Double Red
6800	D	Red
6959	D	Red
7800	D	Blue
4-4-0		
9000	B	Yellow
2-8-0		
2800	E	Blue
R.O.D.	D	Blue
4700	D	Red
2-6-0		
4300	D	Blue
9300-19		Red
0-6-0		
2251	B	Yellow
2301	A	—
(844)	A	Yellow
2-8-2T		
7200	E	Red
2-8-0T		
4200	E	Red
2-6-2T		
3100	E	Red
3150	D	Red
4400	C	—
4500	C	Yellow
5100	D	Blue
6100	D	Blue
8100	D	Blue
(1205)	C	Yellow
(7)	—	—
0-6-2T		
5600	D	Red
(35)	D	Red

Class	Power Class	Route Restriction Colour
(56)	C	Blue
(82)	B	Blue
(77)	B	Blue
(204)	C	Blue
(303)	C	Red
0-6-0T		
850	—	—
1361	—	—
1366	—	—
1500	C	Red
1600	A	—
2021	A	—
2181	A	—
5400	—	Yellow
5700	C	Yellow
9700-10		Blue
6400	A	Yellow
7400	A	Yellow
9400	C	Red
(666)	B	Blue
(2196)	A	—
(2176)	A	—
(2198)	A	—
(2162)	A	Yellow
(681)	C	Yellow
(93)	C	Red
0-4-2T		
1400	—	—
5800	—	—
0-4-0T		
1101	B	Red
(1338)	—	—
(1151)	—	—
(1153)	A	Yellow
(1140)	—	—
(1143)	—	Blue
(1144)	—	Yellow
(1142)	A	Yellow

APPLICATION TO JOIN THE LOCOSPOTTERS CLUB

(see inside front cover for more details.)

To Join: Note and sign the Club Promise, fill in details below, and post with necessary remittance and stamped addressed envelope (2½d.) to :

IAN ALLAN LOCOSPOTTERS CLUB (LSE),
Craven House, The Green, Hampton Court, Surrey.

THE CLUB RULE: Members of the Locospotters Club will not in any way interfere with railway working or material, nor be a nuisance or hindrance to railway staff, nor, above all, trespass on railway property. No one will be admitted a member of the Club unless he solemnly agrees to keep this rule.

I, the undersigned, do hereby make application to join the Ian Allan Locospotters Club, and undertake on my honour, if this application is accepted, to keep the rule of the Club ; I understand that if I break this rule in any way I cease to be a member and forfeit the right to wear the badge and take part in the Club's activities.

Date.................................195.. Signed...

These details to be completed in BLOCK LETTERS .

SURNAME...DATE OF BIRTH...................19......

CHRISTIAN NAMES ....

ADDRESS ....

....

....

PLEASE MARK WITH CROSS (X) THE BADGE OR BADGES YOU REQUIRE. Remember membership costs 1/3 and entitles you to ONE badge. EACH EXTRA BADGE 6d.

Western Region	...	... Brown	
Southern Region	...	... Green	
London Midland Region	...	Red	
Eastern Region	...	Dark Blue	
North-Eastern Region		Tangerine	
Scottish Region	...	Light Blue	

POSTAL ORDER enclosed, value............... ..:............a.

WHEN SENDING YOUR APPLICATION, AND IN ALL FUTURE CORRESPONDENCE REQUIRING A REPLY, DON'T FORGET THE STAMPED ADDRESSED ENVELOPE.

CUT OUT ALONG THIS LINE

TI DIRECT SUBSCRIPTION SERVICE

By placing a subscription order with the Publisher, a copy of TRAINS ILLUSTRATED printed on art paper will be posted to you direct to reach you on the first of each month. ART PAPER copies are available only by direct subscription.

RATES : Yearly 18/- : 6 months 9/-

NO EXTRA CHARGE IS MADE FOR POSTAGE

* * *

Please supply Trains Illustrated by direct mail for .... issues, for which I enclose remittance for £ : s. d.

Name ....

Address ....

....

....

Ian Allan Ltd

CRAVEN HOUSE
HAMPTON COURT
SURREY

~RAILWAY BOOKS FOR~ CONNOISSEURS

LOCOMOTIVES OF THE PREMIER LINE
O. S. NOCK

It was always the proud boast of the L.N.W.R. that it was the Premier Line; as such it had to have first-class engines. The author here describes the various types, their practice and development, and the reasons for their design. **25/-**

4,000 MILES ON THE FOOTPLATE
O. S. NOCK

This book is really the sequel to *British Locomotives from the Footplate*, and in it the author describes further runs, this time diverging to some extent from the well-known main lines. **17/6**

TITLED TRAINS OF GREAT BRITAIN
CECIL J. ALLEN

This is the fourth edition, and a very much enlarged one, of a book first published in 1946, describing all the named trains which ran and run on British Railways, from their instigation until the present day. **15/-**

THE MIDLAND RAILWAY
C. HAMILTON ELLIS

Describing the growth and operation of the Midland Railway. Fully bound, with colour plates and many black and white illustrations. **25/-**

LOCOMOTIVES OF THE NORTH EASTERN RAILWAY
O. S. NOCK

The North Eastern was the middle partner of the East Coast route partnership and apart from its express services had a most intense coal traffic. This book is a fascinating history of the locomotives of this highly individual railway. **25/-**

Ian Allan Ltd

~CRAVEN HOUSE · HAMPTON COURT · SURREY~

NOTES ON THE USE OF THIS BOOK

1. This book lists and describes British Railways locomotives numbered between 10000 and 39999 and Southern Region electric units. Some British Railways standard locomotives numbered between 70000 and 90000 are in service on the Southern Region and are listed in Parts 1, 3 or 4 of the *ABC of British Railways Locomotives*. The following notes are a guide to the system of reference marks and other details given in the lists of dimensions shown for each class in the alphabetical list of classes.

    (*a*) In the lists of dimensions " Su " indicates a superheated locomotive

    (*b*) Locomotives are fitted with two inside cylinders, slide valves and Stephenson link motion, except where otherwise shown, *e.g.*, (O) indicates outside cylinders and " P.V." piston valves.

    (*c*) The letter " S " following a number indicates a Service Locomotive. On the S.R. (only) this marking appears on the locomotive.

    (*d*) (W) before a number indicates an Isle of Wight locomotive. The " W " is no longer painted on the locomotives, but may still be seen on the bunker numberplate of some of them.

    (*e*) The date on which a design of locomotive first appeared is indicated by " Introduced." Differences between subdivisions of a class can be followed by tracing the appropriate reference mark throughout the details given for that class.

    (*f*) The code given in smaller bold type at the head of each class, *e.g.*, " 4MT " denotes its British Railways power classification.

2. Southern electric units are listed on pp. 60-66.

3. The details given in this book are correct to May 13th, 1954.

THE **ABC** OF
BRITISH RAILWAYS
LOCOMOTIVES

PART 2—Nos. 10000-39999

also S.R. Electric Train Units.

SUMMER
1954
EDITION

LONDON :

Ian Allan Ltd

BRITISH RAILWAYS
MOTIVE POWER DEPOTS AND CODES

**(ALL B.R. LOCOMOTIVES CARRY THE CODE OF THEIR HOME DEPOT
ON SMALL PLATES AFFIXED TO THEIR SMOKEBOX DOORS.)**

LONDON MIDLAND REGION

1A	**Willesden**	9B	Stockport	19A	**Sheffield**
1B	Camden		(Edgeley)	19B	Millhouses
1C	Watford	9C	Macclesfield	19C	Canklow
1D	Devons Road (Bow)	9D	Buxton	20A	**Leeds (Holbeck)**
1E	Bletchley	9E	Trafford Park	20B	Stourton
2A	**Rugby**	9F	Heaton Mersey	20C	Royston
2B	Nuneaton	9G	Northwich	20D	Normanton
2C	Warwick	10A	**Springs Branch**	20E	Manningham
2D	Coventry		**(Wigan)**	20F	Skipton
2E	Northampton	10B	Preston	20G	Hellifield
3A	**Bescot**	10C	Patricroft	21A	**Saltley**
3B	Bushbury	10D	Plodder Lane	21B	Bournville
3C	Walsall	10E	Sutton Oak	21C	Bromsgrove
3D	Aston	11A	**Carnforth**	22A	**Bristol**
3E	Monument Lane	11B	Barrow	22B	Gloucester
5A	**Crewe North**	11C	Oxenholme	24A	**Accrington**
5B	Crewe South	11D	Tebay	24B	Rose Grove
5C	Stafford	11E	Lancaster	24C	Lostock Hall
5D	Stoke	12A	**Carlisle**	24D	Lower Darwen
5E	Alsager		**(Upperby)**	24E	Blackpool
5F	Uttoxeter	12C	Penrith	24F	Fleetwood
6A	**Chester**	12D	Workington	25A	**Wakefield**
6B	Mold Junction	12E	Moor Row	25B	Huddersfield
6C	Birkenhead	14A	**Cricklewood**	25C	Goole
6D	Chester	14B	Kentish Town	25D	Mirfield
	(Northgate)	14C	St. Albans	25E	Sowerby Bridge
6E	Wrexham	15A	**Wellingborough**	25F	Low Moor
6F	Bidston	15B	Kettering	25G	Farnley Junction
6G	Llandudno	15C	Leicester	26A	**Newton Heath**
	Junction	15D	Bedford	26B	Agecroft
6H	Bangor	16A	**Nottingham**	26C	Bolton
6J	Holyhead	16C	Kirkby	26D	Bury
6K	Rhyl	16D	Mansfield	26E	Bacup
8A	**Edge Hill**	17A	**Derby**	26F	Lees
8B	Warrington	17B	Burton	26G	Belle Vue
8C	Speke Junction	17C	Coalville	27A	**Bank Hall**
8D	Widnes	17D	Rowsley	27B	Aintree
8E	Brunswick (L'pool)	18A	**Toton**	27C	Southport
8F	Warrington	18B	Westhouses	27D	Wigan (L. & Y.)
	(C.L.C.)	18C	Hasland	27E	Walton
9A	**Longsight**	18D	Staveley		

MOTIVE POWER DEPOTS AND CODES—*continued*

EASTERN REGION

30A	**Stratford**	32F	Yarmouth Beach	36E	Retford
30B	Hertford East	32G	Melton Constable	37A	**Ardsley**
30C	Bishops Stortford	33A	**Plaistow**	37B	Copley Hill
30D	Southend (Victoria)	33B	Tilbury	37C	Bradford
30E	Colchester	33C	Shoeburyness	38A	**Colwick**
30F	Parkeston	34A	**Kings Cross**	38B	Annesley
31A	**Cambridge**	34B	Hornsey	38C	Leicester
31B	March	34C	Hatfield	38D	Staveley
31C	Kings Lynn	34D	Hitchin	38E	Woodford Halse
31D	South Lynn	34E	Neasden	39A	**Gorton**
31E	Bury St. Edmunds	35A	**New England**	39B	Sheffield (Darnall)
32A	**Norwich**	35B	Grantham	40A	**Lincoln**
32B	Ipswich	35C	Peterborough	40B	Immingham
32C	Lowestoft		(Spital)	40C	Louth
32D	Yarmouth	36A	**Doncaster**	40D	Tuxford
	(South Town)	36B	Mexborough	40E	Langwith Junction
32E	Yarmouth	36C	Frodingham	40F	Boston
	(Vauxhall)	36D	Barnsley		

NORTH EASTERN REGION

50A	**York**	51E	Stockton	52F	North Blyth
50B	Leeds (Neville Hill)	51F	West Auckland	53A	**Hull**
50C	Selby	51G	Haverton Hill		(Dairycoates)
50D	Starbeck	51H	Kirkby Stephen	53B	Hull
50E	Scarborough	51J	Northallerton		(Botanic Gardens)
50F	Malton	51K	Saltburn	53C	Hull (Springhead)
50G	Whitby	52A	**Gateshead**	53D	Bridlington
51A	**Darlington**	52B	Heaton	54A	**Sunderland**
51B	Newport	52C	Blaydon	54B	Tyne Dock
51C	West Hartlepool	52D	Tweedmouth	54C	Borough Gardens
51D	Middlesbrough	52E	Percy Main	54D	Consett

SCOTTISH REGION

60A	**Inverness**	63E	Oban	65H	Helensburgh
60B	Aviemore	64A	**St. Margarets**	65 I	Balloch
60C	Helmsdale		(Edinburgh)	66A	**Polmadie**
60D	Wick	64B	Haymarket		(Glasgow)
60E	Forres	64C	Dalry Road	66B	Motherwell
61A	**Kittybrewster**	64D	Carstairs	66C	Hamilton
61B	Aberdeen	64E	Polmont	66D	Greenock
	(Ferryhill)	64F	Bathgate	67A	**Corkerhill**
61C	Keith	64G	Hawick		(Glasgow)
62A	**Thornton**	65A	**Eastfield**	67B	Hurlford
62B	Dundee		(Glasgow)	67C	Ayr
	(Tay Bridge)	65B	St. Rollox	67D	Ardrossan
62C	Dunfermline	65C	Parkhead	68A	**Carlisle**
	(Upper)	65D	Dawsholm		(Kingmoor)
63A	**Perth South**	65E	Kipps	68B	Dumfries
63B	Stirling	65F	Grangemouth	68C	Stranraer
63C	Forfar	65G	Yoker	68D	Beattock
63D	Fort William			68E	Carlisle (Canal)

3

SOUTHERN REGION

70A	**Nine Elms**	72B	Salisbury
70B	Feltham	72C	Yeovil
70C	Guildford	72D	Plymouth
70D	Basingstoke		Callington
70E	Reading	72E	Barnstaple Junction
71A	**Eastleigh**		Torrington
	Winchester		Ilfracombe
	Lymington	72F	Wadebridge
	Andover Junction	73A	**Stewarts Lane**
71B	Bournemouth	73B	Bricklayers' Arms
	Swanage	73C	Hither Green
	Hamworthy Junction	73D	Gillingham (Kent)
	Branksome	73E	Faversham
71C	Dorchester	74A	**Ashford (Kent)**
	Weymouth		Canterbury West
71D	Fratton	74B	Ramsgate
	Midhurst	74C	Dover
71E	Newport (I.O.W.)		Folkestone
71F	Ryde (I.O.W.)	74D	Tonbridge
71G	Bath (S. & D.)	74E	St. Leonards
	Radstock	75A	**Brighton**
71H	Templecombe		Newhaven
71I	Southampton Docks	75B	Redhill
71J	Highbridge	75C	Norwood Junction
72A	**Exmouth Junction**	75D	Horsham
	Seaton	75E	Three Bridges
	Lyme Regis	75F	Tunbridge Wells West
	Exmouth		
	Okehampton		
	Bude		

WESTERN REGION

81A	**Old Oak Common**	84B	Oxley	86J	Aberdare
		84C	Banbury	86K	Abergavenny
81B	Slough	84D	Leamington Spa	87A	**Neath**
81C	Southall	84E	Tyseley	87B	Duffryn Yard
81D	Reading	84F	Stourbridge	87C	Danygraig
81E	Didcot	84G	Shrewsbury	87D	Swansea
81F	Oxford	84H	Wellington (Salop)		East Dock
82A	**Bristol (Bath Rd.)**	84J	Croes Newydd	87E	Landore
82B	Bristol	84K	Chester	87F	Llanelly
	(St. Philip's Marsh)	85A	**Worcester**	87G	Carmarthen
82C	Swindon	85B	Gloucester	87H	Neyland
82D	Westbury	85C	Hereford	87J	Goodwick
82E	Yeovil	85D	Kidderminster	87K	Swansea (Victoria)
82F	Weymouth	86A	**Newport**	88A	**Cardiff (Cathays)**
83A	**Newton Abbot**		**(Ebbw Jcn.)**	88B	Cardiff East Dock
83B	Taunton	86B	Newport (Pill)	88C	Barry
83C	Exeter	86C	Cardiff (Canton)	88D	Merthyr
83D	Laira (Plymouth)	86D	Llantrisant	88E	Abercynon
83E	St. Blazey	86E	Severn Tunnel	88F	Treherbert
83F	Truro		Junction	89A	**Oswestry**
83G	Penzance	86F	Tondu	89B	Brecon
84A	**Wolverhampton (Stafford Road)**	86G	Pontypool Road	89C	Machynlleth
		86H	Aberbeeg		

BRITISH RAILWAYS NON-STEAM LOCOMOTIVE CLASSES

INTERNAL COMBUSTION LOCOMOTIVES

Co-Co   Diesel Electric

Introduced 1947: English Electric Co. and H. A. Ivatt, main line passenger design for L.M.S.R.
Weight: 121 tons 10 cwt.
Driving Wheels: 3′ 6″.
T.E.: 41,400 lb.
Engine: English Electric Co. 16 cyls. 1,600 h.p.
Motors: Six nose-suspended motors, single reduction gear drive.

10000   10001   **Total 2**

4-8-4   Diesel Mechanical

Introduced 1951: H. G. Ivatt and Fell design for L.M.S.R.
Engines: Four 500 h.p., 12-cylinder.
Transmission: Fell patent differential drive and fluid couplings.
Weight : 120 tons.
Driving Wheels : 4′ 3″.
T.E. : 25,000 lb.

10100   **Total 1**

I Co-Co I   Diesel Elec.

Introduced 1951: English Electric Co. and Bulleid main line passenger design for S.R.
Introduced 1954: Modernised version of above. Engine: English Electric Co. 16 cyls. 1,750 h.p. (2,000 h.p.)
Weight : 135 tons.
Driving Wheels : 3′ 7″.
T.E. : { 48,000 lb.
         { 50,000 lb.*

10201   10202   10203
                              Total 3

Bo-Bo   Diesel Electric

Introduced 1950: N.B. Loco. Co., B.T.H. Co. and H. A. Ivatt, branch line design for L.M.S.R.
Weight: 69 tons 16 cwt.
Driving Wheels: 3′ 6″.
T.E.: 34,500 lb.
Engine: Davey Paxman 16 cyls. 827 h.p.
Motors: Four nose-suspended motors, single reduction gear drive.

10800   **Total 1**

0-6-0   Diesel Mechanical

Introduced 1950: Bulleid S.R. design for shunting and transfer work.
Weight: 49 tons 9 cwt.
Driving Wheels: 4′ 6″.
T.E.: 33,500 lb. (max. in lowgear).
Engine: Davey Paxman 12 cyls. 500 h.p.
Transmission: S.S.S. Powerflow three-speed gearbox and fluid coupling.

11001   **Total 1**

0-6-0   Diesel Mech. DMSI

Introduced 1952 : 200 h.p. locomotives to replace ex-L.N.E.R. tram engines.
Weight : 29 tons 15 cwt.
Driving Wheels : 3′ 3″
T.E. : 16,850 lb.
Engine : Gardner 8L3 type.

11100	11105	11109	11113
11101	11106	11110	11114
11102	11107	11111	11115
11103	11108	11112	

N.B.—Locos of this type are still being delivered.

0-4-0 Diesel Mechanical

To be introduced 1954. 153 h.p. locomotives for E.R. and S.R.

11500	11501	11502	11503

0-4-0 Diesel Hydraulic

Introduced 1953 : N.B. Loco. Co. for North Eastern Region.
Engine : Davey Paxman G.R.P.H.L. 200 h.p.
Weight : 32 tons
Driving Wheels : 3′ 6″.
T.E. : 22,000 lb.

11700	11703	11706
11701	11704	11707
11702	11705	

N.B.—Locos of this type are still being delivered

0-6-0 Diesel Electric

Introduced 1936: English Electric-Hawthorn Leslie design for L.M.S.R.
Weight: ⎰51 tons.*
⎱47 tons.†
Driving Wheels: 4′ 0½″.
T.E.: 30,000 lb.
Engine: English Electric 6 cyls. 350 h.p.
Motors: Two nose-suspended motors, single reduction gear drive.

12000* 12001* 12002† **Total 3**

0-6-0 Diesel Electric

Introduced 1939: English Electric and Stanier design for L.M.S.R., development of previous design with jackshaft drive.
Weight: 54 tons 16 cwt.
Driving Wheels: 4′ 3″
T.E.: 33,000 lb.
Engine: English Electric, 6 cyls. 350 h.p.
Motors: Single motor; jackshaft drive.

12003	12011	12019	12027
12004	12012	12020	12028
12005	12013	12021	12029
12006	12014	12022	12030
12007	12015	12023	12031
12008	12016	12024	12032
12009	12017	12025	**Total**
12010	12018	12026	**30**

0-6-0 Diesel Electric

Introduced 1945: English Electric and Fairburn design for L.M.S.R., development of previous design with double reduction gear drive.

Weight: 50 tons.

Driving Wheels: 4′ 0½″.

T.E.: 33,000 lb.

Engine: English Electric, 6 cyls. 350 h.p.

Motors: Two nose-suspended motors double reduction gear drive.

12033	12060	12087	12114
12034	12061	12088	12115
12035	12062	12089	12116
12036	12063	12090	12117
12037	12064	12091	12118
12038	12065	12092	12119
12039	12066	12093	12120
12040	12067	12094	12121
12041	12068	12095	12122
12042	12069	12096	12123
12043	12070	12097	12124
12044	12071	12098	12125
12045	12072	12099	12126
12046	12073	12100	12127
12047	12074	12101	12128
12048	12075	12102	12129
12049	12076	12103	12130
12050	12077	12104	12131
12051	12078	12105	12132
12052	12079	12106	12133
12053	12080	12107	12134
12054	12081	12108	12135
12055	12082	12109	12136
12056	12083	12110	12137
12057	12084	12111	12138
12058	12085	12112	**Total**
12059	12086	12113	**106**

0-6-0 Diesel Electric

Introduced 1953. B.R. standard design.
Weight : 49 tons.
Driving Wheels : 4′ 6″.
T.E. : 35,000 lb.
Engine : English Electric 6 cyls. 400 h.p.
Motors : Two nose-suspended motors, double reduction gear drive.

13000	13036	13072	13108
13001	13037	13073	13109
13002	13038	13074	13110
13003	13039	13075	13111
13004	13040	13076	13112
13005	13041	13077	13113
13006	13042	13078	13114
13007	13043	13079	13115
13008	13044	13080	13116
13009	13045	13081	13117
13010	13046	13082	13118
13011	13047	13083	13119
13012	13048	13084	13120
13013	13049	13085	13121
13014	13050	13086	13122
13015	13051	13087	13123
13016	13052	13088	13124
13017	13053	13089	13125
13018	13054	13090	13126
13019	13055	13091	13127
13020	13056	13092	13128
13021	13057	13093	13129
13022	13058	13094	13130
13023	13059	13095	13131
13024	13060	13096	13132
13025	13061	13097	13133
13026	13062	13098	13134
13027	13063	13099	13135
13028	13064	13100	13136
13029	13065	13101	13137
13030	13066	13102	13138
13031	13067	13103	13139
13032	13068	13104	
13033	13069	13105	
13034	13070	13106	
13035	13071	13107	

N.B.—Locos of this class are still being delivered.

0-6-0 Diesel Electric DES 1

Introduced 1944: English Electric and Thompson design for L.N.E.R., (L.N.E.R. version of L.M.S. 12033 series).
Weight: 51 tons.
Driving Wheels: 4′ 0″.
T.E.: 32,000 lb.
Engine: English Electric, 6 cyls. 350 h.p.
Motors: Two nose-suspended motors, double reduction gear drive.

15000	15001	15002	15003

Total 4

0-6-0 Diesel Electric DES 2

Introduced 1949: Brush design for E.R.
Weight: 51 tons.
Driving Wheels: 4′ 0″.
T.E.: 32,000 lb.
Engine: Petter 4 cyls. 360 h.p.

15004   **Total 1**

0-4-0 Petrol Class Y11

Introduced 1921: Motor, Rail and Tram Car Co., design (purchased by N.B.R. and L.N.E.R.).
Weight: 8 tons.
Driving Wheels: 3′ 1″.
Engine: 4 cyls. 40 h.p. petrol.
Drive: Chains and two-speed gear box.

15093   15099   **Total 2**

0-6-0 Diesel Electric

Introduced 1936: Hawthorn Leslie and English Electric design for G.W.R. (G.W.R. version of L.M.S.R. Nos. 12000/1).
Weight: 51 tons 10 cwt.
Driving Wheels: 4′ 1″.
T.E.: 30,000 lb.
Engine: English Electric 6 cyls. 350 h.p.
Motors: Two nose-suspended motors, single reduction gear drive.

15100   **Total 1**

0-6-0   Diesel Electric

Introduced 1948: English Electric and Hawksworth design for Western Region (W.R. version of L.M.S. 12033 series).
Weight: 46 tons 9 cwt.
Driving Wheels: 4' 0½".
T.E.: 33,500 lb.
Engine: English Electric 6 cyls. 350 h.p.
Motors: Two nose-suspended motors, single reduction gear drive.

15101	15103	15105	
15102	15104	15106	**Total 6**

0-6-0   Diesel Electric

Introduced 1949: Brush design for W.R.

15107   **Total I**

0-6-0   Diesel Electric

Introduced 1937: English Electric and Bulleid design for S.R.
Weight: 55 tons 5 cwt.
Driving Wheels: 4' 6".
T.E.: 30,000 lb.
Engine: English Electric 6 cyls. 350 h.p.
Motors: Two nose-suspended motors, single reduction gear drive.

15201   15202   15203   **Total 3**

0-6-0   Diesel Electric

Introduced 1949: English Electric and Bulleid design for S.R. (S.R. version of L.M.S.R. 12033 series, but designed for higher speeds).
Weight: 49 tons.
Driving Wheels: 4' 6".
T.E.: 24,000 lb.
Engine: English Electric 6 cyls. 350 h.p.
Motors: Two nose-suspended motors, double reduction gear drive.

15211	15218	15225	15232
15212	15219	15226	15233
15213	15220	15227	15234
15214	15221	15228	15235
15215	15222	15229	15236
15216	15223	15230	
15217	15224	15231	

Total 26

A-I-A-A-I-A   Gas Turbine

Introduced 1949: Brown Boveri (Switzerland) design for W.R.
Weight: 115 tons.
Driving Wheels: 4' 0½".
T.E.: 31,500 lb. at 21 m.p.h.
Engine: 2,500 h.p. gas turbine.
Motors: Four independently mounted motors with spring drive.

18000   **Total I**

Co-Co   Gas Turbine

Introduced 1951.
Metropolitan-Vickers and Hawksworth design for G.W.R.
Weight: 129 tons 10 cwt.
Driving Wheels: 3' 8".
T.E.: maximum 60,000 lb. Continuous rating : 30,000.lb
Motors: Six nose-suspended motors with single reduction gear drive.

18100   **Total I**

ELECTRIC LOCOMOTIVES

Co-Co   Class CC

*Introduced 1941: Raworth & Bulleid design for S.R.
†Introduced 1948: Later design with detail differences.
Weight: { 99 tons 14 cwt.*
{ 104 tons 14 cwt.†
Driving Wheels: 3′ 7″.
T.E.: { 40,000 lb.*
{ 45,000 lb.†
Voltage: 660 D.C.
Current Collection: Overhead and third rail, with flywheel-driven generator for gaps in third rail.

20001*	20002*	20003†
		Total 3

Bo-Bo   Class EM1

*Introduced 1941: Metropolitan-Vickers and Gresley design for L.N.E.R.
Remainder. Introduced 1950.
Production design with detail alterations.
Weight: 87 tons 18 cwt.
Driving Wheels: 4′ 2″.
T.E.: 45,000 lb.   Voltage: 1,500 D.C.
Current Collection : overhead.

26000*	26015	26030	26045
26001	26016	26031	26046
26002	26017	26032	26047
26003	26018	26033	26048
26004	26019	26034	26049
26005	26020	26035	26050
26006	26021	26036	26051
26007	26022	26037	26052
26008	26023	26038	26053
26009	26024	26039	26054
26010	26025	26040	26055
26011	26026	26041	26056
26012	26027	26042	26057
26013	26028	26043	**Total**
26014	26029	26044	**58**

Bo-Bo   Class ES1

Built 1902: Brush & Thomson-Houston shunting design for N.E.R.
Weight: 46 tons.
Voltage: 600 D.C.   T.E.: 25,000 lb.

26500	26501 **Total 2**

Bo-Bo   Class EB1

EB1 Introduced 1946: L.N.E.R. rebuild of N.E.R. Raven freight design (Introduced 1914) for banking work on Manchester-Wath line.
Weight: 74 tons 8 cwt.
Driving Wheels: 4′ 0″.
T.E.: 37,600 lb.   Voltage: 1,500 D.C.
Current collection: overhead.

26510   **Total 1**

Co-Co   Class EM2

Introduced 1954: Metropolitan-Vickers and L.N.E.R. design, development of E.M.I. with six axles and higher speed range.
Weight: 102 tons.
Driving Wheels: 4′ 2″.
T.E.: 45,000 lb.   Voltage: 1,500 D.C.
Current Collection: Overhead.

27000	27007	27014	27021
27001	27008	27015	27022
27002	27009	27016	27023
27003	27010	27017	27024
27004	27011	27018	27025
27005	27012	27019	27026
27006	27013	27020	

NOTE: Locomotives of this class are still being delivered.

SUMMARY OF SOUTHERN REGION STEAM LOCOMOTIVE CLASSES
IN ALPHABETICAL ORDER
WITH HISTORICAL NOTES AND DIMENSIONS

Classes
0-6-0T OP A1 & A1X

*A1 Introduced 1872: Stroudley L.B.S.C. "Terrier," later fitted with Marsh boiler, retaining original type smokebox.

†A1X Introduced 1911: Rebuild of A1 with Marsh boiler and extended smokebox.

‡A1X Loco. with increased cylinder diameter.

Weight: { 27 tons 10 cwt.*†
         { 28 tons 5 cwt.†‡
Pressure: 150 lb. Cyls. { 12″ × 20″*†
                        { 14¾″ × 20″‡
Driving Wheels: 4′ 0″.
T.E.: { 7,650 lb.*†
      { 10,695 lb.‡

*DS680

†DS377 DS681, 32640/6/50/5/61 /2/70/7/8.

‡32636

Totals: A1 1
A1X 12

0-4-0T 1F Class B4

*Introduced 1891: Adams L.S.W. design for dock shunting.
†Introduced 1908: Drummond K14 locos., with smaller boiler and detail alterations.
‡Adams locos. fitted with Drummond boiler.
§Drummond loco. fitted with Adams boiler.

Weight: { 33 tons 9 cwt.*‡
         { 32 tons 18 cwt.†§
Pressure: 140 lb. Cyls. (O): 16″ × 22″.
Driving Wheels: 3′ 9¾″.
T.E.: 14,650 lb.

*30086/7/9/93/4/6, 30102.
†30082/3   ‡30088   §30084

Total 11

0-6-0 2F Class C

Introduced 1900: Wainwright S.E.C. design.
Weight: Loco. 43 tons 16 cwt.
Pressure: 160 lb. Cyls.: 18¼″ × 26″
Driving Wheels: 5′ 2″.
T.E.: 19,520 lb.

31004/18/33/7/54/9/61 /3/8/71/ 86, 31102/12/3/50/91, 31218/9 /21/3/5/7/9/42—5/52/3/5/6/67 /8/70—2/7/80/7/93/4/7/8, 31317, 31461/80/1/95/8, 31508/10/3/73 /5/6/8/9/81—5/3—90/2/3,31681 —4/6—95, 31711—25.

Total 96

0-6-0 2F Class C2X

C2X Introduced 1908: Marsh rebuild of R. J. Billinton L.B.S.C. C.2 with larger C3-type boiler, extended smokebox, etc.
Weight: Loco. 45 tons 5 cwt.
Pressure: 170 lb.
Cyls.: 17½″ × 26″.
Driving Wheels: 5′ 0″.
T.E.: 19,175 lb.

32434/7/8/40—51, 32521—9/32/4— 41/3—54.

Total 45

0-4-0T OP Class C14

Introduced 1923: Urie rebuild as shunting locos. of Drummond L.S.W. motor-train 2-2-0T (originally introduced 1906).
Weight: 25 tons 15 cwt.
Pressure: 150 lb.
Cyls.: (O) 14″ × 14″.
Driving Wheels: 3′ 0″.
T.E.: 9,720 lb.
Walschaerts gear.

DS77, 30588/9.   **Total 3**

Classes D & DI

4-4-0 $\begin{Bmatrix} 2PD \\ 3PDI \end{Bmatrix}$

*D Introduced 1901: Wainwright S.E.C. design, with round-top fire box, some later fitted with extended smokebox.
†DI Introduced 1921: Maunsell rebuild of Class D, with superheated Belpaire boiler, and long-travel piston valves.
Weights: $\begin{cases} 50 \text{ tons.*} \\ 52 \text{ tons 4 cwt.†} \end{cases}$
Pressure: $\begin{cases} 175 \text{ lb.*} \\ 180 \text{ lb. Su.†} \end{cases}$
Cyls.: 19″ × 26″.
Driving Wheels: 6′ 8″.
T.E.: $\begin{cases} 17,450 \text{ lb.*} \\ 17,950 \text{ lb.†} \end{cases}$

*31075, 31488/96, 31549/74/7/86/91, 317/34/7/46.

†31145, 31246/7, 31470/87/9/92/4, 31505/9/45, 31727/35/9/41/3/9.

Totals: Class D 11
Class DI 17

0-4-4T   1P   **Class D3**

Introduced 1892: R. J. Billinton L.B.S.C. design, later reboilered by Marsh and fitted from 1934 for push-and-pull working.
Weight: 52 tons.
Pressure: 170 lb. Cyls.: 17½″ × 26″.
Driving Wheels: 5′ 6″.
T.E.: 17,435 lb.

32390.

Total 1

4-4-0   3P   **Class D15**

Introduced 1912: Drummond L.S.W. design, superheated by Urie from 1915.
Weight: Loco. 61 tons 11 cwt.
Pressure: 180 lb. Su.
Cyls.: 20″ × 26″.
Driving Wheels: 6′ 7″.
T.E.: 20,140 lb.
Walschaerts gear, P.V.

30464/5/7. **Total 3**

Classes E & EI

4-4-0 $\begin{Bmatrix} 2P E \\ 3P EI \end{Bmatrix}$

*E Introduced 1905: Wainwright S.E.C. design with Belpaire boiler.
‡EI Introduced 1919 : Maunsell rebuild of E. with larger superheated Belpaire boiler and long-travel piston valves.
Weight: Loco. $\begin{cases} 52 \text{ tons 5 cwt.*} \\ 53 \text{ tons 9 cwt.‡} \end{cases}$
Pressure: 180 lb.
Cyls.: 19″ × 26″.
Driving Wheels: 6′ 6″.
T.E.: 18,410 lb.

*31166.

‡31019/67,   31165,   31497, 31504/6/7.

Totals: Class E 1
Class EI 7

0-6-0T   2F   **Class EI**

Introduced 1874: Stroudley L.B.S.C. design, reboilered by Marsh.
Weight: 44 tons 3 cwt.
Pressure: 170 lb. Cyls.: 17″ × 24″.
Driving Wheels: 4′ 6″.
T.E.: 18,560 lb.

32113/38/9/51   32606/89/94. (W) 1–4.

Total 11

0-6-2T   1P2F   **Class EI/R**

Introduced 1927: Maunsell rebuild of Stroudley EI, with radial trailing axle and larger bunker for passenger service in West of England.
Weight: 50 tons 5 cwt.
Pressure: 170 lb. Cyls.: 17″ × 24″.
Driving Wheels: 4′ 6″.
T.E.: 18,560 lb.

32094–6, 32124/35, 32608/10/95–7.

Total 10

Classes E2–E6 & E6X

0-6-0T   3F   Class E2

*Introduced 1913: L. B. Billinton L.B.S.C. design.

†Introduced 1915: Later locos. with tanks extended further forward.

Weight: $\begin{cases} 52 \text{ tons } 15 \text{ cwt.*} \\ 53 \text{ tons } 10 \text{ cwt.†} \end{cases}$

Pressure: 170 lb.   Cyls.: $17\frac{1}{2}'' \times 26''$

Driving Wheels: 4′ 6″.

T.E.: 21,305 lb.

*32100–4.
†32105–9.

Total 10

0-6-2T   2F   Class E3

Introduced 1894: R. J. Billinton L.B.S.C. design, development of Stroudley " West Brighton " (introduced 1891), reboilered and fitted with extended smokebox, 1918 onwards; cylinder diameter reduced from 18″ by S.R.

Weight: 56 tons 10 cwt.

Pressure: $\begin{cases} 160 \text{ lb.} \\ 170 \text{ lb.*} \end{cases}$

Cyls.: $17\frac{1}{2}'' \times 26''$.

Driving Wheels: 4′ 6″.

T.E.: $\begin{cases} 20,055 \text{ lb.} \\ 21,305 \text{ lb.*} \end{cases}$

*32165–70.
32453–6/8–62

Total 15

Classes
0-6-2T   2MT   E4 & E4X

*E4 Introduced 1910: R. J. Billinton L.B.S.C. design, development of E3 with larger wheels, reboilered with Marsh boiler and extended smokebox, cylinder diameter reduced from 18″ by S.R.

†E4X Introduced 1909: E4 reboilered with larger 12 4-4-2T type boiler.

Weights: $\begin{cases} 57 \text{ tons } 10 \text{ cwt.*} \\ 59 \text{ tons } 5 \text{ cwt.†} \end{cases}$

Pressure: 170 lb.   Cyls.: $17\frac{1}{2}'' \times 26''$

Driving Wheels: 5′ 0″.

T.E.: 19,175 lb.

*32463–5/7–76/9–82/4–8/90–9, 32500–20/56–66/77–82.
†32466/77/8/89.

Totals: E4 70
E4X 4

Classes
0-6-2T   2MT   E5 & E5X

*‡E5 Introduced 1902: R. J. Billinton L.B.S.C. design, development of E4 with larger wheels and firebox, cylinder diameter reduced from 18″ by S.R.

†E5X Introduced 1911: E5 reboilered with larger C3-type boiler.

Weights: $\begin{cases} 60 \text{ tons.*} \\ 64 \text{ tons } 5 \text{ cwt.†} \end{cases}$

Pressure: $\begin{cases} 160 \text{ lb.*} \\ 175 \text{ lb.‡} \\ 170 \text{ lb.†} \end{cases}$

Cyls.: $17\frac{1}{2}'' \times 26''$.

Driving Wheels: 5′ 6″.

T.E.: $\begin{cases} 16,410 \text{ lb.*} \\ 17,945 \text{ lb.‡} \\ 17,435 \text{ lb.†} \end{cases}$

*‡32568/71/83/5/7/91/3.
†32401, 32570/6/86.

Totals: E5 7
E5X 4

Classes
0-6-2T   3F   E6 & E6X

*‡E6 Introduced 1904: R. J. Billinton L.B.S.C. design, development of E5 with smaller wheels.

†E6X Introduced 1911: E6 reboilered with larger C3-type boiler.

Weights: $\begin{cases} 61 \text{ tons.*} \\ 63 \text{ tons.†} \end{cases}$

Pressure: $\begin{cases} 160 \text{ lb.*} \\ 175 \text{ lb.‡} \\ 170 \text{ lb.†} \end{cases}$

Cyls.: $18'' \times 26''$.

Driving Wheels: 4′ 6″.

T.E.: $\begin{cases} 21,215 \text{ lb.*} \\ 23,205 \text{ lb.‡} \\ 22,540 \text{ lb.†} \end{cases}$

*‡32408–10/2–8.   †32407/11.

Totals: E6 10
E6X 2

0-6-0T 2F Class G6

*Introduced 1894: Adams L.S.W. design, later additions by Drummond, but with Adams type boiler.
†Introduced 1925: Fitted with Drummond type boiler.
Weight: 47 tons 13 cwt.
Pressure: 160 lb. Cyls.: $17\frac{1}{2}'' \times 24''$.
Driving Wheels: 4' 10".
T.E.: 17,235 lb.

*30162, 30238/58/60/6/70/7, 30349, DS3152
†30160, 30274.

Total 11

4-8-0T 8F Class G16

Introduced 1921: Urie L.S.W. " Hump " loco.
Weight: 95 tons 2 cwt.
Pressure: 180 lb. Su.
Cyls. (O): $22'' \times 28''$
Driving Wheels: 5' 1"
T.E.: 33,990 lb.
Walschaerts gear, P.V.

30492–5 **Total 4**

0-4-4T 1P Class H

Introduced 1904. Wainwright S.E.C. design.
*Introduced 1949. Fitted for push-and-pull working.
Weight: 54 tons 8 cwt.
Pressure: 160 lb. Cyls.: $18'' \times 26''$.
Driving Wheels: 5' 6".
T.E.: 17,360 lb.

31005, 31259/61/3/5/6/78,
31305-7/9/11/21/4/6/8/9,
31500/3/31/3/40/2/4/50-3.

*31158/61/2/4/9/77/84/93, 31239/
69/74/6/9/95, 31303/10/9/20/
2/7,31512/7—23/30/43/8/54.

Total 60

4-4-2 4P Class H2

Introduced 1911: Marsh L.B.S.C. design, superheated development of H1 with larger cylinders.
Weight: Loco. 68 tons 5 cwt.
Pressure: 200 lb. Su.
Cyls.: (O) $21'' \times 26''$.
Driving Wheels: 6' 7½".
T.E.: 24,520 lb.
P.V.

32421/2/4–6. **Total 5**

4-6-0 4P5F Class H15

*Introduced 1914: Urie L S.W. design, fitted with " Maunsell " superheater from 1927, replacing earlier types (30490 built saturated).
†Introduced 1915: Urie rebuild with two outside cylinders of Drummond E14, 4 cyl. 4–6–0 introduced 1907, retaining original boiler retubed and fitted with superheater.
‡Introduced 1924: Maunsell locos. with N15 type boiler and smaller tenders.
§Introduced 1924: Maunsell rebuild of Drummond F13 4-cyl. 4–6–0 introduced 1905, with detail differences from rebuild of E14.
¶Introduced 1927: Urie loco. (built 1914 saturated) rebuilt with later N15 class boiler, with smaller firebox.
Weight: Loco. $\begin{cases} 81 \text{ tons } 5 \text{ cwt.*} \\ 82 \text{ tons } 1 \text{ cwt.†} \\ 79 \text{ tons } 19 \text{ cwt.‡¶} \\ 80 \text{ tons } 11 \text{ cwt. §} \end{cases}$
Pressure: $\begin{cases} 180 \text{ lb. Su.*‡¶} \\ 175 \text{ lb. Su.*§} \end{cases}$
Cyls.: $21'' \times 28''$
Driving Wheels: 6' 0".
T.E.: $\begin{cases} 26,240 \text{ lb.*‡¶} \\ 25,510 \text{ lb.†§} \end{cases}$
Walschaerts gear, P.V

*30482–90
†30335
‡30473–8, 30521–4
§30330–4
¶30491 **Total 26**

Classes H16–M7

4-6-2T 6F Class H16

Introduced 1921: Urie L.S.W. design for heavy freight traffic.
Weight: 96 tons 8 cwt.
Pressure: 180 lb. Su.
Cyls.: (O) 21″ × 28″.
Driving Wheels: 5′ 7″.
T.E.: 28,200 lb.
Walschaerts valve gear, P.V.

30516–20   **Total 5**

2-6-0 4P5F Class K

Introduced 1913: L. B. Billinton L.B.S.C. design.
Weight: Loco. 63 tons 15 cwt.
Pressure: 180 lb. Su.
Cyls.: (O) 21″ × 26″.
Driving Wheels: 5′ 6″.
T.E.: 26,580 lb.
P.V.

32337–53   **Total 17**

4-4-0 3P Class L

Introduced 1914: Wainwright S.E.C. design, with detail alterations by Maunsell.
Weight: Loco. 57 tons 9 cwt.
Pressure: 160 lb. Su.
Cyls.: 20½″ × 26″.
Driving Wheels: 6′ 8″.
T.E.: 18,575 lb.
P.V.

31760–81   **Total 22**

4-4-0 3P Class L1

Introduced 1926: Post-grouping development of L, with long-travel valves, side window cab and detail alterations
Weight: Loco. 57 tons 16 cwt.
Pressure: 180 lb. Su.
Cyls: 19½″ × 26″.
Driving Wheels: 6′ 8″.
T.E.: 18,910 lb.
P.V.

31753–9/82–9   **Total 15**

4-4-0 3P Class L12

Introduced 1904: Drummond L.S.W. design, development of T9 with larger boiler, superheated from 1915.
Weight: Loco. 55 tons 5 cwt.
Pressure: 175 lb. Su.
Cyls.: 19″ × 26″.
Driving Wheels: 6′ 7″.
T.E.: 17,675 lb.

30434

                            Total 1

4-6-0 7P Class LN

*Introduced 1926: Maunsell design, cylinders and tender modified by Bulleid from 1938, and fitted with multiple-jet blastpipes and large chimney.
†Introduced 1929: Loco. fitted experimentally with smaller driving wheels.
‡Introduced 1929: Loco. fitted experimentally with longer boiler.
Weights: Loco. {83 tons 10 cwt.*†
{84 tons 16 cwt.‡
Pressure: 220 lb. Su.
Cyls.: (4) 16½″ × 26″.*
Driving Wheels: {6′ 7″ *‡
{6′ 3″ †
T.E.: {33,510 lb.*‡
{35,300 lb.†
Walschaerts gear, P.V.

*30850–8/61–5.
†30859   ‡30860
                            Total 16

0-4-4T 2P Class M7

*Introduced 1897: Drummond L.S.W. M7 design.
†Introduced 1903: Drummond X14 design, with increased front overhang, steam reverser and detail alterations, now classified M7 (30254 originally M7).

‡Introduced 1925 X14 design fitted for push-and-pull working.

Weights: { 60 tons 4 cwt.*
{ 60 tons 3 cwt.†
{ 62 tons 0 cwt.‡

Pressure: 175 lb.
Cyls.: 18½″ × 26″.
Driving Wheels: 5′ 7″.
T.E.: 19.755 lb.

*30022–6/31–44, 30112, 30241–53/5/6, 30318–24/56/7, 30667–71/3–6.
†30030, 30123/4/7/30/2/3, 30254, 30374–8, 30479.
‡30021/7/8/9/45–60, 30104–11/25/8/9/31, 30328/79, 30480/1.

Total 103

4-6-2   8P   Class MN

*Introduced 1941: Bulleid design.
†Introduced 1951: Modified with single blastpipe and chimney.

Weight: Loco. 94 tons 15 cwt.
Pressure: 280 lb. Su.
Cyl.: (3) 18″ × 24″.
Driving Wheels: 6′ 2″.
T.E.: 37,515 lb.
Bulleid valve gear, P.V.

*35001–18/20–30
†35019

Total 30

2-6-0   4P5F   Classes N & N1

*N Introduced 1917: Maunsell S.E.C. mixed traffic design.
†N1 Introduced 1922: 3-cylinder development of N.

Weight: Loco. { 61 tons 4 cwt.*
{ 64 tons 5 cwt.†

Pressure: 200 lb. Su.
Cyls.: { (O) 19″ × 28″*
{ (3) 16″ × 28″†
Driving Wheels: 5′ 6″

T.E.: { 26,035 lb.*
{ 27,695 lb.†

Walschaerts gear, P.V.

*31400–14, 31810–21/3–75
†31822/76–80

**Totals: Class N 80
Class N1 6**

4-6-0   5P   Class N15

*Introduced 1918: Urie L.S.W. design.
†Introduced 1928: Urie Locos. modified with cylinders of reduced diameter.
‡Introduced 1925: Maunsell Locos. with long-travel valves, increased boiler pressure, smaller fireboxes, and tenders from Drummond G14 4–6–0's.
§Introduced 1925: Later locos. with detail alterations and increased weight.
‖Introduced 1925: Locos. with modified cabs to suit Eastern Section and new bogie tenders.
¶Introduced 1926: Locos. with detail alterations and six-wheeled tenders for Central Section.

Weight: Loco. { 80 tons 7 cwt.*†
{ 79 tons 18 cwt.‡
{ 80 tons 19 cwt.§‖
{ 81 tons 17 cwt.¶

Pressure: { 180 lb. Su.*†
{ 200 lb. Su.‡§‖¶
Cyls.: { (O) 22″ × 28″*
{ (O) 21″ × 28″†
{ (O) 20½″ × 28″‡§‖¶
Driving Wheels: 6′ 7″
T.E.: { 26,245 lb.*
{ 23,915 lb.†
{ 25,320 lb.§‡‖¶

Walschaerts gear, P.V.

NOTE: Nos. 30736/7/41/52/5 are fitted with multiple jet blastpipe and large diameter chimney.

*30755   †30736–53
‡30453–7   §30448–52
‖30763–92   ¶30793–30806

Total 73

Classes NI5X–R & RI

4-6-0   4P   Class NI5X

Introduced 1934: Maunsell rebuild of
L. B. Billinton L.B.S.C. Class L
4–6–4T (introduced 1914).
Weight: Loco. 73 tons 2 cwt.
Pressure: 180 lb. Su.
Cyls.: (O) 21″ × 28″.
Driving Wheels: 6′ 9″.
T.E.: 23,325 lb.
Walschaerts gear, P.V.

32327–33   **Total 7**

0-6-0   2F   Class OI

*Introduced 1903: Wainwright rebuild
with domed boiler and new cab of
Stirling S.E.R. Class O 0–6–0 (intro-
duced 1878).
†Introduced 1903: Locos. with smaller
driving wheels.
Weight: Loco. 41 tons 1 cwt.
Pressure: 150 lb. Cyls.: 18″ × 26″.
Driving Wheels: $\begin{cases} 5′2″* \\ 5′1″† \end{cases}$
T.E.: $\begin{cases} 17,325 \text{ lb.}* \\ 17,610 \text{ lb.}† \end{cases}$

*31064/5,   31258,   31370,
31425/30/4
†31048

     Total 8

0-4-4T   0P   Class O2

*Introduced 1889: Adams L.S.W.
design.
†Introduced 1923: Fitted with West-
inghouse brake for I.O.W., bunkers
enlarged from 1932.
‡Fitted with Drummond-type boiler.
§Fitted for push-and-pull working.
Weight: $\begin{cases} 46 \text{ tons } 18 \text{ cwt.}*‡ \\ 48 \text{ tons } 8 \text{ cwt.}† \end{cases}$
Pressure: 160 lb. Cyls.: 17½″ × 24″.
Driving Wheels: 4′ 10″.
T.E.· 17,235 lb.

*30177/9/92/3/9,   30200/12/6/
24/5/9/30/2/6.
† (W)14–34 †§ (W)35/6.
‡30203/23/33.
‡§30182/3, 30207.

     Total 43

0-6-0T   Unclass   Class P

Introduced 1909: Wainwright S.E.C.
design for push-and-pull work, now
used for shunting.
Weight: 28 tons 10 cwt.
Pressure: 160 lb. Cyls.: 12″ × 18″.
Driving Wheels: 3′ 9⅝″.
T.E.: 7,810 lb.

31027, 31178, 31323/5, 31555–8.
     Total 8

0-6-0   4F   Class Q

Introduced 1938: Maunsell design, later
fitted with multiple-jet blastpipe and
large chimney.
Weight: Loco. 49 tons 10 cwt.
Pressure: 200 lb. Su.
Cyls.: 19″ × 26″.
Driving Wheels: 5′ 1″.
T.E.: 26,160 lb.
P.V.

30530–49   **Total 20**

0-6-0   5F   Class QI

Introduced 1942: Bulleid " Austerity "
design.
Weight: Loco. 51 tons 5 cwt.
Pressure: 230 lb. Su.
Cyls.: 19″ × 26″.
Driving Wheels: 5′ 1″.
T.E.: 30,080 lb.
P.V.

33001–40   **Total 40**

0-4-4T   1P   Classes R & RI

*R Introduced 1891: Kirtley L.C.D.
design, since rebuilt with H. class
boiler.

†RI Introduced 1900: Locos. built for
S.E.C. with enlarged bunkers, since
rebuilt with H class boiler

Class M7 0-4-4T No. 30676. [D. Kelk

Class M7 0-4-4T No. 30028 (push-and-pull fitted). [G. Wheeler

Class O2 0-4-4T No. 30182 (with Drummond-type boiler). [L. Elsey

Class T9 4-4-0 No. 30721.

[F. W. Day

Class S11 4-4-0 No. 30400.

[G. Wheeler

Class L12 4-4-0 No. 30434.

[G. Wheeler

Above: Class D15
4-4-0 No. 30465.
[P. Ransome-Wallis

Right: Class G6 0-6-0T
No. 30160 (with
Drummond-type
boiler).
[H. C. Casserley

Below: Class H2 4-4-2
No. 32424 Beachy
Head.
[F. W. Day

Class D 4-4-0 No. 31574.   [A. B. Crompton

Class D1 4-4-0 No. 31489.   [F. J. Saunders

Class E 4-4-0 No. 31166.   [P. Ransome-Wallis

Class E1 4-4-0 No. 31507.   [L. Marshall

Class L 4-4-0 No. 31774.   [R. E. Vincen

Class L1 4-4-0 No. 31789.   [R. Griffiths

Class U 2-6-0 No. 31806 (rebuilt from Class K 2-6-4T). [F. J. Saunders

Class U 2-6-0 No. 31621. [P. Ransome-Wallis

Class U1 2-6-0 No. 31896. [F. J. Saunders

Class N 2-6-0 No. 31842. [L. Marshall

Class K 2-6-0 No. 32345. [G. Wheeler

Class S15 4-6-0 No. 30510 (Urie design). [L. Marshall

Left: **Class 757 0-6-2T**
No. 30757 *Earl of Mount Edgecumbe.*

[*M. A. Arnold*

Centre: **Class H 0-4-4T**
No. 31309.

[*F. J. Saunders*

Bottom: **Class R 0-4-4T**
No. 31666 (fitted for push-and-pull working).

[*G. Wheeler*

‡Fitted for push-and-pull working.
Weight: { 48 tons 15 cwt.*
{ 52 tons 3 cwt.†
Pressure: 160 lb. Cyls.: 17½″ × 24″.
Driving Wheels: 5′ 6″.
T.E.: 15,145 lb.

*31661.
†31698.
*‡31666/71.
†‡31704.

Totals: Class R 3
Class RI 2

0-6-0T   2F   Class RI

*Introduced 1888: Stirling S.E. design,
  later rebuilt with domed boiler.
†Introduced 1938: Fitted with Urie
  type short chimney for Whitstable
  branch, and fitted with or retaining
  original Stirling-type cab.
‡ Introduced 1952.   Rebuilt with
  domed boiler but retaining Stirling
  Cab.
Weight: { 46 tons 15 cwt.*
{ 46 tons 8 cwt.†‡
Pressure: 160 lb. Cyls.: 18″ × 26″.
Driving Wheels: { 5′ 2″*
{ 5′ 1″†‡
T.E.: { 18,480 lb.*
{ 18,780 lb.†‡
*31047, 31128/54/74, 31335/7/40
†31010, 31107/47, 31339.
‡31069

Total 12

4-4-0   3P   Class S11

Introduced 1903: Drummond L.S.W.
  design, development of T9 with larger
  boiler and smaller wheels for West
  of England, superheated from 1920.
Weight: Loco. 53 tons, 15 cwt.
Pressure: 175 lb. Su.
Cyls.: 19″ × 26″.
Driving Wheels: 6′ 0″.
T.E.: 19,390 lb.
30400
Total 1

4-6-0   6F   Class S15

*Introduced 1920: Urie L.S.W. design,
  development of N15 for mixed traffic
  work.

Classes R & RI–U & UI

†Introduced 1927: Post-grouping locos.
  with higher pressure, smaller grate,
  modified footplating and other detail
  differences.   30833-7 with 6-wheel
  tenders for Central Section.
‡Introduced 1936: Later locos. with
  detail differences and reduced weight
Weight Loco. { 79 tons 16 cwt.*
{ 80 tons 14 cwt.†
{ 79 tons 5 cwt.‡
Pressure: { 180 lb. Su.*
{ 200 lb. Su.†‡
Cyls.: { (O) 21″ × 28″*
{ (O) 20½″ × 28″†‡
Driving Wheels: 5′ 7″
T.E.: { 28,200 lb.*
{ 29,855 lb.†‡
Walschaerts gear, P.V.

*30496–30515   †30823–37
‡30838–47

Total 45

4-4-0   3P   Class T9

*Introduced 1899: Drummond L.S.W.
  design, fitted with superheater and
  larger cylinders by Urie from 1922.
†Introduced 1899: Locos. with detail
  differences (originally fitted with firebox watertubes).
‡Introduced 1900: Locos. with wider
  cab and splashers, and without
  coupling rod splashers (originally
  fitted with firebox watertubes.)
Weight: Loco. { 51 tons 18 cwt.*
{ 51 tons 16 cwt.†
{ 51 tons 7 cwt.‡
Pressure: 175 lb. Su.
Cyls.: 19″ × 26″.
Driving Wheels: 6′ 7″.
T.E.: 17,675 lb.

*30117/20, 30283–5/7–9
†30702/5–12/5/7–9/21/4/6–30/2
‡30300/1/4/10/3/37/8

Total 36

Classes
U & UI

2-6-0   4P3F

*U Introduced 1928:   Rebuild of
  Maunsell S.E.C. Class K (" River ")
  2–6–4T (introduced 1917).
†U Introduced 1928: Locos. built as
  Class U, with smaller splashers and
  detail alterations.

25

Classes U & UI–Z, 700

‡**UI Introduced** 1928: 3-cylinder development of Class U (prototype 31890, rebuilt from 2–6–4T, originally built 1925).

Weight: Loco. $\begin{cases} 63 \text{ tons*} \\ 62 \text{ tons 6 cwt.†} \\ 65 \text{ tons 6 cwt.‡} \end{cases}$

Pressure: 200 lb. Su.
Cyls.: $\begin{cases} (O) \ 19'' \times 28''*† \\ (3) \ 16'' \times 28''‡ \end{cases}$
Driving Wheels: 6′ 0″.
T.E.: $\begin{cases} 23,865 \text{ lb.*†} \\ 25,385 \text{ lb.‡} \end{cases}$
Walschaerts gear, P.V.

*31790–31809   †31610–39
‡31890–31910

Totals: Class U 50
Class UI 21

0-6-0T   3F   Class USA

Introduced 1942: U.S. Army Transportation Corps design, purchased by S.R. 1946, and fitted with modified cab and bunker and other detail alterations.
Weight: 46 tons 10 cwt.
Pressure: 210 lb.
Cyls.: (O) $16\frac{1}{2}'' \times 24''$.
Driving Wheels: 4′ 6″.
T.E.: 21,600 lb.
Walschaerts gear, P.V.

30061–74   **Total 14**

4-4-0   5P   Class V

*Introduced 1930: Maunsell design.
†Introduced 1938: Fitted with multiple jet blastpipe and larger chimney by Bulleid.
Weight: Loco. 67 tons 2 cwt.
Pressure: 220 lb. Su.
Cyls.: (3) $16\frac{1}{2}'' \times 26''$.
Driving Wheels: 6′ 7″.
T.E.: 25,135 lb.
Walschaerts gear, P.V.

*30902–6/8/10–2/6/22/3/5–8/32/5/6.
†30900/1/7/9/13–3/7–21/4/29–31/3/4/7–9.
Total 40

2-6-4T   6F   Class W

Introduced 1931: Maunsell design, developed from Class NI 2–6–0.
Weight: 90 tons 14 cwt.
Pressure: 200 lb. Su.
Cyls.: (3) $16\frac{1}{2}'' \times 28''$.
Driving Wheels: 5′ 6″.
T.E.: 29,450 lb.
Walschaerts gear, P.V.

31911–25   **Total 15**

4-6-2   7P5F   Classes WC & BB

*Introduced 1945: Bulleid " West Country " Class.
†Introduced 1946: Bulleid " Battle of Britain " Class.
‡Introduced 1948: Locos. with larger tenders.
Weight: Loco. 86 tons 0 cwt.
Pressure: 280 lb. Su.
Cyls.: (3) $16\frac{3}{8}'' \times 24''$.
Driving Wheels: 6′ 2″.
T.E.: 31,050 lb.
Bulleid valve gear, P.V.

*34001–48   †34049–70
†‡34071–90, 34109/10
*‡34091–34108   **Total 110**

0-8-0T   6F   Class Z

Introduced 1929: Maunsell design for heavy shunting.
Weight: 71 tons 12 cwt.
Pressure: 180 lb. Cyls.: (3) $16'' \times 18''$.
Driving Wheels: 4′ 8″.
T.E.: 29,375 lb.
Walschaerts gear, P.V.

30950–7   **Total 8**

0-6-0   3F   Class 700

Introduced 1897: Drummond L.S.W. design, superheated from 1921.
Weight: Loco. 46 tons 14 cwt.
Pressure: 180 lb. Su.
Cyls.: $19'' \times 26''$.
Driving Wheels: 5′ 1″.
T.E.: 23,540 lb.

30306/8/9/15–7/25–7/39/46/50/2/5/68, 30687–30701.
Total 30

0-6-2T   1P2F   **Class 757**

Introduced 1907: Hawthorn Leslie
design for P.D.S.W.J.
Weight: 49 tons 19 cwt.
Pressure: 170 lb.
Cyls.: (O) 16″ × 24″.
Driving Wheels: 4′ 0″.
T.E.: 18,495 lb.

30757–8   **Total 2**

2-4-0WT   0P   **Class 0298**

Introduced 1874: Beattie L.S.W.
design, rebuilt by Adams (1884-92),
Urie (1921-2) and Maunsell (1931-5)
Weight: 37 tons 16 cwt.
Pressure: 160 lb.
Cyls.: (O) 16½″ × 20″.
Driving Wheels: 5′ 7″.
T.E.: 11,050 lb.

30585–7   **Total 3**

0-6-0   2F   **Class 0395**

*Introduced 1881: Adams L.S.W.
design.
†Introduced 1885: Adams " 496 "
class with longer front overhang.
‡Introduced 1928: Reboilered with
ex-S.E.C. Class M3 4-4-0 boiler.
§Fitted with Drummond type boiler.
Weight: Loco. { 37 tons 12 cwt.*
{ 38 tons 14 cwt.†
Pressure: { 140 lb.*
{ 150 lb.†

Driving Wheels: 5′ 1″.
T.E.: { 15,535 lb.*
{ 16,645 lb†.

*30568–70/2/4/5/7/8
†30566/79   *‡30573
*§30567   †‡30580   †§30564

                    Total 14

4-4-2T   1P   **Class 0415**

Introduced 1882: Adams L.S.W.
design later reboilered.
Weight: 55 tons 2 cwt.
Pressure: 160 lb.
Cyls.: (O) 17½″ × 24″.
Driving Wheels: 5′ 7″.
T.E.: 14,920 lb.

30582–4   **Total 3**

0-4-0ST   Unclass   **Class 0458**

Introduced 1890: Hawthorn Leslie
design for Southampton Docks Co.,
absorbed by L.S.W., 1892.
Weight: 21 tons 2 cwt.
Pressure: 120 lb
Cyls.: (O) 12″ × 20″.
Driving Wheels: 3′ 2″.
T.E.: 7,730 lb.

30458   **Total 1**

You have bought your ABC and now, to be the complete railway
enthusiast, you MUST get

TRAINS ILLUSTRATED
monthly

=====THE RAILFAN'S OWN MAGAZINE=====

BRITISH RAILWAYS' LOCOMOTIVES

Nos. 30021-35030, W1-36

Named Engines are indicated by an asterisk (*)

No.	Class	No.	Class	No.	Class	No.	Class
30021	M7	30056	M7	30109	M7	30232	O2
30022	M7	30057	M7	30110	M7	30233	O2
30023	M7	30058	M7	30111	M7	30236	O2
30024	M7	30059	M7	30112	M7	30238	G6
30025	M7	30060	M7	30117	T9	30241	M7
30026	M7	30061	U.S.A.	30120	T9	30242	M7
30027	M7	30062	U.S.A.	30123	M7	30243	M7
30028	M7	30063	U.S.A.	30124	M7	30244	M7
30029	M7	30064	U.S.A.	30125	M7	30245	M7
30030	M7	30065	U.S.A.	30127	M7	30246	M7
30031	M7	30066	U.S.A.	30128	M7	30247	M7
30032	M7	30067	U.S.A.	30129	M7	30248	M7
30033	M7	30068	U.S.A.	30130	M7	30249	M7
30034	M7	30069	U.S.A.	30131	M7	30250	M7
30035	M7	30070	U.S.A.	30132	M7	30251	M7
30036	M7	30071	U.S.A.	30133	M7	30252	M7
30037	M7	30072	U.S.A.	30160	G6	30253	M7
30038	M7	30073	U.S.A.	30162	G6	30254	M7
30039	M7	30074	U.S.A.	30177	O2	30255	M7
30040	M7	30082	B4	30179	O2	30256	M7
30041	M7	30083	B4	30182	O2	30258	G6
30042	M7	30084	B4	30183	O2	30260	G6
30043	M7	30086	B4	30192	O2	30266	G6
30044	M7	30087	B4	30193	O2	30270	G6
30045	M7	30088	B4	30199	O2	30274	G6
30046	M7	30089	B4	30200	O2	30277	G6
30047	M7	30093	B4	30203	O2	30283	T9
30048	M7	30094	B4	30207	O2	30284	T9
30049	M7	30096	B4	30212	O2	30285	T9
30050	M7	30102	B4	30216	O2	30287	T9
30051	M7	30104	M7	30223	O2	30288	T9
30052	M7	30105	M7	30224	O2	30289	T9
30053	M7	30106	M7	30225	O2	30300	T9
30054	M7	30107	M7	30229	O2	30301	T9
30055	M7	30108	M7	30230	O2	30304	T9

No.	Class	No.	Class	No.	Class	No.	Class
30306	700	30434	L12	30501	S15	30549	Q
30308	700	30448*	N15	30502	S15	30564	0395
30309	700	30449*	N15	30503	S15	30566	0395
30310	T9	30450*	N15	30504	S15	30567	0395
30313	T9	30451*	N15	30505	S15	30568	0395
30315	700	30452*	N15	30506	S15	30569	0395
30316	700	30453*	N15	30507	S15	30570	0395
30317	700	30454*	N15	30508	S15	30572	0395
30318	M7	30455*	N15	30509	S15	30573	0395
30319	M7	30456*	N15	30510	S15	30574	0395
30320	M7	30457*	N15	30511	S15	30575	0395
30321	M7	30458*	0458	30512	S15	30577	0395
30322	M7	30464	D15	30513	S15	30578	0395
30323	M7	30465	D15	30514	S15	30579	0395
30324	M7	30467	D15	30515	S15	30580	0395
30325	700	30473	H15	30516	H16	30582	0415
30326	700	30474	H15	30517	H16	30583	0415
30327	700	30475	H15	30518	H16	30584	0415
30328	M7	30476	H15	30519	H16	30585	0298
30330	H15	30477	H15	30520	H16	30586	0298
30331	H15	30478	H15	30521	H15	30587	0298
30332	H15	30479	M7	30522	H15	30588	C14
30333	H15	30480	M7	30523	H15	30589	C14
30334	H15	30481	M7	30524	H15	30667	M7
30335	H15	30482	H15	30530	Q	30668	M7
30337	T9	30483	H15	30531	Q	30669	M7
30338	T9	30484	H15	30532	Q	30670	M7
30339	700	30485	H15	30533	Q	30671	M7
30346	700	30486	H15	30534	Q	30673	M7
30349	G6	30487	H15	30535	Q	30674	M7
30350	700	30488	H15	30536	Q	30675	M7
30352	700	30489	H15	30537	Q	30676	M7
30355	700	30490	H15	30538	Q	30687	700
30356	M7	30491	H15	30539	Q	30688	700
30357	M7	30492	G16	30540	Q	30689	700
30368	700	30493	G16	30541	Q	30690	700
30374	M7	30494	G16	30542	Q	30691	700
30375	M7	30495	G16	30543	Q	30692	700
30376	M7	30496	S15	30544	Q	30693	700
30377	M7	30497	S15	30545	Q	30694	700
30378	M7	30498	S15	30546	Q	30695	700
30379	M7	30499	S15	30547	Q	30696	700
30400	S11	30500	S15	30548	Q	30697	700

29

No.	Class	No.	Class	No.	Class	No.	Class
30698	700	30755*	N15	30803*	N15	30864*	LN
30699	700	30757*	757	30804*	N15	30865*	LN
30700	700	30758*	757	30805*	N15	30900*	V
30701	700	30763*	N15	30806*	N15	30901*	V
30702	T9	30764*	N15	30823	S15	30902*	V
30705	T9	30765*	N15	30824	S15	30903*	V
30706	T9	30766*	N15	30825	S15	30904*	V
30707	T9	30767*	N15	30826	S15	30905*	V
30708	T9	30768*	N15	30827	S15	30906*	V
30709	T9	30769*	N15	30828	S15	30907*	V
30710	T9	30770*	N15	30829	S15	30908*	V
30711	T9	30771*	N15	30830	S15	30909*	V
30712	T9	30772*	N15	30831	S15	30910*	V
30715	T9	30773*	N15	30832	S15	30911*	V
30717	T9	30774*	N15	30833	S15	30912*	V
30718	T9	30775*	N15	30834	S15	30913*	V
30719	T9	30776*	N15	30835	S15	30914*	V
30721	T9	30777*	N15	30836	S15	30915*	V
30724	T9	30778*	N15	30837	S15	30916*	V
30726	T9	30779*	N15	30838	S15	30917*	V
30727	T9	30780*	N15	30839	S15	30918*	V
30728	T9	30781*	N15	30840	S15	30919*	V
30729	T9	30782*	N15	30841	S15	30920*	V
30730	T9	30783*	N15	30842	S15	30921*	V
30732	T9	30784*	N15	30843	S15	30922*	V
30736*	N15	30785*	N15	30844	S15	30923*	V
30737*	N15	30786*	N15	30845	S15	30924*	V
30738*	N15	30787*	N15	30846	S15	30925*	V
30739*	N15	30788*	N15	30847	S15	30926*	V
30740*	N15	30789*	N15	30850*	LN	30927*	V
30741*	N15	30790*	N15	30851*	LN	30928*	V
30742*	N15	30791*	N15	30852*	LN	30929*	V
30743*	N15	30792*	N15	30853*	LN	30930*	V
30744*	N15	30793*	N15	30854*	LN	30931*	V
30745*	N15	30794*	N15	30855*	LN	30932*	V
30746*	N15	30795*	N15	30856*	LN	30933*	V
30747*	N15	30796*	N15	30857*	LN	30934*	V
30748*	N15	30797*	N15	30858*	LN	30935*	V
30749*	N15	30798*	N15	30859*	LN	30936*	V
30750*	N15	30799*	N15	30860*	LN	30937*	V
30751*	N15	30800*	N15	30861*	LN	30938*	V
30752*	N15	30801*	N15	30862*	LN	30939*	V
30753*	N15	30802*	N15	30863*	LN	30950	Z

No.	Class	No.	Class	No.	Class	No.	Class
30951	Z	31166	E	31287	C	31413	N
30952	Z	31174	RI	31293	C	31414	N
30953	Z	31177	H	31294	C	31425	OI
30954	Z	31178	P	31295	H	31430	OI
30955	Z	31184	H	31297	C	31434	OI
30956	Z	31191	C	31298	C	31461	C
30957	Z	31193	H	31305	H	31470	DI
31004	C	31218	C	31306	H	31480	C
31005	H	31219	C	31307	H	31481	C
31010	RI	31221	C	31308	H	31487	DI
31018	C	31223	C	31309	H	31488	D
31019	EI	31225	C	31310	H	31489	DI
31027	P	31227	C	31311	H	31492	DI
31033	C	31229	C	31317	C	31494	DI
31037	C	31239	H	31319	H	31495	C
31047	RI	31242	C	31320	H	31496	D
31048	OI	31243	C	31321	H	31497	EI
31054	C	31244	C	31322	H	31498	C
31059	C	31245	C	31323	P	31500	H
31061	C	31246	DI	31324	H	31503	H
31063	C	31247	DI	31325	P	31504	EI
31064	OI	31252	C	31326	H	31505	DI
31065	OI	31253	C	31327	H	31506	EI
31067	EI	31255	C	31328	H	31507	EI
31068	C	31256	C	31329	H	31508	C
31069	RI	31258	OI	31335	RI	31509	DI
31071	C	31259	H	31337	RI	31510	C
31075	D	31261	H	31339	RI	31512	H
31086	C	31263	H	31340	RI	31513	C
31102	C	31265	H	31370	OI	31517	H
31107	RI	31266	H	31400	N	31518	H
31112	C	31267	C	31401	N	31519	H
31113	C	31268	C	31402	N	31520	H
31128	RI	31269	H	31403	N	31521	H
31145	DI	31270	C	31404	N	31522	H
31147	RI	31271	C	31405	N	31523	H
31150	C	31272	C	31406	N	31530	H
31154	RI	31274	H	31407	N	31531	H
31158	H	31276	H	31408	N	31533	H
31161	H	31277	C	31409	N	31540	H
31162	H	31278	H	31410	N	31542	H
31164	H	31279	H	31411	N	31543	H
31165	EI	31280	C	31412	N	31544	H

No.	Class	No.	Class	No.	Class	No.	Class
31545	DI	31622	U	31717	C	31778	L
31548	H	31623	U	31718	C	31779	L
31549	D	31624	U	31719	C	31780	L
31550	H	31625	U	31720	C	31781	L
31551	H	31626	U	31721	C	31782	LI
31552	H	31627	U	31722	C	31783	LI
31553	H	31628	U	31723	C	31784	LI
31554	H	31629	U	31724	C	31785	LI
31555	P	31630	U	31725	C	31786	LI
31556	P	31631	U	31727	DI	31787	LI
31557	P	31632	U	31734	D	31788	LI
31558	P	31633	U	31735	DI	31789	LI
31573	C	31634	U	31737	D	31790	U
31574	D	31635	U	31739	DI	31791	U
31575	C	31636	U	31741	DI	31792	U
31576	C	31637	U	31743	DI	31793	U
31577	D	31638	U	31746	D	31794	U
31578	C	31639	U	31749	DI	31795	U
31579	C	31661	R	31753	LI	31796	U
31581	C	31666	R	31754	LI	31797	U
31582	C	31671	R	31755	LI	31798	U
31583	C	31681	C	31756	LI	31799	U
31584	C	31682	C	31757	LI	31800	U
31585	C	31683	C	31758	LI	31801	U
31586	D	31684	C	31759	LI	31802	U
31588	C	31686	C	31760	L	31803	U
31589	C	31687	C	31761	L	31804	U
31590	C	31688	C	31762	L	31805	U
31591	D	31689	C	31763	L	31806	U
31592	C	31690	C	31764	L	31807	U
31593	C	31691	C	31765	L	31808	U
31610	U	31692	C	31766	L	31809	U
31611	U	31693	C	31767	L	31810	N
31612	U	31694	C	31768	L	31811	N
31613	U	31695	C	31769	L	31812	N
31614	U	31698	RI	31770	L	31813	N
31615	U	31704	RI	31771	L	31814	N
31616	U	31711	C	31772	L	31815	N
31617	U	31712	C	31773	L	31816	N
31618	U	31713	C	31774	L	31817	N
31619	U	31714	C	31775	L	31818	N
31620	U	31715	C	31776	L	31819	N
31621	U	31716	C	31777	L	31820	N

Above: Class R1 0-6-0T
No. 31339 (with cut
down boiler mountings).
[*F. J. Saunders*

Right: Class U.S.A. 0-6-0T
No. 30064.
[*F. W. Day*

Below: Class P 0-6-0T
No. 31178.
[*F. W. Day*

Class S15 4-6-0 No. 30836 (1927 series with six-wheel tender). [*G. H. Robin*

Class H15 4-6-0 No. 30335 (rebuilt from Class E14). [*G. Wheeler*

Class H15 4-6-0 No. 30334 (rebuilt from Class F13). [*L. Elsey*

Class H15 4-6-0 No. 30490 (Urie design, originally saturated). [*G. Wheeler*

Class H15 4-6-0 No. 30491 (rebuilt with N15-type boiler). [*G. Wheeler*

Class H15 4-6-0 No. 30476 (Maunsell design with N15-type boiler). [*G. Wheeler*

Class N15 4-6-0 No. 30456 *Sir Galahad* (Maunsell design with Drummond-type tender).
[*G. Wheeler*

Class N15 4-6-0 No. 30741 *Joyous Gard* (Urie design with modified cylinders).
[*R. Eckersley*

Class N15 4-6-0 No. 30800 *Sir Meleaus de Lile* (with six-wheel tender and later-type cab).
[*L. Elsey*

No.	Class	No.	Class	No.	Class	No.	Class
31821	N	31864	N	31916	W	32338	K
31822	NI	31865	N	31917	W	32339	K
31823	N	31866	N	31918	W	32340	K
31824	N	31867	N	31919	W	32341	K
31825	N	31868	N	31920	W	32342	K
31826	N	31869	N	31921	W	32343	K
31827	N	31870	N	31922	W	32344	K
31828	N	31871	N	31923	W	32345	K
31829	N	31872	N	31924	W	32346	K
31830	N	31873	N	31925	W	32347	K
31831	N	31874	N	32094	E1/R	32348	K
31832	N	31875	N	32095	E1/R	32349	K
31833	N	31876	NI	32096	E1/R	32350	K
31834	N	31877	NI	32100	E2	32351	K
31835	N	31878	NI	32101	E2	32352	K
31836	N	31879	NI	32102	E2	32353	K
31837	N	31880	NI	32103	E2	32390	D3
31838	N	31890	UI	32104	E2	32401	E5X
31839	N	31891	UI	32105	E2	32407	E6X
31840	N	31892	UI	32106	E2	32408	E6
31841	N	31893	UI	32107	E2	32409	E6
31842	N	31894	UI	32108	E2	32410	E6
31843	N	31895	UI	32109	E2	32411	E6X
31844	N	31896	UI	32113	E1	32412	E6
31845	N	31897	UI	32124	E1/R	32413	E6
31846	N	31898	UI	32135	E1/R	32414	E6
31847	N	31899	UI	32138	E1	32415	E6
31848	N	31900	UI	32139	E1	32416	E6
31849	N	31901	UI	32151	E1	32417	E6
31850	N	31902	UI	32165	E3	32418	E6
31851	N	31903	UI	32166	E3	32421*	H2
31852	N	31904	UI	32167	E3	32422*	H2
31853	N	31905	UI	32168	E3	32424*	H2
31854	N	31906	UI	32169	E3	32425*	H2
31855	N	31907	UI	32170	E3	32426*	H2
31856	N	31908	UI	32327*	N15X	32434	C2X
31857	N	31909	UI	32328*	N15X	32437	C2X
31858	N	31910	UI	32329*	N15X	32438	C2X
31859	N	31911	W	32330*	N15X	32440	C2X
31860	N	31912	W	32331*	N15X	32441	C2X
31861	N	31913	W	32332*	N15X	32442	C2X
31862	N	31914	W	32333*	N15X	32443	C2X
31863	N	31915	W	32337	K	32444	C2X

No.	Class	No.	Class	No.	Class	No.	Class
32445	C2X	32491	E4	32537	C2X	32593	E5
32446	C2X	32492	E4	32538	C2X	32606	E1
32447	C2X	32493	E4	32539	C2X	32608	E1/R
32448	C2X	32494	E4	32540	C2X	32610	E1/R
32449	C2X	32495	E4	32541	C2X	32636	AIX
32450	C2X	32496	E4	32543	C2X	32640	AIX
32451	C2X	32497	E4	32544	C2X	32646	AIX
32453	E3	32498	E4	32545	C2X	32650	AIX
32454	E3	32499	E4	32546	C2X	32655	AIX
32455	E3	32500	E4	32547	C2X	32661	AIX
32456	E3	32501	E4	32548	C2X	32662	AIX
32458	E3	32502	E4	32549	C2X	32670	AIX
32459	E3	32503	E4	32550	C2X	32677	AIX
32460	E3	32504	E4	32551	C2X	32678	AIX
32461	E3	32505	E4	32552	C2X	32689	E1
32462	E3	32506	E4	32553	C2X	32694	E1
32463	E4	32507	E4	32554	C2X	32695	E1/R
32464	E4	32508	E4	32556	E4	32696	E1/R
32465	E4	32509	E4	32557	E4	32697	E1/R
32466	E4X	32510	E4	32558	E4	33001	Q1
32467	E4	32511	E4	32559	E4	33002	Q1
32468	E4	32512	E4	32560	E4	33003	Q1
32469	E4	32513	E4	32561	E4	33004	Q1
32470	E4	32514	E4	32562	E4	33005	Q1
32471	E4	32515	E4	32563	E4	33006	Q1
32472	E4	32516	E4	32564	E4	33007	Q1
32473	E4	32517	E4	32565	E4	33008	Q1
32474	E4	32518	E4	32566	E4	33009	Q1
32475	E4	32519	E4	32568	E5	33010	Q1
32476	E4	32520	E4	32570	E5X	33011	Q1
32477	E4X	32521	C2X	32571	E5	33012	Q1
32478	E4X	32522	C2X	32576	E5X	33013	Q1
32479	E4	32523	C2X	32577	E4	33014	Q1
32480	E4	32524	C2X	32578	E4	33015	Q1
32481	E4	32525	C2X	32579	E4	33016	Q1
32482	E4	32526	C2X	32580	E4	33017	Q1
32484	E4	32527	C2X	32581	E4	33018	Q1
32485	E4	32528	C2X	32582	E4	33019	Q1
32486	E4	32529	C2X	32583	E5	33020	Q1
32487	E4	32532	C2X	32585	E5	33021	Q1
32488	E4	32534	C2X	32586	E5X	33022	Q1
32489	E4X	32535	C2X	32587	E5	33023	Q1
32490	E4	32536	C2X	32591	E5	33024	Q1

No.	Class	No.	Class	No.	Class	No.	Class
33025	QI	34025*	WC	34065*	BB	34105*	WC
33026	QI	34026*	WC	34066*	BB	34106*	WC
33027	QI	34027*	WC	34067*	BB	34107*	WC
33028	QI	34028*	WC	34068*	BB	34108*	WC
33029	QI	34029*	WC	34069*	BB	34109*	BB
33030	QI	34030*	WC	34070*	BB	34110*	BB
33031	QI	34031*	WC	34071*	BB	35001*	MN
33032	QI	34032*	WC	34072*	BB	35002*	MN
33033	QI	34033*	WC	34073*	BB	35003*	MN
33034	QI	34034*	WC	34074*	BB	35004*	MN
33035	QI	34035*	WC	34075*	BB	35005*	MN
33036	QI	34036*	WC	34076*	BB	35006*	MN
33037	QI	34037*	WC	34077*	BB	35007*	MN
33038	QI	34038*	WC	34078*	BB	35008*	MN
33039	QI	34039*	WC	34079*	BB	35009*	MN
33040	QI	34040*	WC	34080*	BB	35010*	MN
34001*	WC	34041*	WC	34081*	BB	35011*	MN
34002*	WC	34042*	WC	34082*	BB	35012*	MN
34003*	WC	34043*	WC	34083*	BB	35013*	MN
34004*	WC	34044*	WC	34084*	BB	35014*	MN
34005*	WC	34045*	WC	34085*	BB	35015*	MN
34006*	WC	34046*	WC	34086*	BB	35016*	MN
34007*	WC	34047*	WC	34087*	BB	35017*	MN
34008*	WC	34048*	WC	34088*	BB	35018*	MN
34009*	WC	34049*	BB	34089*	BB	35019*	MN
34010*	WC	34050*	BB	34090*	BB	35020*	MN
34011*	WC	34051*	BB	34091*	WC	35021*	MN
34012*	WC	34052*	BB	34092*	WC	35022*	MN
34013*	WC	34053*	BB	34093*	WC	35023*	MN
34014*	WC	34054*	BB	34094*	WC	35024*	MN
34015*	WC	34055*	BB	34095*	WC	35025*	MN
34016*	WC	34056*	BB	34096*	WC	35026*	MN
34017*	WC	34057*	BB	34097*	WC	35027*	MN
34018*	WC	34058*	BB	34098*	WC	35028*	MN
34019*	WC	34059*	BB	34099*	WC	35029*	MN
34020*	WC	34060*	BB	34100*	WC	35030*	MN
34021*	WC	34061*	BB	34101*	WC		
34022*	WC	34062*	BB	34102*	WC		
34023*	WC	34063*	BB	34103*	WC		
34024*	WC	34064*	BB	34104*	WC		

Isle of Wight & Service Locos.

ISLE OF WIGHT LOCOMOTIVES

W1*	E1	W17*	O2	W24*	O2	W31*	O2
W2*	E1	W18*	O2	W25*	O2	W32*	O2
W3*	E1	W19*	O2	W26*	O2	W33*	O2
W4*	E1	W20*	O2	W27*	O2	W34*	O2
W14*	O2	W21*	O2	W28*	O2	W35*	O2
W15*	O2	W22*	O2	W29*	O2	W36*	O2
W16*	O2	W23*	O2	W30*	O2		

SOUTHERN REGION SERVICE LOCOMOTIVES

No.	Old No.	Class	Station
*DS 74	—	Bo-Bo	Durnsford Road Power Station
*DS 75	—	Bo	Waterloo & City
DS 77	0745	C14	Redbridge Sleeper Depot
†DS 377	2635	A1X	Brighton Works
DS 600	—	0-4-0 Diesel	Eastleigh Carriage Works
DS 680	L.B.S.C. 654 S.E.C. 751	A1	Lancing Carriage Works
DS 681	L.B.S.C. 659 I.W.9	A1X	Lancing Carriage Works
DS 1173	2217	0-6-0 Diesel	Engineer's Department
DS 3152	30272	G 6	Meldon Quarry

* Electric   † Repainted 1947 in Stroudley livery

SOUTHERN RAILWAY LOCOMOTIVE SUPERINTENDENTS AND CHIEF MECHANICAL ENGINEERS OF CONSTITUENT COMPANIES

LONDON & SOUTH WESTERN RAILWAY

J. Woods ...	... ...	1835–1841
J. V. Gooch	... ...	1841–1850
J. Beattie ...	... ...	1850–1871
W. G. Beattie	... ...	1871–1878
W. Adams ...	... ...	1878–1895
D. Drummond	... ...	1895–1912
R. W. Urie...	... ...	1912–1922

LONDON, BRIGHTON AND SOUTH COAST RAILWAY

—. Statham	... ...	? –1845
J. Gray ...	... ...	1845–1847
S. Kirtley ...	... ...	1847
J. C. Craven	... ...	1847–1869
W. Stroudley	... ...	1870–1889
R. J. Billinton	... ...	1890–1904
D. Earle Marsh	... ...	1905–1911
L. B. Billinton	... ...	1911–1922

SOUTH EASTERN RAILWAY

B. Cubitt ...	... ...	? –1845
J. Cudworth	... ...	1845–1876
A. M. Watkin	... ...	1876
R. Mansell	... ...	1877–1878
J. Stirling ...	... ...	1878–1898

LONDON, CHATHAM AND DOVER RAILWAY

W. Cubitt ...	... ...	? –1860
W. Martley	... ...	1860–1874
W. Kirtley ...	... ...	1874–1898

SOUTH EASTERN AND CHATHAM RAILWAY

H. S. Wainwright ...	...	1899–1913
R. E. L. Maunsell ...	...	1913–1922

SOUTHERN RAILWAY

R. E. L. Maunsell ...	...	1923–1937
O. V. Bulleid	... ...	1937–1949

BRITISH RAILWAYS' LOCOMOTIVES

Nos. 26000-35030

NAMED LOCOMOTIVES

CLASS EM1 BO-BO ELECTRIC

26000 Tommy

CLASS N15 "KING ARTHUR" 4-6-0

30448	Sir Tristram	30453	King Arthur
30449	Sir Torre	30454	Queen Guinevere
30450	Sir Kay	30455	Sir Launcelot
30451	Sir Lamorak	30456	Sir Galahad
30452	Sir Meliagrance	30457	Sir Bedivere

CLASS 0458 0-4-0ST

30458 Ironside

CLASS N15 "KING ARTHUR" 4-6-0

30736	Excalibur	30746	Pendragon
30737	King Uther	30747	Elaine
30738	King Pellinore	30748	Vivien
30739	King Leodegrance	30749	Iseult
30740	Merlin	30750	Morgan le Fay
30741	Joyous Gard	30751	Etarre
30742	Camelot	30752	Linette
30743	Lyonnesse	30753	Melisande
30744	Maid of Astolat	30755	The Red Knight
30745	Tintagel		

CLASS 757 0-6-2T

30757 Earl of Mount Edgcumbe | 30758 Lord St. Levan

NAMED LOCOMOTIVES—cont.

CLASS N15 "KING ARTHUR" 4-6-0

30763	Sir Bors de Ganis	30785	Sir Mador de la Porte
30764	Sir Gawin	30786	Sir Lionel
30765	Sir Gareth	30787	Sir Menadeuke
30766	Sir Gera nt	30788	Sir Urre of the Mount
30767	Sir Valence	30789	Sir Guy
30768	Sir Balin	30790	Sir Villiars
30769	Sir Balan	30791	Sir Uwaine
30770	Sir Prianius	30792	Sir Hervis de Revel
30771	Sir Sagramore	30793	Sir Ontzlake
30772	Sir Percivale	30794	Sir Ector de Maris
30773	Sir Lavaine	30795	Sir Dinadan
30774	Sir Gaheris	30796	Sir Dodinas le Savage
30775	Sir Agravaine	30797	Sir Blamor de Ganis
30776	Sir Galagars	30798	Sir Hectimere
30777	Sir Lamiel	30799	Sir Ironside
30778	Sir Pelleas	30800	Sir Meleaus de Lile
30779	Sir Colgrevance	30801	Sir Meliot de Logres
30780	Sir Persant	30802	Sir Durnore
30781	Sir Aglovale	30803	Sir Harry le Fise Lake
30782	Sir Brian	30804	Sir Cador of Cornwall
30783	Sir Gillemere	30805	Sir Constantine
30784	Sir Nerovens	30806	Sir Galleron

CLASS LN "LORD NELSON" 4-6-0

30850	Lord Nelson	30858	Lord Duncan
30851	Sir Francis Drake	30859	Lord Hood
30852	Sir Walter Raleigh	30860	Lord Hawke
30853	Sir Richard Grenville	30861	Lord Anson
30854	Howard of Effingham	30862	Lord Collingwood
30855	Robert Blake	30863	Lord Rodney
30856	Lord St. Vincent	30864	Sir Martin Frobisher
30857	Lord Howe	30865	Sir John Hawkins

CLASS V "SCHOOLS" 4-4-0

30900	Eton	30903	Charterhouse
30901	Winchester	30904	Lancing
30902	Wellington	30905	Tonbridge

NAMED LOCOMOTIVES—*cont.*

30906	Sherborne	30923	Bradfield
30907	Dulwich	30924	Haileybury
30908	Westminster	30925	Cheltenham
30909	St. Paul's	30926	Repton
30910	Merchant Taylors	30927	Clifton
30911	Dover	30928	Stowe
30912	Downside	30929	Malvern
30913	Christ's Hospital	30930	Radley
30914	Eastbourne	30931	King's Wimbledon
30915	Brighton	30932	Blundells
30916	Whitgift	30933	King's Canterbury
30917	Ardingly	30934	St. Lawrence
30918	Hurstpierpoint	30935	Sevenoaks
30919	Harrow	30936	Cranleigh
30920	Rugby	30937	Epsom
30921	Shrewsbury	30938	St. Olave's
30922	Marlborough	30939	Leatherhead

CLASS N15X " REMEMBRANCE " 4-6-0

32327	Trevithick	32331	Beattie
32328	Hackworth	32332	Stroudley
32329	Stephenson	32333	Remembrance
32330	Cudworth		

CLASS H2 4-4-2

32421	South Foreland	32425	Trevose Head
32422	North Foreland	32426	St. Alban's Head
32424	Beachy Head		

CLASSES WC & BB 4-6-2
" WEST COUNTRY " and " BATTLE OF BRITAIN "

34001	Exeter	34005	Barnstaple
34002	Salisbury	34006	Bude
34003	Plymouth	34007	Wadebridge
34004	Yeovil	34008	Padstow

43

34009	Lyme Regis	34053	Sir Keith Park
34010	Sidmouth	34054	Lord Beaverbrook
34011	Tavistock	34055	Fighter Pilot
34012	Launceston	34056	Croydon
34013	Okehampton	34057	Biggin Hill
34014	Budleigh Salterton	34058	Sir Frederick Pile
34015	Exmouth	34059	Sir Archibald Sinclair
34016	Bodmin	34060	25 Squadron
34017	Ilfracombe	34061	73 Squadron
34018	Axminster	34062	17 Squadron
34019	Bideford	34063	229 Squadron
34020	Seaton	34064	Fighter Command
34021	Dartmoor	34065	Hurricane
34022	Exmoor	34066	Spitfire
34023	Blackmore Vale	34067	Tangmere
34024	Tamar Valley	34068	Kenley
34025	Whimple	34069	Hawkinge
34026	Yes Tor	34070	Manston
34027	Taw Valley	34071	601 Squadron
34028	Eddystone	34072	257 Squadron
34029	Lundy	34073	249 Squadron
34030	Watersmeet	34074	46 Squadron
34031	Torrington	34075	264 Squadron
34032	Camelford	34076	41 Squadron
34033	Chard	34077	603 Squadron
34034	Honiton	34078	222 Squadron
34035	Shaftesbury	34079	141 Squadron
34036	Westward Ho	34080	74 Squadron
34037	Clovelly	34081	92 Squadron
34038	Lynton	34082	615 Squadron
34039	Boscastle	34083	605 Squadron
34040	Crewkerne	34084	253 Squadron
34041	Wilton	34085	501 Squadron
34042	Dorchester	34086	219 Squadron
34043	Combe Martin	34087	145 Squadron
34044	Woolacombe	34088	213 Squadron
34045	Ottery St. Mary	34089	602 Squadron
34046	Braunton	34090	Sir Eustace Missenden, Southern Railway
34047	Callington		
34048	Crediton	34091	Weymouth
34049	Anti-Aircraft Command	34092	City of Wells
34050	Royal Observer Corps	34093	Saunton
34051	Winston Churchill	34094	Mortehoe
34052	Lord Dowding	34095	Brentor

Class V 4-4-0 No. 30902 *Wellington*.　　　　　　　　　　　　[R. E. Vincent

Class N15X 4-6-0 No. 32332 *Stroudley*.　　　　　　　　　　　　[P. J. Lynch

Class LN 4-6-0 No. 30857 *Lord Howe*.　　　　　　　　　　　　[G. Wheeler

Class BB 4-6-2 No. 34067 *Tangmere* [*W. A. Corkill*

Class MN 4-6-2 No. 35008 *Orient Line* (with original tender design and front end).
[*R. Russell*

Class MN 4-6-2 No. 35014 *Nederland Line* (with later-type tender). [*G. Wheeler*

Class Q1 0-6-0 No. 33040.   [P. Ransome-Wallis

Class C 0-6-0 No. 31589.   [A. B. Crompton

Class O1 0-6-0 No. 31048.   [A. B. Crompton

Class 700 0-6-0 No. 30688. *[E. D. Bruton*

Class 0395 0-6-0 No. 30567 (with Drummond-type boiler). *[C. G. Pearson*

Class C2X 0-6-0 No. 32547. *[C. G. Pearson*

Class G16 4-8-0T No. 30494.   [G. Wheeler

Class H16 4-6-2T No. 30519.   [G. Wheeler

Class Z 0-8-0T No. 30953.   [R. E. Vincent

Above: Class E1/R
0-6-2T No. 32697.
[*G. Wheeler*

Left: Class E1
0-6-0T No. 32151.
[*L. Elsey*

Below: Class E2
0-6-0T No. 32103
(of original series).
[*R. J. Buckley*

Above: Class E4X No. 32489.
[*C. G. Pearson*

Right: Class E4 0-6-2T No. 32500.
[*A. T. H. Tayler*

Below: Class A1X 0-6-0T No. 32677.
[*W. M. J. Jackson*

Above: Class 0458
0-4-0ST No. 30458
Ironside.
[*H. C. Casserley*

Left: Class C14 0-4-0T
No. 77S.
[*L. Elsey*

Below: Class B4 0-4-0T
No. 30088 (with
Drummond boiler).
[*H. C. Casserley*

NAMED LOCOMOTIVES—cont.

34096	Trevone	34104	Bere Alston
34097	Holsworthy	34105	Swanage
34098	Templecombe	34106	Lydford
34099	Lynmouth	34107	Blandford Forum
34100	Appledore	34108	Wincanton
34101	Hartland	34109	Sir Trafford
34102	Lapford		Leigh-Mallory
34103	Calstock	34110	66 Squadron

CLASS MN " MERCHANT NAVY " 4-6-2

35001	Channel Packet	35015	Rotterdam Lloyd
35002	Union Castle	35016	Elders Fyffes
35003	Royal Mail	35017	Belgian Marine
35004	Cunard White Star	35018	British India Line
35005	Canadian Pacific	35019	French Line CGT
35006	Peninsular & Oriental S.N. Co.	35020	Bibby Line
		35021	New Zealand Line
35007	Aberdeen Commonwealth	35022	Holland-America Line
		35023	Holland-Afrika Line
35008	Orient Line	35024	East Asiatic Company
35009	Shaw Savill	35025	Brocklebank Line
35010	Blue Star	35026	Lamport & Holt Line
35011	General Steam Navigation	35027	Port Line
		35028	Clan Line
35012	United States Line	35029	Ellerman Lines
35013	Blue Funnel	35030	Elder Dempster Lines
35014	Nederland Line		

CLASS E1 0-6-0T

W 1	Medina	W 3	Ryde
W 2	Yarmouth	W 4	Wroxall

CLASS O2 0-4-4T

W14	Fishbourne	W22	Brading	W30	Shorwell
W15	Cowes	W23	Totland	W31	Chale
W16	Ventnor	W24	Calbourne	W32	Bonchurch
W17	Seaview	W25	Godshill	W33	Bembridge
W18	Ningwood	W26	Whitwell	W34	Newport
W19	Osborne	W27	Merstone	W35	Freshwater
W20	Shanklin	W28	Ashey	W36	Carisbrooke
W21	Sandown	W29	Alverstone		

SOME S.R. LOCOMOTIVE HEAD SIGNALS

This list is not complete and gives only the principle one and two disc (or lamp) codes.

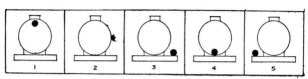

No. I

Victoria and Dover via Chatham
Victoria and Norwood Yard via Selhurst
Loughborough Sidings to Holborn
Ashford and Hastings
Reading and Margate via Redhill
Eastleigh and Bulford via Chandlers Road and Andover
Southampton Terminus and Brockenhurst and Weymouth via Wimborne
Plymouth Friary and Tavistock
Woking and Reading via Virginia Water West Curve
Exeter Central and Ilfracombe
Bodmin and Wadebridge
Petersfield and Midhurst
Exeter Central and Exmouth

NO. 2

Victoria or Clapham Junction and Holborn (L.L.)
London Bridge or Bricklayers' Arms and Portsmouth via Quarry line and Horsham
Via Mid Kent Line and Beckenham Junction
Ashford and Eastbourne direct
Waterloo or Nine Elms and Southampton Terminus, direct (not boat trains)
Willesden and Feltham Yard via Gunnersbury
Waterloo or Nine Elms and Windsor via Twickenham
Southampton Central to Lymington
Yeovil Junction and Yeovil Town
Seaton Junction and Seaton
Barnstaple Junction and Torrington
Halwill and Bude

NO. 3

Victoria or Clapham Junction and Holborn
London Bridge or Bricklayers' Arms and Brighton via Quarry Line
Tonbridge and Brighton via Eridge
Hastings via Mid Kent Line, Oxted, Crowhurst Junction and Tonbridge
Dunton Green and Westerham
Ashford and Margate via Canterbury West
Lydd Branch
Canterbury West and Whitstable Harbour
Folkestone Junction and Folkestone Harbour
Crowhurst and Bexhill
Swanley Junction and Gravesend West Street
Sittingbourne and Sheerness
Deal and Kearsney
Gravesend Central and Allhallows-on-Sea or Port Victoria
All stations to Feltham (except via Mortlake)

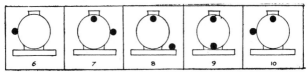

| 6 | 7 | 8 | 9 | 10 |

Weymouth and Portland and Easton (goods trains)
Bournemouth West and Brockenhurst via Wimborne

NO. 4

Victoria or Battersea Yard and Brighton via Redhill
Oxted and Eastbourne via Eridge
London Bridge and New Cross via Bricklayers' Arms Junction
Horsham and Brighton
Alton and Fareham
Bentley and Bordon
Salisbury and Bulford
Axminster and Lyme Regis
Tipton St. John's and Exmouth
Wareham and Swanage
Brockenhurst and Lymington Pier
Bere Alston and Callington

NO. 5

Victoria or Stewarts Lane and Clapham Junction
Oxted and Tunbridge Wells West via East Grinstead (H.L.)
Pulborough, Midhurst and Chichester
Havant and Hayling Island
London Bridge and Bricklayers' Arms
Tonbridge and Maidstone West
Ashford (Kent) and Dover via Minster and Deal
Stewarts Lane to Victoria
Southampton Docks and Nine Elms via main line (market goods, fruit or potato
train)

NO. 6

London Bridge or Bricklayers' Arms and Dover or Ramsgate via East Croydon,
Oxted and Tonbridge
Tonbridge and Hawkhurst
Battersea Yard and Kensington
Waterloo or Nine Elms and Reading via Twickenham
Willesden and Feltham Yard via Kew East Junction
Exeter Central and Sidmouth
Plymouth Friary and Turnchapel
Eastleigh or Southampton and Fawley
Bournemouth Central and Brockenhurst via Wimbourne
Torrington and Halwill

NO. 7

Victoria or Battersea Yard and Portsmouth via Quarry Line and Horsham
Via Maidstone East line to Victoria or Holborn
Waterloo or Nine Elms and Southampton Docks via Brentford, Chertsey and
Woking

NO. 8

London Bridge or Bricklayers' Arms and Eastbourne or Hastings via Quarry line
Victoria or West London line and Ramsgate via Herne Hill or Catford Loop
London Bridge or Bricklayers' Arms and Hastings via Chislehurst and Tunbridge
Wells Central

55

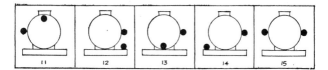

West London line to East Croydon via Crystal Palace (L.L.)
Special boat trains Waterloo and Southampton Docks via Northam
Special boat trains from Southampton Docks to Waterloo via Millbrook
Southampton and Andover via Redbridge

NO. 9

Victoria or Battersea Yard and Eastbourne or Hastings via Quarry line
London and Hither Green Sidings
Victoria and Folkestone Harbour or Dover Marine via Swanley, Otford and Tonbridge
Waterloo or Nine Elms and Plymouth
Bournemouth Central and Dorchester goods trains
Battersea Yard and Brent via New Kew Junction
Southampton Terminus and Portsmouth Harbour via Netley

NO. 10

London Bridge or Bricklayers' Arms and Portsmouth via Redhill and Horsham
Victoria or Battersea Yard and Norwood Yard via Crystal Palace (L.L.)
London Bridge and New Cross Gate to Eardley Sidings via Peckham Rye
Deptford Wharf and New Cross Gate
London Bridge or Bricklayers' Arms and Folkestone or Dover via Chislehurst, Tonbridge and Ashford
Dover and Margate via Deal and Minster Loop
Special boat trains Waterloo to Southampton Docks via Millbrook
Feltham to Durnsford Road via Chertsey

NO. 11

Victoria or Battersea Yard and Portsmouth via Redhill and Horsham
Via Dartford Loop line
Victoria or Holborn and Hastings Branch via Orpington Loop and Tunbridge Wells Central
Bricklayers' Arms and Guildford via Leatherhead and Effingham Junction
Waterloo or Nine Elms and Southampton Terminus via Alton
Salisbury and Bournemouth West via Wimbourne
Fareham and Gosport
Ballast trains to Meldon Quarry from Exeter Central and stations West thereof

NO. 12

Victoria or Battersea Yard and Portsmouth via Mitcham Junction
London Bridge or Bricklayers' Arms and Eastbourne or Hastings via Redhill
Victoria, Stewarts Lane or Holborn to North Kent lines via Nunhead line
Nine Elms and Feltham via Mortlake
Exeter Central to Nine Elms (market goods and fish)
Down main line goods terminating at Woking
Southampton Docks and Salisbury via Eastleigh

NO. 13

London Bridge or Bricklayers' Arms and Brighton via Redhill
Oxted and Brighton via East Grinstead (L.L.) and Lewes
Three Bridges and Tunbridge Wells West
West London line to Norwood Yard via Thornton Heath
Victoria or Holborn to Dover via Nunhead line and Maidstone East
Parcels and empty trains Waterloo to Clapham Junction (Kensington sidings)

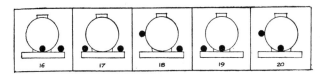

| 16 | 17 | 18 | 19 | 20 |

Feltham Yard and Neasden via Kew East Junction
Portsmouth Harbour or Portsmouth and Southsea to Fratton Loco. Depot
Exeter Central and Exmouth Junction
Bournemouth West to Dorchester
Southampton and Salisbury via Redbridge

NO. 14

London Bridge and Portsmouth via Mitcham Junction
London Bridge, Oxted and Tunbridge Wells West via Hever
Oxted and Lewes or Seaford or Eastbourne via Haywards Heath and Keymer Junction (change to No. 5 or No. 21 code at Lewes)
London Bridge or Bricklayers' Arms and Dover via Chislehurst Loop and Maidstone East
Waterloo or Nine Elms and Brockenhurst and Bournemouth West via Sway

NO. 15

Via Bexley Heath line
Victoria, Stewarts Lane or Holborn via Nunhead line and Bexley Heath
Oxted and Brighton via Haywards Heath
Waterloo or Nine Elms and Reading via Loop line
All trains terminating at Portsmouth and Southsea (trains from Salisbury to carry No. 17 to Eastleigh)
Exeter Central and Padstow
Light engines, Bournemouth Central or Bournemouth West to Bournemouth Central via triangle to turn
Light engines Eastleigh Loco. to Portsmouth and Southsea.
Light engines to Guildford Loco. via Woking (except via Staines)

NO. 16

London Bridge or Bricklayers' Arms and Portsmouth via West Croydon
Victoria or Battersea Yard and Eastbourne or Hastings via Redhill
Oxted and Brighton via Eridge
London Bridge or Bricklayers' Arms and Ramsgate via Tonbridge and Canterbury West
Waterloo or Nine Elms and Woking via Richmond and Chertsey
Milk and empty trains to Clapham Junction via Byfleet curve and Richmond

NO. 17

London Bridge or Bricklayers' Arms and Tonbridge or Reading via East Croydon and Redhill (also Tonbridge and Reading)
Brighton and Hove via Preston Park Spur
Three Bridges and Eridge
Victoria or Holborn and Folkestone or Dover via Orpington Loop, Tonbridge and Ashford
London Bridge or Bricklayers' Arms and Gillingham, Faversham, Ramsgate or Dover via Chislehurst Loop and Chatham
Waterloo or Nine Elms and Clapham Junction (empty trains and light engines)
Passenger trains Bournemouth Central and Weymouth

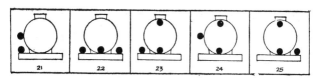

| 21 | 22 | 23 | 24 | 25 |

NO 18.

London Bridge or Bricklayers' Arms and Dover, Ramsgate or Hastings via
  Chislehurst, Swanley, Otford and Sevenoaks
Victoria, Oxted and Tunbridge Wells West via Hever
Holborn and Ramsgate via Herne Hill or Catford Loop
Light engines and trains requiring to run to up main loop, Clapham Junction,
  from stations westward
Southampton and Andover via Eastleigh
Light engines or engines with vehicles attached running round the triangle at
  Bournemouth West to turn

NO. 19

Victoria to Battersea Yard and Brighton via Quarry line
London Bridge or New Cross Gate and Norwood Yard
Tunbridge Wells West and Eastbourne
Victoria or Holborn and Ramsgate, Dover or Hastings via Nunhead line and
  Tonbridge
Horsham and Guildford
Waterloo or Nine Elms and Southampton Docks via East Putney
Salisbury and Portsmouth Harbour via Eastleigh
Portsmouth and Southsea to Salisbury via Eastleigh

NO. 20

Victoria, Stewarts Lane or Holborn to Ramsgate via Nunhead line, Chislehurst
  and Chatham
London Bridge or Bricklayers' Arms and North Kent line via Greenwich
Via Streatham Spur
Feltham Yard and Brent via Kew East Junction
Clapham Junction and Kensington
Portsmouth and Southsea to Salisbury via Redbridge
Salisbury and Portsmouth Harbour via Redbridge

NO. 21

Victoria and Newhaven Harbour
Victoria or Holborn to Ramsgate via Nunhead line and Maidstone East
Waterloo or Nine Elms and Portsmouth via Woking and Guildford
Light engines from all stations to Feltham Loco.
Light engines from all stations West of Basingstoke to Eastleigh Loco.

NO. 22

Waterloo and Portsmouth Harbour via Eastleigh
Feltham and Brent via Richmond
S.R. and W.R. trains Hither Green Sidings, Stewarts Lane or South Lambeth to
  Old Oak Common
L.M. (Western Division) trains between Willesden and Redhill via Clapham
  Junction
L.M. (Midland Division) and E.R. (G.N.) trains to or from Hither Green Sidings
W.R. trains, Norwood Yard to Old Oak Common
W.R. trains Cattewater Junction and Plymstock

58

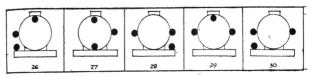

| 26 | 27 | 28 | 29 | 30 |

NO. 23
Nine Elms and Willesden via New Kew Junction
Brighton and Salisbury via Southampton Central
Eastleigh and Micheldever or Basingstoke (light engines for testing)
Windsor and Hastings Excursion trains
Windsor and Margate or Dover Excursion trains or between Windsor and Redhill
W.R. trains to South Lambeth
E.R. trains to or from Lower Sydenham

NO. 24
Waterloo and Guildford via Leatherhead (except light engines Nine Elms to Raynes Park)
Southampton and Willesden via Richmond and Gunnersbury
Southampton or Salisbury and Willesden via Chertsey and Kew East Junction (or from Basingstoke)
Reading to Willesden

NO. 25
Nine Elms and Brent via New Kew Junction
Kingston and Shepperton
Brighton and Salisbury through trains via Eastleigh
Windsor and Bognor Regis Excursion trains
To L.M.R. via West London line

NO. 26
Brighton and Bournemouth
Waterloo and Wimbledon Park Sidings via East Putney (empty trains and light engines)
Merstham and Staines Moor via Guildford, Byfleet Junction and Staines
Victoria (E. or C.), Stewarts Lane, Clapham Junction or Holborn and Eardley Sidings via Herne Hill

NO. 27
Hither Green Sidings and Feltham via Brentford
Feltham to Wimbledon West Yard
London Bridge or Bricklayers' Arms and Brighton via Oxted, Eridge and Lewes

NO. 28
Hither Green Sidings and Feltham via Richmond
London Bridge or Bricklayers' Arms and Brighton via Oxted, East Grinstead and Lewes

NO. 29
Plumstead and Feltham via Brentford
Victoria or Battersea Yard and Brighton via Oxted, Eridge and Lewes

NO. 30
Plumstead and F ltham via Richmond
Victoria or Battersea Yard and Brighton via Oxted, East Grinstead and Lewes

NUMERICAL LIST OF SOUTHERN REGION ELECTRIC MOTOR UNITS

(Number to be seen on front and rear of each set)

TWO-CAR MOTOR UNITS
(for South London and Wimbledon-West Croydon services)

1801	1805	1810
1803	1806	1811
1804	1808	1812

TWO-CAR NON-CORRIDOR MOTOR UNITS
(2-NOL.)

1813*	1833*	1853	1873
1814*	1834*	1854	1874
1815*	1835*	1856	1875
1816*	1836*	1857	1876
1817*	1837*	1858	1877
1818*	1839*	1859	1878
1819*	1840*	1860	1879
1820*	1841*	1861	1880
1821*	1842*	1862	1881
1822*	1843*	1863	1882
1823*	1844*	1864	1883†
1824*	1845*	1865	1884†
1825*	1846*	1866	1885†
1826*	1847*	1867	1886†
1827*	1848*	1868	1887†
1829*	1849	1869	1888†
1830*	1850	1870	1889†
1831*	1851	1871	1890†
1832*	1852	1872	

* With 1st and 3rd class compartments.

† With electro-pneumatic control gear.

TWO-CAR MOTOR LAVATORY UNITS
(2-BIL.)

2001†	2003†	2005†	2007†
2002†	2004†	2006†	2008†

2009†	2045	2080	2116
2010†	2046	2081	2117
2011	2047	2082	2118
2012	2048	2083	2120
2013	2049	2084	2121
2015	2050	2085	2122
2016	2051	2086	2123
2017	2052	2087	2124
2018	2053	2088*	2125
2019	2054	2089	2126
2020	2055	2090	2127
2021	2056*	2091	2128
2022	2057	2092	2129
2023	2058	2093	2130
2024	2059	2094	2132
2025	2060	2095	2134
2026	2061	2096	2135
2027	2062	2097	2136
2028	2063	2098	2137
2029	2064	2099	2138
2030	2065	2100	2139
2031	2066	2101	2140
2032	2067	2103	2141
2033	2068	2104	2142
2034	2069	2105	2143
2035	2070	2106	2144
2036	2071	2107	2145
2037	2072	2108	2146
2038	2073	2109	2147
2039	2074	2110	2148
2040	2075	2111	2149
2041	2076	2112	2150
2042	2077	2113	2151
2043	2078	2114	2152
2044	2079	2115	

†88 3rd seats instead of 84 and all-electric control gear.

*BIL Motor Coach and HAL trailer.

TWO-CAR MOTOR LAVATORY UNITS

(with one corridor and one non-corridor coach).

(2-HAL.)

2601	2626	2652	2677
2602	2627	2653	2678
2603	2628	2654	2679
2604	2629	2655	2680
2605	2630	2656	2681
2606	2631	2657	2682
2607	2632	2658	2683
2608	2633	2659	2684
2609	2634	2660	2685
2610	2635	2661	2686
2611	2636	2662	2687
2612	2637	2663	2688
2613	2638	2664	2689
2614	2639	2665	2690
2615	2640	2666	2691
2616	2641	2667	2692
2617	2642	2668	2693
2618	2643	2669	2694
2619	2644	2670	2695
2620	2645	2671	2696
2621	2647	2672	2697
2622	2648	2673	2698
2623	2649	2674	2699
2624	2650	2675	
2625	2651	2676	

FOUR-CAR MOTOR LAVATORY UNITS

(with three non-corridor 3rd and one 3rd/1st corridor coach).

(4-LAV.)

2921	2928	2935	2942
2922	2929	2936	2943
2923	2930	2937	2944
2924	2931	2938	2945
2925	2932	2939	2946
2926*	2933	2940	2947
2927	2934	2941	2948

2949	2951	2953	2955†
2950	2952	2954†	

*One motor coach with electro-pneumatic control gear.

†With electro-pneumatic control gear.

SIX-CAR MOTOR CORRIDOR UNITS *(with Pullman Car)*

(6-PUL.)

3001	3007	3013	3019
3002	3008	3014	3020
3003	3009	3015	3041*
3004	3010	3016	3042*
3005	3011	3017	3043*
3006	3012	3018	

*Ex-" 6-CIT " Units.

SIX-CAR MOTOR CORRIDOR UNITS *(with Pantry Car)*

(6-PAN.)

3021	3026	3030	3034
3022	3027	3031	3035
3023	3028	3032	3036
3024	3029	3033	3037
3025			

FIVE-CAR PULLMAN MOTOR UNITS
(For "Brighton Belle" Service)

(5-BEL.)

3051	3052	3053

FOUR-CAR KITCHEN CORRIDOR MOTOR UNITS

(4-RES.)

3054	3059	3065	3069
3055	3061	3066	3070
3056	3062	3067	3071
3057	3064	3068	3072

FOUR-CAR BUFFET CORRIDOR MOTOR UNITS

(4-BUF.)

3073	3077	3080	3083
3074	3078	3081	3084
3075	3079	3082	3085
3076			

FOUR-CAR CORRIDOR MOTOR UNITS

(4-COR.)

3101	3116	3131	3145
3102	3117	3132	3146
3103	3118	3133	3147
3104	3119	3134	3148
3105	3120	3135	3149
3106	3121	3136	3150
3107	3122	3137	3151
3108	3123	3138	3152
3109	3124	3139	3153
3110	3125	3140	3154
3111	3126	3141	3155
3112	3127	3142	3156
3113	3128	3143	3157
3114	3129	3144	3158
3115	3130		

FOUR-CAR DOUBLE DECK SUBURBAN UNITS

(4-DD.)

4001	4002

FOUR-CAR NON CORRIDOR SUBURBAN UNITS

(4-SUB.)

4101	4108	4115	4122
4102	4109	4116	4123
4103	4110	4117	4124
4104	4111	4118	4125
4105	4112	4119	4126
4106	4113	4120	4127
4107	4114	4121	4128
4129	4195	4279	4324
4130	4196	4280	4325
4131	4197	4281	4326
4132	4198	4282	4327
4133	4199	4283	4328
4134	4200	4284	4329
4135	4201	4285	4330
4136	4203	4286	4331
4137	4204	4287	4332
4138	4205	4288	4333
4140	4206	4289	4334
4141	4207	4290	4335
4142	4208	4291	4336
4143	4209	4292	4337
4144	4210	4293	4338
4145	4211	4294	4339
4146	4212	4295	4340
4147	4213	4296	4341
4148	4214	4297	4342
4149	4215	4298	4343
4150	4216	4299	4344
4151	4217	4300	4345
4152	4218	4301	4346
4153	4219	4302	4347
4156	4220	4303	4348
4157	4221	4304	4349
4158	4223	4305	4351
4159	4224	4306	4352
4160	4225	4307	4353
4162	4226	4308	4354
4163	4227	4309	4355
4164	4228	4310	4356
4165	4229	4311	4357
4166	4230	4312	4358
4167	4231	4313	4359
4168	4232	4314	4360
4169	4234	4315	4361
4170	4238	4316	4362
4171	4239	4317	4363
4176	4247	4318	4364
4178	4250	4319	4365
4181	4251	4320	4366
4182	4254	4321	4367
4187	4277	4322	4368
4190	4278	4323	4369

4370	4537	4607	4661	4702	4716	4730	4744
4371	4538	4621	4662	4703	4717	4731	4745
4372	4539	4622	4663	4704	4718	4732	4746
4373	4540	4623	4664	4705	4719	4733	4747
4374	4541	4624	4665	4706	4720	4734	4748
4375	4542	4625	4666	4707	4721	4735	4749
4376	4543	4626	4667	4708	4722	4736	4750
4377	4544	4627	4668	4709	4723	4737	4751
4378	4545	4628	4669	4710	4724	4738	4752
4379	4546	4629	4670	4711	4725	4739	4753
4380	4547	4630	4671	4712	4726	4740	4754
4381	4548	4631	4672	4713	4727	4741	
4382	4549	4632	4673	4714	4728	4742	
4383	4550	4633	4674	4715	4729	4743	
4384	4551	4634	4675				
4385	4552	4635	4676				
4386	4553	4636	4677				
4387	4554	4637	4678				
4409	4555	4638	4679				
4411	4556	4639	4680				
4420	4557	4640	4681				
4424	4558	4641	4682				
4425	4559	4642	4683				
4426	4560	4643	4684				
4427	4561	4644	4685				
4428	4564	4645	4686				
4429	4565	4646	4687				
4503	4566	4647	4688				
4515	4567	4648	4689				
4519	4571	4649	4690				
4520	4572	4650	4691				
4526	4573	4651	4692				
4527	4579	4652	4693				
4528	4586	4653	4694				
4529	4590	4654	4695				
4530	4601	4655	4696				
4531	4602	4656	4697				
4532	4603	4657	4698				
4533	4604	4658	4699				
4534	4605	4659	4700				
4535	4606	4660	4701				

FOUR-CAR NON-CORRIDOR SUBURBAN UNITS

(4–EPB)

5001	5017	5033	5049
5002	5018	5034	5050
5003	5019	5035	5051
5004	5020	5036	5052
5005	5021	5037	5053
5006	5022	5038	5054
5007	5023	5039	5101
5008	5024	5040	5102
5009	5025	5041	5103
5010	5026	5042	5104
5011	5027	5043	5105
5012	5028	5044	5106
5013	5029	5045	5107
5014	5030	5046	5108
5015	5031	5047	5109
5016	5032	5048	5110

TWO-CAR NON-CORRIDOR SUBURBAN UNITS

(2-EPB)

5701	5730	5759	5788
5702	5731	5760	5789
5703	5732	5761	5790
5704	5733	5762	5791
5705	5734	5763	5792
5706	5735	5764	5793
5707	5736	5765	5794
5708	5737	5766	5795
5709	5738	5767	5796
5710	5739	5768	5797
5711	5740	5769	5798
5712	5741	5770	5799
5713	5742	5771	5800
5714	5743	5772	5801
5715	5744	5773	5802
5716	5745	5774	5803
5717	5746	5775	5804
5718	5747	5776	5805
5719	5748	5777	5806
5720	5749	5778	5807
5721	5750	5779	5808
5722	5751	5780	5809
5723	5752	5781	5810
5724	5753	5782	5811
5725	5754	5783	5812
5726	5755	5784	5813
5727	5756	5785	5814
5728	5757	5786	5815
5729	5758	5787	5816

N.B.—These units are still being delivered.

FOUR-CAR BUFFET UNITS

(B.R. Standard under-frames)

To be delivered in the 6001 series.

FOUR-CAR CORRIDOR UNITS

(B.R. Standard under-frames)

To be delivered in the 6101 series.

WATERLOO AND CITY LINE MOTOR COACH NOS.

51	54	57	60
52	55	58	61
53	56	59	62

FOUR-CAR SUBURBAN (4 SUB) UNITS
Make-up, Seating Capacity, etc.

Unit Nos.	Type	Motor Coaches	Trailer Coaches	Seating Capacity
4101– 4110	All-Steel Built 1942	9 compt.	1 10 compt. 1 11 compt.	468
4111– 4120	All-Steel Built 1946	8 compt.	1 9 compt. 1 10 compt.	420
4121– 4129	All-Steel Built 1946	Semi-Saloon	1 Semi-Saloon 1 9 compt.	382
4130	All-Steel Built 1946	Semi-Saloon Lightweight Motors	1 Semi-Saloon 1 9 compt.	382
4131–8 4140–53 4156–60/ 2-71	Original L.S.W.R. Units	1 8 compt. 1 7 compt.	2 10 compt.	350
4176/8/ 81/2/7/90	L.S.W.R. Stock converted S.R.	1 8 compt. 1 7 compt.	2 10 compt.	350
4195– 4234	Original L.S.W.R. Units	7½ compt.	1 11 compt. 1 9 compt. (with saloon)	352 or 354
4238/9/ 47/50	L.S.W.R. Stock converted S.R.	1 8 compt. 1 7 compt.	1 11 compt. 1 10 compt.	360
4251	L.B.S.C. Stock converted S.R.	1 7 compt. 1 8 compt.	2 10 compt.	350
4254	L.B.S.C., L.S.W. and S.E.C.R. Stock converted S.R.	1 L.B.S.C. 7 compt. 1 L.S.W. 7½ compt.	1 L.B.S.C. 10 compt. 1 S.E.C.R. 8 compt.	340
4277– 4299	All-Steel Built 1949	Saloon ; Lightweight Motors	1 Saloon 1 10 compt.	386
4300– 4319 4321– 4325	Augmented W-Section Built 1925	7 compt.	1 9 compt. * 1 All-Steel 10 compt.	350
4320	Augmented W-Section Built 1925	7 compt.	1 10 compt. 1 All-Steel 9 compt.	350
4326– 4349/ 51-4	Augmented E-Section Built 1925/6	8 compt.	1 9 compt. 1 All-Steel 10 compt.	370
4355– 4363	All-Steel Built 1947/8	8 compt.	2 10 compt.	432

* No. 4313 has a 9 compt. all steel trailer.

4364–4376	All-Steel Built 1947/8	8 compt.	1 9 compt. 1 10 compt.	420
4377	All-Steel Built 1947	8 compt.	1 9 compt. 1 Saloon	402
4378–4387	All-Steel Built 1948	Saloon	1 Saloon 1 10 compt.	386
4409	Augmented L.S.W.R. Stock converted S.R.	8 compt.	1 9 compt. 1 All-Steel 10 compt.	370
4411/20	Augmented L.S.W.R. Stock converted S.R.	7½ compt.	1 9 compt. 1 All-Steel 10 compt.	360
4424–4429	Augmented L.S.W.R. Stock converted S.R.	8 compt. Electro-pneumatic Control	1 9 compt. 1 All-Steel 10 compt.	370
4503/15/86	Augmented S.E.C.R. Stock converted S.R.	8 compt. (No. 4515, 1 L.B.S.C. motor)	1 9 compt. 1 All-Steel 10 compt.	370
4519/20/6–61/4–7/71/2/3/9	Augmented L.S.W.R. and L.B.S.C.R. converted S.R.†	1 8 compt. 1 7 compt.†	1 10 compt. 1 All Steel 9 compt. or 10 compt.†	368 or 370
4590	Augmented L.B.S.C.R. Stock converted S.R.	1 L.B.S.C.R. 7 compt. 1 Saloon	1 L.B.S.C.R. 9 compt. 1 All-Steel 9 compt.	350
4601–4607	All-Steel bodies on original underframes Rebuilt 1949/50	Saloon	2 10 compt.	404
4621–4666		Saloon	1 Saloon 1 10 compt.	386
4667–4754	New all-steel bodies (1951-3) on original underframes.	Saloon	1 Saloon 1 10 compt.*	386
5001–48		Saloon	1 Saloon 1 10 compt.*	386

* Except Nos. 4688/96, 4723/8/33/9, 5005 which have 9 compt. trailers.   † Except **4520**—2 8-compt. L.B.S.C. motors, 1 9-compt. S.E.C.R. trailer, and 1 10 compt. all-steel trailer ; **4526**—1 8-compt. L.S.W.R. motor, 1 7-compt. L.B.S.C. motor, 1 L.S.W.R. 10-compt. trailer and 1 L.S.W.R. 9-compt. trailer ; **4551**—1 L.B.S.C. 7-compt. and 1 8-compt. motor, 1 all-steel 10-compt. and 1 L.S.W.R. 10-compt. trailer ; **4567**—1 L.B.S.C. 7-compt. and 1 8-compt. motor, 1 L.B.S.C. 10-compt. trailer, 1 L.S.W.R. 9-compt. trailer ; **4571**—1 L.B.S.C. 8-compt. and 1 7-compt. motors, 2 L.B.S.C. 10-compt. trailers ; **4573**—1 L.B.S.C. 8-compt. and 1 L.S.W.R. 7-compt. motor, 1.L.S.W.R. 10-compt. and 1 L.S.W.R. 9-compt. trailer.

PULLMAN CARS ALLOCATED
TO THE SOUTHERN REGION
K — Kitchen Car
B — Brake Car

STEAM CARS
First Class

ALICANTE	(K)	MONTANA	(B)
AQUKA	(K)	MYRTLE	(K)
ARGUS	(K)	NEPTUNE ●	(K)
ARIES	(K)	NEW CENTURY BAR	
AURELIA ●	(K)	OCTAVIA ●	(K)
AURORA	(B)	ONYX ●	
CAMILLA	(K)	ORION	
CARINA	(K)	ORPHEUS	(K)
CASSANDRA	(K)	PALERMO	(K)
CECILIA	(K)	PALMYRA	(K)
CHLORIA	(K)	PEGASUS	
CLEMENTINA	(K)	PENELOPE	(K)
CORAL		PERSEUS	
CORUNNA	(K)	PHILOMEL	(K)
CYGNUS	(K)	PHOENIX	
DAPHNE	(K)	PLATO	(K)
EMERALD	(K)	PORTIA ●	(K)
FINGALL	(K)	RAINBOW	(K)
FLORA	(B)	REGINA	(K)
FLORENCE	(K)	ROSALIND	(K)
GLENCOE		ROSAMUND	(K)
GROSVENOR	(K)	ROSEMARY ●	
HAWTHORN	(K)	RUBY	(K)
HERCULES		SAPPHIRE	(K)
HIBERNIA	(K)	SAPPHO	(K)
IBIS	(K)	SAVONA	(K)
ISLE OF THANET	(B)	SCOTIA	(K)
JUNO	(B)	SEVILLE	(K)
LATONA	(K)	SORRENTO	(K)
LEGHORN		SUNBEAM	
MAID OF KENT	(K)	THEODORA	(K)
MALAGA	(K)	TOPAZ	
MEDUSA	(K)	VALENCIA	(K)
MIMOSA	(K)	ZENA	
MINERVA ●	(B)	ZENOBIA ●	(K)
MONACO	(K)		

Third Class

Car No. 5	(Now *Trianon Bar*)	Car. No. 27 ●	(B)
,, ,, 6	(K)	,, ,, 30	
,, ,, 7	(K)	,, ,, 31	(K)
,, ,, 8	(K)	,, ,, 34 ●	
,, ,, 11	(K)	,, ,, 35	
,, ,, 13 ⎫	Observation Cars	,, ,, 36	(B)
,, ,, 14 ⎭		,, ,, 41	(B)
,, ,, 15	(B)	,, ,, 45	(K)
,, ,, 16	(B)	,, ,, 47	(K)
,, ,, 17	(K)	,, ,, 54	(B)
,, ,, 19	(K)	,, ,, 55 ●	(B)

67

STEAM CARS—*(cont.)*

Third Class

Car No.	60	(K)	Car No. 166	(K)
,, ,,	61	(K)	,, ,, 167	(K)
,, ,,	95	(B)	,, ,, 169	(K)
,, ,,	96		,, ,, 171	(K)
,, ,,	97		,, ,, 182	(K)
,, ,,	98		,, ,, 183	(K)
,, ,,	99	(B)	,, ,, 185	(K)
,, ,,	132	(K)	,, ,, 208	(B)
,, ,,	133	(K)	,, ,, 249	(K)
,, ,,	135	(K)	,, ,, 294	
,, ,,	137	(K)	,, ,, 303	(K)

ELECTRIC CARS

First Class

AUDREY	(K)	HAZEL	(K)
DORIS	(K)	MONA	(K)
GWEN	(K)	VERA	(K)

Third Class

Car No. 85		Car No. 90	(B)
,, ,, 86		,, ,, 91	(B)
,, ,, 87		,, ,, 92	(B)
,, ,, 88	(B)	,, ,, 93	(B)
,, ,, 89	(B)		

Composite First and Third Class

ALICE	(K)	IRIS	(K)
ANNE	(K)	JOYCE	(K)
BERTHA	(K)	LONRA	(K)
BRENDA	(K)	MAY	(K)
CLARA	(K)	NAOMI	(K)
DAISY	(K)	OLIVE	(K)
ELINOR	(K)	PEGGY	(K)
ENID	(K)	RITA	(K)
ETHEL	(K)	ROSE	(K)
GRACE	(K)	RUTH	(K)
GWLADYS	(K)	VIOLET	(K)
IDA	(K)		

DIRECT SUBSCRIPTION SERVICE

By placing a subscription order with the Publisher, a copy of TRAINS ILLUSTRATED printed on art paper will be posted to you direct to reach you on the first of each month. ART PAPER copies are available only by direct subscription.

RATES : Yearly 18/- : 6 months 9/-

NO EXTRA CHARGE IS MADE FOR POSTAGE

* * *

Please supply Trains Illustrated by direct mail for .... issues, for which I enclose remittance for £ : s. d.

Name ....

Address ....

....

....

Ian Allan Ltd

**CRAVEN HOUSE
HAMPTON COURT
SURREY**

THE **ABC** OF
BRITISH RAILWAYS
LOCOMOTIVES

PART 3—Nos. 40000-59999
B.R. STANDARD LOCOMOTIVES
and L.M.R. Electric Motor Coaches

SUMMER
1954
EDITION

LONDON

Ian Allan Ltd

FOREWORD

THIS booklet lists all British Railways locomotives numbered between 40000 and 59999 and London Midland electric motor coaches. This series of numbers includes all London Midland Region and Scottish (ex-L.M.S.) Region steam locos. For convenience a complete list of the B.R. standard locomotives has also been included in this edition.

1. At the head of each class will be found a list of any important sub-divisions of the class, usually in order of introduction. Each sub-division is given a reference mark, by which its relevant dimensions (if differing from those of other sub-divisions) and the locomotives it comprises (if known) may be identified.

2. The lists of dimensions at the head of each class show locomotives fitted with two inside cylinders unless otherwise stated, e.g. (O)= two outside cylinders.

3. Superheated locos. are denoted by the letters " Su " after the boiler pressure. " SS " denotes that some are superheated.

4. The date on which the first locomotive of a class was built is denoted by " Introduced."

5. S denotes Service (Departmental) locomotive. This reference letter is introduced only for the reader's guidance and is not borne by the locomotive concerned.

6. The numbers of locomotives in service have been checked to **April 24th 1954.**

CHIEF MECHANICAL ENGINEERS

BRITISH RAILWAYS (L.M. Region)

H.G. Ivatt   ...   1948–1951

L.M.S.

George Hughes ...	...	1923–1925	Sir William Stanier	...	1932–1944
Sir Henry Fowler	...	1925–1931	Charles E. Fairburn	...	1944–1945
E.H.J. Lemon			H. G. Ivatt	...	1945–1947
(Sir Ernest Lemon)		1931–1932			

LOCOMOTIVE SUPERINTENDENTS AND C.M.E.'S—L.M.S. CONSTITUENT COMPANIES

CALEDONIAN RAILWAY

Robert Sinclair		
(First loco. engineer)*		1847–1856
Benjamin Connor	...	1856–1876
George Brittain ...	...	1876–1882
Dugald Drummond	...	1882–1890
Hugh Smellie	...	1890
J. Lambie	...	1890–1895
J. F. McIntosh	...	1895–1914
William Pickersgill	...	1914–1923

FURNESS RAILWAY

R. Mason ...	...	1890–1897
W. F. Pettigrew ...	...	1897–1918
D. J. Rutherford ...	...	1918–1923

GLASGOW AND SOUTH WESTERN RLY.

Patrick Stirling	...	1853–1866
James Stirling	...	1866–1878
Hugh Smellie	...	1878–1890
James Manson	...	1890–1912
Peter Drummond	...	1912–1918
R. H. Whitelegg	...	1918–1923

HIGHLAND RAILWAY

William Stroudley		
(First loco. engineer)...		1866–1869
David Jones	...	1869–1896
Peter Drummond	...	1896–1911
F. G. Smith	...	1912–1915
C. Cumming	...	1915–1923

L. & Y.R.

Sir John Hawkshaw (Consultant),*		
Hurst and Jenkins successively to 1868		
W. Hurst ...	...	1868–1876
W. Barton Wright	...	1876–1886
John A. F. Aspinall	...	1886–1899
H. A. Hoy ...	...	1899–1904
George Hughes	...	1904–1921
The L. & Y. amalgamated with L.N.W.R. in 1921.		

L.N.W.R.

Francis Trevithick and J. E. McConnell, first loco. engineers, 18?6, with Alexander Allan largely responsible for design at Crewe.*

John Ramsbottom	...	1857–1871
Francis William Webb ...		1871–1903
George Whale	...	1903–1909
Charles John Bowen-Cooke ...	...	1909–1920
Capt. Hewitt Pearson Montague Beames	...	1920–1921
George Hughes ...	...	1922

L.T. & S.R.

Thomas Whitelegg	...	1880–1910
Robert Harben Whitelegg	...	1910–1912

(L.T. & S.R. absorbed by M.R., control of locos. transferred to Derby as from Aug., 1912.)

---

* Exclusive of previous service with constituent company.

LOCOMOTIVE SUPERINTENDENTS
AND C.M.E.'S (*continued*)

MARYPORT & CARLISLE

Hugh Smellie	1870–1878
J. Campbell	1878–
William Coulthard ...	* –1904
J. B. Adamson	1904–1923

MIDLAND RAILWAY

Matthew Kirtley (First loco. engineer)...	1844–1873
Samuel Waite Johnson ...	1873–1903
Richard Mountford Deeley	1903–1909
Henry Fowler	1909–1923

SOMERSET AND DORSET JOINT RAILWAY

Until leased by Mid. and L. & S.W. (as from 1st Nov., 1875) locomotives were bought from outside builders, principally George England of Hatcham Iron Works, S.E. After the above date, Derby and its various Loco. Supts. and C.M.E.'s have acted for S. & D.J., aided by a resident Loco. Supt. stationed at Highbridge works.

NORTH STAFFORDSHIRE RAILWAY

L. Clare	1876–1882
L. Longbottom	1882–1902
J. H. Adams	1902–1915
J. A. Hookham	1915–1923

W. Angus was Loco. Supt. at Stoke prior to 1876. No earlier records can be traced.

WIRRAL

Eric G. Barker	1892–1902
T. B. Hunter	1903–1923

Barker of the Wirral Railway is noteworthy for originating the 4-4-4 tank type in this country (1896).

NORTH LONDON RAILWAY

(Worked by L. & N.W. by agreement dated Dec., 1908.)

William Adams	1853–1873
J. C. Park	1873–1893
Henry J. Pryce	1893–1903

HISTORIC LOCOMOTIVES PRESERVED IN STORE

Type	Originating Company	Pre-Grouping No.	L.M.S. No.	Name	Place of Preservation
4–2–2	M.R.	118	(673)	—	Derby
2–4–0	M.R.	158A	—	—	Derby
2–2–2	L.N.W.	(49)	—	Columbine	York Museum
2–2–2	L.N.W.	3020	—	Cornwall	Crewe
2–4–0	L.N.W.	790	(5031)	Hardwicke	Crewe
*0–4–0T	L.N.W.	—	—	Pet	Crewe
0–4–0	F.R.	3	—	Coppernob	Horwich
0–4–2	Liverpool & Manchester	—	—	Lion	Crewe
4–2–2	C.R.	123	(14010)	—	St. Rollox
4–6–0	H.R.	103	(17916)	—	St. Rollox

The un-bracketed numbers are the ones at present carried by the locos.
*18*in*. gauge works shunter.

---

* Date of actual entry into office not known.

BRITISH RAILWAYS LOCOMOTIVE SHEDS AND SHED CODES

LONDON MIDLAND REGION

1A	**Willesden**	9A	**Longsight**	19A	**Sheffield**
1B	Camden	9B	Stockport (Edgeley)	19B	Millhouses
1C	Watford	9C	Macclesfield	19C	Canklow
1D	Devons Road (Bow)	9D	Buxton		
1E	Bletchley	9E	Trafford Park	20A	**Leeds (Holbeck)**
	Leighton Buzzard	9F	Heaton Mersey	20B	Stourton
	Newport Pagnell	9G	Northwich	20C	Royston
				20D	Normanton
2A	**Rugby**	10A	**Springs Branch**	20E	Manningham
	Market		**(Wigan)**		Ilkley
	Harborough	10B	Preston	20F	Skipton
	Seaton	10C	Patricroft		Keighley
2B	Nuneaton	10D	Plodder Lane	20G	Hellifield
2C	Warwick		**(Bolton)**		
2D	Coventry	10E	Sutton Oak	21A	**Saltley**
2E	Northampton	11A	**Carnforth**	21B	Bournville
3A	**Bescot**	11B	Barrow	21C	Bromsgrove
3B	Bushbury		Coniston		
3C	Walsall	11C	Oxenholme	22A	**Bristol**
3D	Aston	11D	Tebay	22B	Gloucester
3E	Monument Lane	11E	Lancaster		Tewkesbury
5A	**Crewe North**				Dursley
	Whitchurch	12A	**Carlisle(Upperby)**		
5B	Crewe South	12C	Penrith	24A	**Accrington**
	Crewe	12D	Workington	24B	Rose Grove
	(Gresty Lane)	12E	Moor Row	24C	Lostock Hall
5C	Stafford	14A	**Cricklewood**	24D	Lower Darwen
5D	Stoke	14B	Kentish Town	24E	Blackpool
5E	Alsager	14C	St. Albans		Blackpool North
5F	Uttoxeter	15A	**Wellingborough**	24F	Fleetwood
6A	**Chester**	15B	Kettering		
6B	Mold Junction	15C	Leicester	25A	**Wakefield**
6C	Birkenhead	15D	Bedford	25B	Huddersfield
6D	Chester (Northgate)	16A	**Nottingham**	25C	Goole
6E	Wrexham		Southwell	25D	Mirfield
6F	Bidston	16C	Kirkby	25E	Sowerby Bridge
6G	Llandudno Junction	16D	Mansfield	25F	Low Moor
6H	Bangor	17A	**Derby**	25G	Farnley Junction
6J	Holyhead	17B	Burton		
6K	Rhyl		Horninglow	26A	**Newton Heath**
	Denbigh		Overseal	26B	Agecroft
8A	**Edge Hill**	17C	Coalville	26C	Bolton
8B	Warrington	17D	Rowsley	26D	Bury
	Warrington		Cromford	26E	Bacup
	(Arpley)		Middleton	26F	Lees
8C	Speke Junction		Sheep Pasture	26G	Belle Vue
8D	Widnes				
	Widnes (C.L.C.)	18A	**Toton**	27A	**Bank Hall**
8E	Brunswick	18B	Westhouses	27B	Aintree
	(Liverpool)	18C	Hasland	27C	Southport
8F	Warrington	18D	Staveley	27D	Wigan (L. & Y.)
	(C.L.C.)		Sheepbridge	27E	**Walton**

EASTERN REGION

30A	**Stratford**	32A	**Norwich**	35C	Peterborough	
	Ilford		Cromer		(Spital)	
	Brentwood		Wells-on-Sea	36A	**Doncaster**	
	Chelmsford		Dereham	36B	Mexborough	
	Epping		Swaffham		Wath	
	Wood St.		Wymondham	36C	Frodingham	
	(Walthamstow)	32B	Ipswich	36D	Barnsley	
	Palace Gates		Felixstowe Beach	36E	Retford	
	Enfield Town		Aldeburgh		Newark	
30B	Hertford East		Stowmarket			
	Ware	32C	Lowestoft	37A	**Ardsley**	
	Buntingford	32D	Yarmouth	37B	Copley Hill	
30C	Bishops Stortford		(South Town)	37C	Bradford	
30D	Southend (Victoria)	32E	Yarmouth (Vauxhall)			
	Southminster	32F	Yarmouth Beach	38A	**Colwick**	
30E	Colchester	32G	Melton Constable		Derby (Friargate)	
	Clacton		Norwich City		Leicester (G.N.)	
	Walton-on-Naze		Cromer Beach	38B	Annesley	
	Maldon			38C	Leicester (G.C.)	
	Braintree	33A	**Plaistow**	38D	Staveley	
30F	Parkeston		Upminster	38E	Woodford Halse	
		33B	Tilbury			
31A	**Cambridge**	33C	Shoeburyness	39A	**Gorton**	
	Ely	34A	**Kings Cross**		Dinting	
	Huntingdon East	34B	Hornsey		Hayfield	
	Saffron Walden	34C	Hatfield	39B	Sheffield (Darnall)	
31B	March	34D	Hitchin			
	Wisbech	34E	Neasden	40A	**Lincoln**	
31C	Kings Lynn		Aylesbury		Lincoln	
	Hunstanton		Chesham		(St. Mark's)	
31D	South Lynn			40B	Immingham	
31E	Bury St. Edmunds	35A	**New England**	40C	Louth	
	Sudbury (Suffolk)		Spalding	40D	Tuxford	
			Stamford	40E	Langwith Junction	
		35B	Grantham	40F	Boston	

NORTH EASTERN REGION

50A	**York**	51E	Stockton	52E	Percy Main	
50B	Leeds (Neville Hill)	51F	West Auckland	52F	North Blyth	
50C	Selby	51G	Haverton Hill		South Blyth	
50D	Starbeck	51H	Kirkby Stephen			
50E	Scarborough	51J	Northallerton	53A	Hull (Dairycoates)	
50F	Malton		Leyburn	53B	Hull	
	Pickering	51K	Saltburn		(Botanic Gardens)	
50G	Whitby			53C	Hull (Springhead)	
		52A	**Gateshead**		Alexandra Dock	
51A	**Darlington**		Bowes Bridge	53D	Bridlington	
	Middleton-in-	52B	Heaton			
	Teesdale	52C	Blaydon	54A	**Sunderland**	
51B	Newport		Hexham		Durham	
51C	West Hartlepool		Alston	54B	Tyne Dock	
51D	Middlesbrough	52D	Tweedmouth		Pelton Level	
	Guisborough		Alnmouth	54C	Borough Gardens	
				54D	Consett	

SCOTTISH REGION

60A	**Inverness**	63A	**Perth South**	65C	Parkhead	
	Dingwall		Aberfeldy	65D	Dawsholm	
	Kyle of Lochalsh		Blair Atholl		Dumbarton	
60B	Aviemore		Crieff	65E	Kipps	
	Boat of Garten	63B	Stirling	65F	Grangemouth	
60C	Helmsdale		Killin	65G	Yoker	
	Dornoch		Stirling	65H	Helensburgh	
	Tain		(Shore Road)		Arrochar	
60D	Wick	63C	Forfar	65I	Balloch	
	Thurso		Brechin	66A	**Polmadie**	
60E	Forres	63D	Fort William		(**Glasgow**)	
			Mallaig	66B	Motherwell	
		63E	Oban		Morningside	
61A	**Kittybrewster**		Ballachulish	66C	Hamilton	
	Ballater	64A	**St. Margarets**	66D	Greenock	
	Fraserburgh		(**Edinburgh**)		(Ladyburn)	
	Peterhead		Dunbar		Greenock	
61B	Aberdeen (Ferryhill)		Galashiels		(Princes Pier)	
61C	Keith		Longniddry	67A	**Corkerhill**	
	Banff		North Berwick		(**Glasgow**)	
	Elgin		Peebles	67B	Hurlford	
			Seafield		Beith	
			South Leith		Muirkirk	
62A	**Thornton**	64B	Haymarket	67C	Ayr	
	Anstruther	64C	Dalry Road	67D	Ardrossan	
	Burntisland	64D	Carstairs	68A	**Carlisle**	
	Ladybank	64E	Polmont		(**Kingmoor**)	
	Methil	64F	Bathgate	68B	Dumfries	
62B	Dundee (Tay Bridge)	64G	Hawick		Kirkcudbright	
	Arbroath		Kelso	68C	Stranraer	
	Montrose		Riccarton		Newton Stewart	
	St. Andrews	65A	**Eastfield**	68D	Beattock	
62C	Dunfermline		(**Glasgow**)	68E	Carlisle Canal	
	(Upper)	65B	St. Rollox		Silloth	
	Alloa					

SOUTHERN REGION

70A	**Nine Elms**	71H	Templecombe	73C	Hither Green	
70B	Feltham	71I	Southampton	73D	Gillingham (Kent)	
70C	Guildford	71J	Highbridge	73E	Faversham	
70D	Basingstoke					
70E	Reading	72A	**Exmouth Junction**	74A	**Ashford (Kent)**	
			Seaton		Canterbury West	
71A	**Eastleigh**		Lyme Regis	74B	Ramsgate	
	Winchester		Exmouth	74C	Dover	
	Lymington		Okehampton		Folkestone	
	Andover Junction		Bude	74D	Tonbridge	
71B	Bournemouth	72B	Salisbury	74E	St. Leonards	
	Swanage	72C	Yeovil			
	Hamworthy Jc.	72D	Plymouth			
	Branksome		Callington	75A	**Brighton**	
71C	Dorchester	72E	Barnstaple Junction		Newhaven	
71D	Fratton		Torrington	75B	Redhill	
	Midhurst		Ilfracombe	75C	Norwood Junction	
71E	Newport (I.O.W.)	72F	Wadebridge	75D	Horsham	
71F	Ryde (I.O.W.)			75E	Three Bridges	
71G	Bath (S. & D.)	73A	**Stewarts Lane**	75F	Tunbridge Wells	
	Radstock	73B	Bricklayers Arms		West	

7

81A	**Old Oak Common**
81B	Slough
	Marlow
	Watlington
81C	Southall
	Staines
81D	Reading
	Henley-on-Thames
81E	Didcot
	Newbury
	Wallingford
81F	Oxford
	Fairford
82A	**Bristol**
	(Bath Road)
	Bath
	Wells
	Weston-Super-
	Yatton [Mare
82B	St. Philip's Marsh
82C	Swindon
	Chippenham
82D	Westbury
	Frome
82E	Yeovil
82F	Weymouth
	Bridport
83A	**Newton Abbot**
	Ashburton
	Kingsbridge
83B	Taunton
	Bridgwater
	Minehead
83C	Exeter
	Tiverton Junction
83D	Laira (Plymouth)
	Princetown
	Launceston
83E	St. Blazey
	Bodmin
	Moorswater
83F	Truro
83G	Penzance
	Helston
	St. Ives

84A	**Wolverhampton**
	(Stafford Road)
84B	Oxley
84C	Banbury
84D	Leamington Spa
84E	Tyseley
	Stratford-on-Avon
84F	Stourbridge
84G	Shrewsbury
	Clee Hill
	Craven Arms
	Knighton
	Builth Road
84H	Wellington (Salop)
84J	Croes Newydd
	Bala
	Trawsfynydd
	Penmaenpool
84K	Chester
85A	**Worcester**
	Evesham
	Kingham
85B	Gloucester
	Cheltenham
	Brimscombe
	Cirencester
	Lydney
	Tetbury
85C	Hereford
	Ledbury
	Leominster
	Ross
85D	Kidderminster
86A	**Newport**
	(Ebbw Junction)
86B	Newport (Pill)
86C	Cardiff (Canton)
86D	Llantrisant
86E	Severn Tunnel
	Junction
86F	Tondu
86G	Pontypool Road
86H	Aberbeeg
86J	Aberdare
86K	Abergavenny
	Tredegar

87A	**Neath**
	Glyn Neath
	Neath (N. & B.)
87B	Duffryn Yard
87C	Danygraig
87D	Swansea East Dock
87E	Landore
87F	Llanelly
	Burry Port
	Pantyfynnon
87G	Carmarthen
87H	Neyland
	Cardigan
	Milford Haven
	Pembroke Dock
	Whitland
87J	Goodwick
87K	Swansea (Victoria)
	Upper Bank
	Gurnos
	Llandovery
88A	**Cardiff (Cathays)**
	Radyr
88B	Cardiff East Dock
88C	Barry
88D	Merthyr
	Cae Harris
	Dowlais Central
	Rhymney
88E	Abercynon
88F	Treherbert
	Ferndale
89A	**Oswestry**
	Llanidloes
	Moat Lane
	Welshpool
	(W. & L.)
89B	Brecon
	Builth Wells
89C	Machynlleth
	Aberayron
	Aberystwyth
	Aberystwyth
	(V. of R.)
	Portmadoc
	Pwllheli

Right: **Class 0F 0-4-0ST No. 41523.**

[*R. Eckersley*

Centre: **Class 1F 0-6-0T No. 41779.**

[*P. J. Lynch*

Bottom: **Class 1F 0-6-0T No. 41814 (rebuilt with Belpaire boiler).**

[*E. Blakey*

Class 3MT (Fowler) 2-6-2T No. 40020 (Push-and-Pull fitted). [R. J. Buckley

Class 3MT (Stanier) 2-6-2T No. 40148 (with large boiler). [H. C. Casserley

Class 3MT (Stanier) 2-6-2T No. 40208. [H. C. Casserley

Class 3MT (Riddles) 2-6-2T No. 82007. [R. J. Buckley

Class 2MT (Riddles) 2-6-2T No. 84008 (Push-and-Pull fitted). [R. J. Buckley

Class 2MT (Ivatt) 2-6-2T No. 41293. [G. Wheeler

Above : Class 2P 0-4-4T
No. 41907.

[R. J. Buckley

Left: Class 3F 0-6-2T
No. 41966.

[B. E. Morrison

Below : Class 3P 4-4-2T
No. 41952.

[C. G. Pearson

Class 4MT (Fairburn) 2-6-4T No. 42093   *[L. Elsey*

Class 4MT (Fowler) 2-6-4T No. 42418 (with side-window cab).   *[A. Murphy*

Class 4MT (Riddles) 2-6-4T No. 80002.   *[J. L. Stevenson*

Class 5MT (Fowler) 2-6-0 No. 42887.

Class 5MT (Fowler) 2-6-0 No. 42825 (with Reidinger rotary valve gear)

Class 4MT (Ivatt) 2-6-0 No. 43047.

Above: Class 3MT (Riddles) 2-6-0 No. 77001.

[*M. Brown*

Right: Class 2MT (Ivatt) 2-6-0 No. 46460 (with cowcatcher for working St. Combs branch).

[*C. L. Kerr*

Below: Class 4MT (Riddles) 2-6-0 No. 76015.

[*T. K. Widd*

Beyer-Garratt 2-6-6-2T No. 47976.

[*Eagle Photos*

Class 7F 0-8-0 No. 49667.

[*R. K. Evans*

Class 7F 0-8-0 No. 49314.

[*J. Davenport*

2-6-2T   3MT

Introduced 1930. Fowler L.M.S. design with parallel boiler.
*Introduced 1930. Condensing locos. for working to Moorgate, London.

Weight: $\begin{cases} 70 \text{ tons 10 cwt.} \\ 71 \text{ tons 16 cwt.*} \end{cases}$

Pressure: 200 lb. Su.
Cyls.: (O) $17\frac{1}{2}'' \times 26''$.
Dr. Wheels: 5' 3".   T.E.: 21,485 lb.
Walschaerts Valve Gear P.V.

40001	40019	40037*	40054
40002	40020	40038*	40055
40003	40021	40039*	40056
40004	40022*	40040*	40057
40005	40023*	40041	40058
40006	40024*	40042	40059
40007	40025*	40043	40060
40008	40026*	40044	40061
40009	40027*	40045	40062
40010	40028*	40046	40063
40011	40029*	40047	40064
40012	40030*	40048	40065
40013	40031*	40049	40066
40014	40032*	40050	40067
40015	40033*	40051	40068
40016	40034*	40052	40069
40017	40035*	40053	40070
40018	40036*		**Total 70**

2-6-2T   3MT

Introduced 1935. Stanier L.M.S. taper boiler development of Fowler design (*above*).
*Introduced 1941. Rebuilt with larger boiler.

Weight: $\begin{cases} 71 \text{ tons 5 cwt.} \\ 72 \text{ tons 10 cwt.*} \end{cases}$

Pressure: 200 lb. Su.
Cyls.: (O) $17\frac{1}{2}'' \times 26''$
Dr. Wheels: 5' 3".   T.E.: 21,485 lb.
Walschaerts Valve Gear P.V.

40071	40075	40079	40083
40072	40076	40080	40084
40073	40077	40081	40085
40074	40078	40082	40086

40087	40118	40149	40180
40088	40119	40150	40181
40089	40120	40151	40182
40090	40121	40152	40183
40091	40122	40153	40184
40092	40123	40154	40185
40093	40124	40155	40186
40094	40125	40156	40187
40095	40126	40157	40188
40096	40127	40158	40189
40097	40128	40159	40190
40098	40129	40160	40191
40099	40130	40161	40192
40100	40131	40162	40193
40101	40132	40163*	40194
40102	40133	40164	40195
40103	40134	40165	40196
40104	40135	40166	40197
40105	40136	40167	40198
40106	40137	40168	40199
40107	40138	40169*	40200
40108	40139	40170	40201
40109	40140	40171	40202
40110	40141	40172	40203*
40111	40142	40173	40204
40112	40143	40174	40205
40113	40144	40175	40206
40114	40145	40176	40207
40115	40146	40177	40208
40116	40147	40178	40209
40117	40148*	40179	
			Total 139

4-4-0   2P

Introduced 1912. Fowler rebuild of Johnson locos. with superheater and piston valves.
*Introduced 1914. Locos. built new to superheated design for S. & D.J.R. (taken into L.M.S. stock, 1930).
Weight: Loco. 53 tons 7 cwt.
Pressure: 160 lb. Su.
Cyls.: $20\frac{1}{2}'' \times 26''$ Dr. Wheels: 7' $0\frac{1}{2}''$
T.E.: 17,585 lb.   P.V.

40323*	40420	40485	40529
40326*	40421	40486	40531
40332	40426	40487	40534
40337	40433	40489	40535
40356	40434	40491	40536
40362	40436	40493	40537
40364	40438	40495	40538
40377	40439	40501	40539
40395	40443	40502	40540
40396	40447	40504	40541
40402	40448	40509	40542
40404	40450	40511	40543
40405	40452	40513	40548
40407	40453	40518	40550
40409	40454	40519	40552
40411	40455	40520	40553
40412	40458	40521	40556
40413	40461	40522	40557
40414	40463	40524	40559
40416	40464	40525	40562
40418	40472	40526	
40419	40482	40527	

Total 86

40604	40628	40653†	40677
40605	40629	40654	40678
40606	40630	40655	40679
40607	40631	40656	40680
40608	40632	40657	40681
40609	40633*†	40658	40682
40610	40634*	40659	40683
40611	40635*	40660	40684
40612	40636	40661	40685
40613	40637	40662	40686
40614	40638	40663	40687
40615	40640	40664	40688
40616	40641	40665	40689
40617	40642	40666	40690
40618	40643	40667	40691
40619	40644	40668	40692
40620	40645	40669	40693
40621	40646	40670	40694
40622	40647	40671	40695
40623	40648	40672	40696
40624	40649	40673	40697
40625	40650	40674	40698
40626	40651	40675	40699
40627	40652	40676	40700

Total 136

4-4-0   2P

Introduced 1928. Post-Grouping development of Midland design, with modified dimensions and reduced boiler mountings.
*Introduced 1928. Locos. built for S. & D.J.R. (taken into L.M.S. stock, 1930).
†Fitted experimentally in 1933 with Dabeg feed-water heater.
Weight: Loco. 54 tons 1 cwt.
Pressure: 180 lb. Su.
Cyls.: 19″ × 26″.
Dr. Wheels: 6′ 9″.   T.E.: 17,730 lb.
P.V.

40563	40573	40583	40594
40564	40574	40584	40595
40565	40575	40585	40596
40566	40576	40586	40597
40567	40577	40587	40598
40568	40578	40588	40599
40569	40579	40589	40600
40570	40580	40590	40601
40571	40581	40592	40602
40572	40582	40593	40603

4-4-0 (3-Cyl. Compd.) 4P

Introduced 1924.   Post-Grouping development of Johnson Midland compound with modified dimensions and (except 41045–64) reduced boiler mountings.
Weight: Loco. 61 tons 14 cwt.
Pressure: 200 lb. Su.
Cyls.: L.P. (2) 21″ × 26″
H.P. (1) 19″ × 26″.
Dr. Wheels: 6′ 9″.
T.E. (of L.P. cyls. at 80% boiler pressure): 22,650 lb.

P.V. (H.P. cyl. only).

40900	40908	40916	40926
40901	40909	40917	40927
40902	40910	40920	40928
40903	40912	40921	40929
40904	40913	40923	40930
40906	40914	40924	40931
40907	40915	40925	40932

40933	41083	41122	41160	41200	41233	41266	41298*
40934	41084	41123	41161	41201	41234	41267	41299*
40935	41085	41124	41162	41202	41235	41268	41300*
40936	41086	41126	41163	41203	41236	41269	41301*
40937	41087	41127	41164	41204	41237	41270	41302*
40938	41088	41128	41165	41205	41238	41271	41303*
40939	41089	41129	41166	41206	41239	41272	41304*
41045	41090	41130	41167	41207	41240	41273	41305*
41048	41091	41131	41168	41208	41241	41274	41306*
41049	41093	41132	41169	41209	41242	41275	41307*
41050	41094	41133	41170	41210	41243	41276	41308*
41051	41095	41134	41172	41211	41244	41277	41309*
41053	41096	41135	41173	41212	41245	41278	41310*
41054	41097	41136	41175	41213	41246	41279	41311*
41059	41098	41137	41176	41214	41247	41280	41312*
41060	41100	41138	41177	41215	41248	41281	41313*
41061	41101	41139	41179	41216	41249	41282	41314*
41062	41102	41140	41180	41217	41250	41283	41315*
41063	41103	41141	41181	41218	41251	41284	41316*
41064	41104	41142	41183	41219	41252	41285	41317*
41065	41105	41143	41185	41220	41253	41286	41318*
41066	41106	41144	41186	41221	41254	41287	41319*
41067	41107	41146	41187	41222	41255	41288	41320*
41068	41108	41147	41188	41223	41256	41289	41321*
41069	41110	41149	41189	41224	41257	41290*	41322*
41070	41111	41150	41190	41225	41258	41291*	41323*
41071	41112	41151	41191	41226	41259	41292*	41324*
41072	41113	41152	41192	41227	41260	41293*	41325*
41073	41114	41153	41193	41228	41261	41294*	41326*
41074	41115	41154	41194	41229	41262	41295*	41327*
41075	41116	41155	41195	41230	41263	41296*	41328*
41076	41117	41156	41196	41231	41264	41297*	41329*
41077	41118	41157	41197	41232	41265		**Total 130**
41078	41119	41158	41198				
41079	41120	41159	41199				
41081	41121						

Total 170

2-6-2T   2MT

Introduced 1946. Ivatt L.M.S. taper boiler design.
Weight: 63 tons 5 cwt.
Pressure: 200 lb. Su.
Cyls.: $\begin{cases} \text{(O)} \ 16'' \times 24'' \\ \text{(O)} \ 16\frac{1}{2}'' \times 24''* \end{cases}$

Dr. Wheels: 5' 0''.   T.E.: $\begin{cases} 17,410 \text{ lb.} \\ 18,510 \text{ lb.}* \end{cases}$

Walschaerts Valve Gear.   P.V.

0-4-0ST   0F

*Introduced 1883. Johnson Midland design.
†‡Introduced 1897. Larger Johnson Midland design.
Dr. Wheels: 3' 10''.
Pressure: $\begin{cases} 140 \text{ lb.}*† \\ 150 \text{ lb.}‡ \end{cases}$

	Weight tons cwt.	Cyls. (O)	T.E.
41516*	23 3	13''×20''	8,745
41518†	32 3	15''×20''	11,640
41523‡	32 3	15''×20''	12,475

Total 3

0-4-0T 0F

Introduced 1907. Deeley Midland design.
Weight: 32 tons 16 cwt.
Pressure: 160 lb.
Cyls.: (O) 15″×22″.
Dr. Wheels: 3′ 9¾″.   T.E.: 14,635 lb.
Walschaerts Valve Gear.

41528	41531	41534	41536
41529	41532	41535	41537
41530	41533		

Total 10

0-6-0T 1F

Introduced 1878. Johnson Midland design.
*Rebuilt with Belpaire boilers.
Weight: 39 tons 11 cwt.
Pressure: { 150 lb.
{ 140 lb.*
Cyls.: 17″×24″.
Dr. Wheels: 4′ 7″.
T.E.: { 16,080 lb.
{ 15,005 lb.*

41661*	41724*	41777	41844*
41671*	41725*	41779	41847*
41672*	41726*	41795*	41853
41682*	41734*	41797*	41855*
41686	41739*	41803*•	41857
41699*	41747*	41804*	41859*
41702*	41748*	41805	41860*
41706*	41749*	41811*	41865
41708*	41752*	41813*	41875*
41710*	41753*	41814*	41878*
41711*	41754*	41826*	41879*
41712*	41763*	41835	41885*
41713	41769*	41838*	41889*
41720*	41773*	41839*	

Total 55

0-4-4T 2P

Introduced: 1932. Stanier L.M.S. design. Push-and-pull fitted
Weight: 58 tons 1 cwt.
Pressure: 160 lb.
Cyls.: 18″×26″.
Dr. Wheels: 5′ 7″.   T.E.: 17,100 lb.

41900	41903	41906	41908
41901	41904	41907	41909
41902	41905		

Total 10

4-4-2T 3P

*Introduced 1909. L.T. & S. Whitelegg "79" Class.
Remainder. Introduced 1923. Midland and L.M.S. development of L.T. & S. "79" Class.
Weight: 71 tons 10 cwt.
Pressure: 170 lb.
Cyls.: (O) 19″×26″.
Dr. Wheels: 6′ 6″.   T.E.: 17,390 lb.

41928	41943	41950	41972
41936	41944	41951	41973
41938	41945	41952	41974
41939	41946	41966*	41975
41940	41947	41969	41976
41941	41948	41970	41977
41942	41949	41971	41978

Total 28

0-6-2T 3F

Introduced 1903. Whitelegg L.T. & S. "69" Class (Nos. 41990-3 built 1912 taken directly into M.R. stock).
Weight: 64 tons 13 cwt.
Pressure: 170 lb.
Cyls.: 18″×26″.
Dr. Wheels: 5′ 3″.   T.E.: 19,320 lb.

41980	41984	41988	41991
41981	41985	41989	41992
41982	41986	41990	41993
41983	41987		

Total 14

2-6-4T   4MT

*Introduced 1927. Fowler L.M.S. parallel boiler design
†Introduced 1933 As earlier engines, but with side-window cabs and doors.
‡Introduced 1934. Stanier taper-boiler 3-cylinder design for L.T & S.
§Introduced 1935. Stanier taper boiler 2-cylinder design.
¶Introduced 1945. Fairburn development of Stanier design with shorter wheelbase and detail alterations.

Weights:
{ 86 tons 5 cwt.*†
{ 92 tons 5 cwt.‡
{ 87 tons 17 cwt.§
{ 85 tons 5 cwt.¶

Pressure (all types): 200 lb. Su.
Cyls.:
{ (O) 19″×26″*†
{ (3) 16″×26″‡
{ (O) 19⅝″×26″§¶

Dr. Wheels (all types): 5′ 9″.
T.E.:
{ 23,125 lb.*†
{ 24,600 lb.‡
{ 24,670 lb.§

Walschaerts valve gear. P.V.

¶FAIRBURN LOCOS.

42050	42074	42098	42122
42051	42075	42099	42123
42052	42076	42100	42124
42053	42077	42101	42125
42054	42078	42102	42126
42055	42079	42103	42127
42056	42080	42104	42128
42057	42081	42105	42129
42058	42082	42106	42130
42059	42083	42107	42131
42060	42084	42108	42132
42061	42085	42109	42133
42062	42086	42110	42134
42063	42087	42111	42135
42064	42088	42112	42136
42065	42089	42113	42137
42066	42090	42114	42138
42067	42091	42115	42139
42068	42092	42116	42140
42069	42093	42117	42141
42070	42094	42118	42142
42071	42095	42119	42143
42072	42096	42120	42144
42073	42097	42121	42145

42146	42185	42224	42263
42147	42186	42225	42264
42148	42187	42226	42265
42149	42188	42227	42266
42150	42189	42228	42267
42151	42190	42229	42268
42152	42191	42230	42269
42153	42192	42231	42270
42154	42193	42232	42271
42155	42194	42233	42272
42156	42195	42234	42273
42157	42196	42235	42274
42158	42197	42236	42275
42159	42198	42237	42276
42160	42199	42238	42277
42161	42200	42239	42278
42162	42201	42240	42279
42163	42202	42241	42280
42164	42203	42242	42281
42165	42204	42243	42282
42166	42205	42244	42283
42167	42206	42245	42284
42168	42207	42246	42285
42169	42208	42247	42286
42170	42209	42248	42287
42171	42210	42249	42288
42172	42211	42250	42289
42173	42212	42251	42290
42174	42213	42252	42291
42175	42214	42253	42292
42176	42215	42254	42293
42177	42216	42255	42294
42178	42217	42256	42295
42179	42218	42257	42296
42180	42219	42258	42297
42181	42220	42259	42298
42182	42221	42260	42299
42183	42222	42261	
42184	42223	42262	

*FOWLER LOCOS.

42300	42305	42310	42315
42301	42306	42311	42316
42302	42307	42312	42317
42303	42308	42313	42318
42304	42309	42314	42319

42320	42339	42358	42377
42321	42340	42359	42378
42322	42341	42360	42379
42323	42342	42361	42380
42324	42343	42362	42381
42325	42344	42363	42382
42326	42345	42364	42383
42327	42346	42365	42384
42328	42347	42366	42385
42329	42348	42367	42386
42330	42349	42368	42387
42331	42350	42369	42388
42332	42351	42370	42389
42333	42352	42371	42390
42334	42353	42372	42391
42335	42354	42373	42392
42336	42355	42374	42393
42337	42356	42375	42394
42338	42357	42376	

† FOWLER LOCOS. WITH SIDE-WINDOW CAB.

42395	42403	42411	42418
42396	42404	42412	42419
42397	42405	42413	42420
42398	42406	42414	42421
42399	42407	42415	42422
42400	42408	42416	42423
42401	42409	42417	42424
42402	42410		

§STANIER 2-CYL. LOCOS.

42425	42440	42455	42470
42426	42441	42456	42471
42427	42442	42457	42472
42428	42443	42458	42473
42429	42444	42459	42474
42430	42445	42460	42475
42431	42446	42461	42476
42432	42447	42462	42477
42433	42448	42463	42478
42434	42449	42464	42479
42435	42450	42455	42480
42436	42451	42466	42481
42437	42452	42467	42482
42438	42453	42468	42483
42439	42454	42469	42484

42485	42488	42491	42493
42486	42489	42492	42494
42487	42490		

‡STANIER 3-CYL. LOCOS.

42500	42510	42519	42528
42501	42511	42520	42529
42502	42512	42521	42530
42503	42513	42522	42531
42504	42514	42523	42532
42505	42515	42524	42533
42506	42516	42525	42534
42507	42517	42526	42535
42508	42518	42527	42536
42509			

§STANIER 2-CYL. LOCOS.

42537	42566	42595	42624
42538	42567	42596	42625
42539	42568	42597	42626
42540	42569	42598	42627
42541	42570	42599	42628
42542	42571	42600	42629
42543	42572	42601	42630
42544	42573	42602	42631
42545	42574	42603	42632
42546	42575	42604	42633
42547	42576	42605	42634
42548	42577	42606	42635
42549	42578	42607	42636
42550	42579	42608	42637
42551	42580	42609	42638
42552	42581	42610	42639
42553	42582	42611	42640
42554	42583	42612	42641
42555	42584	42613	42642
42556	42585	42614	42643
42557	42586	42615	42644
42558	42587	42616	42645
42559	42588	42617	42646
42560	42589	42618	42647
42561	42590	42619	42648
42562	42591	42620	42649
42563	42592	42621	42650
42564	42593	42622	42651
42565	42594	42623	42652

42653	42658	42663	42668
42654	42659	42664	42669
42655	42660	42665	42670
42656	42661	42666	42671
42657	42662	42667	42672

¶FAIRBURN LOCOS.

42673	42680	42687	42694
42674	42681	42688	42695
42675	42682	42689	42696
42676	42683	42690	42697
42677	42684	42691	42698
42678	42685	42692	42699
42679	42686	42693	

Total 645

2-6-0   5MT

Introduced 1926. Hughes L.M.S. design built under Fowler's direction. Walschaerts Valve Gear. P.V.
*Introduced 1953. Locos. rebuilt experimentally with Lentz R.C. poppet valves in 1931; rebuilt with Reidinger rotary poppet valve gear in 1953.
Weight: Loco. 66 tons 0 cwt.
Pressure: 180 lb. Su.
Cyls.: (O) 21″ × 26″.
Dr. Wheels: 5′ 6″.   T.E.: 26,580 lb.

42700	42717	42734	42751
42701	42718	42735	42752
42702	42719	42736	42753
42703	42720	42737	42754
42704	42721	42738	42755
42705	42722	42739	42756
42706	42723	42740	42757
42707	42724	42741	42758
42708	42725	42742	42759
42709	42726	42743	42760
42710	42727	42744	42761
42711	42728	42745	42762
42712	42729	42746	42763
42713	42730	42747	42764
42714	42731	42748	42765
42715	42732	42749	42766
42716	42733	42750	42767

42768	42813	42857	42901
42769	42814	42858	42902
42770	42815	42859	42903
42771	42816	42860	42904
42772	42817	42861	42905
42773	42818*	42862	42906
42774	42819	42863	42907
42775	42820	42864	42908
42776	42821	42865	42909
42777	42822*	42866	42910
42778	42823	42867	42911
42779	42824*	42868	42912
42780	42825*	42869	42913
42781	42826	42870	42914
42782	42827	42871	42915
42783	42828	42872	42916
42784	42829*	42873	42917
42785	42830	42874	42918
42786	42831	42875	42919
42787	42832	42876	42920
42788	42833	42877	42921
42789	42834	42878	42922
42790	42835	42879	42923
42791	42836	42880	42924
42792	42837	42881	42925
42793	42838	42882	42926
42794	42839	42883	42927
42795	42840	42884	42928
42796	42841	42885	42929
42797	42842	42886	42930
42798	42843	42887	42931
42799	42844	42888	42932
42800	42845	42889	42933
42801	42846	42890	42934
42802	42847	42891	42935
42803	42848	42892	42936
42804	42849	42893	42937
42805	42850	42894	42938
42806	42851	42895	42939
42807	42852	42896	42940
42808	42853	42897	42941
42809	42854	42898	42942
42810	42855	42899	42943
42811	42856	42900	42944
42812			

Total 245

2-6-0   5MT

Introduced 1933. Stanier L.M.S. taper boiler design, some with safety valves mounted on the top feed.
Weight: Loco. 69 tons 2 cwt.
Pressure: 225 lb. Su.
Cyls.: (O) 18″ × 28″.
Dr. Wheels: 5′ 6″.   T.E.: 26,290 lb.
Walschaerts Valve Gear. P.V.

42945	42955	42965	42975
42946	42956	42966	42976
42947	42957	42967	42977
42948	42958	42968	42978
42949	42959	42969	42979
42950	42960	42970	42980
42951	42961	42971	42981
42952	42962	42972	42982
42953	42963	42973	42983
42954	42964	42974	42984

Total 40

2-6-0   4MT

Introduced 1947. Ivatt L.M.S. taper boiler design with double chimney. Later engines introduced with single chimney, with which earlier engines are being rebuilt.
Weight: Loco. 59 tons 2 cwt.
Pressure: 225 lb. Su.
Cyls.: (O) 17½″ × 26″.
Dr. Wheels: 5′ 3″.   T.E.: 24,170 lb.
Walschaerts Valve Gear. P.V.

43000	43018	43036	43054
43001	43019	43037	43055
43002	43020	43038	43056
43003	43021	43039	43057
43004	43022	43040	43058
43005	43023	43041	43059
43006	43024	43042	43060
43007	43025	43043	43061
43008	43026	43044	43062
43009	43027	43045	43063
43010	43028	43046	43064
43011	43029	43047	43065
43012	43030	43048	43066
43013	43031	43049	43067
43014	43032	43050	43068
43015	43033	43051	43069
43016	43034	43052	43070
43017	43035	43053	43071

43072	43095	43118	43140
43073	43096	43119	43141
43074	43097	43120	43142
43075	43098	43121	43143
43076	43099	43122	43144
43077	43100	43123	43145
43078	43101	43124	43146
43079	43102	43125	43147
43080	43103	43126	43148
43081	43104	43127	43149
43082	43105	43128	43150
43083	43106	43129	43151
43084	43107	43130	43152
43085	43108	43131	43153
43086	43109	43132	43154
43087	43110	43133	43155
43088	43111	43134	43156
43089	43112	43135	43157
43090	43113	43136	43158
43091	43114	43137	43159
43092	43115	43138	43160
43093	43116	43139	43161
43094	43117		

Total 162

0-6-0   3F

Introduced 1885. Johnson Midland locos., rebuilt from 1916 by Fowler with Belpaire boilers.
*Introduced 1885. Johnson Midland locos., rebuilt from 1920 by Fowler with Belpaire boilers.
†Introduced 1896. Locos. built for S. & D.J. (taken into L.M.S. stock 1930).
Weight: Loco. 43 tons 17 cwt.
Pressure: 175 lb.
Cyls.: 18″ × 26″.
Dr. Wheels: $\begin{cases} 5′ \ 3″. \\ 4′ \ 11″.* \end{cases}$ T.E.: $\begin{cases} 19,890 \text{ lb.} \\ 21,240 \text{ lb.*} \end{cases}$

43174*	43187*	43200	43210
43178*	43188*	43201†	43211†
43180*	43189*	43203	43212
43181*	43191	43204†	43213
43183*	43192	43205	43214
43185*	43193	43207	43216†
43186*	43194†	43208	43218†

43219	43286	43361	43459	43580	43627	43675	43728
43222	43287	43367	43462	43581	43629	43676	43729
43223	43290	43368	43463	43583	43630	43678	43731
43224	43292	43369	43464	43584	43631	43679	43734
43225	43294	43370	43468	43585	43633	43680	43735
43226	43295	43371	43469	43586	43634	43681	43737
43231	43298	43373	43474	43587	43636	43682	43742
43232	43299	43374	43476	43593	43637	43683	43745
43233	43300	43378	43482	43594	43638	43684	43748
43234	43301	43379	43484	43595	43639	43686	43749
43235	43305	43381	43490	43596	43644	43687	43750*
43237	43306	43386	43491	43598	43645	43690	43751
43239	43307	43387	43494	43599	43650	43693	43753
43240	43308	43388	43496	43600	43651	43698	43754
43241	43309	43389	43497	43605	43652	43705	43755
43242	43310	43392	43499	43607	43656	43709	43756
43243	43312	43394	43502	43608	43657	43710	43757
43244	43313	43395	43506	43612	43658	43711	43759
43245	43314	43396	43507	43615	43660	43712	43760
43246	43315	43398	43509	43618	43661	43714	43762
43247	43317	43399	43510	43619	43664	43715	43763
43248†	43318	43400	43514	43620	43665	43717	43766
43249	43321	43401	43515	43621	43668	43721	43770
43250	43323	43402	43520	43622	43669	43723	43771
43251	43324	43405	43521	43623	43673	43727	43773
43252	43325	43406	43522	43624	43674		
43253	43326	43410	43523				
43254	43327	43411	43524				
43256	43329	43419	43529				
43257	43330	43427	43531				
43258	43331	43428	43538				
43259	43332	43429	43544				
43261	43333	43431	43546				
43263	43334	43433	43548				
43266	43335	43435	43550				
43267	43337	43436	43553				
43268	43339	43440	43558				
43271	43340	43441	43562				
43273	43341	43443	43565				
43274	43342	43444	43568				
43275	43344	43446	43570				
43277	43351	43449	43572				
43278	43355	43453	43574				
43281	43356	43454	43575				
43282	43357	43456	43578				
43284	43359	43457	43579				

Total 314

0-6-0   3F

Introduced 1906. Deeley Midland design, rebuilt by Fowler with Belpaire boiler.

Weight: Loco. 46 tons 3 cwt.

Pressure: 175 lb.

Cyls.: $18\frac{1}{2}'' \times 26''$.

Dr. Wheels: 5' 3".   T.E.: 21,010 lb.

43775	43784	43789	43795
43776	43785	43790	43798
43778	43786	43791	43799
43781	43787	43793	43800

43803	43810	43817	43826
43806	43812	43822	43828
43808	43814	43823	43829
43809	43815	43825	43832

Total 32

0-6-0   4F

Introduced 1911. Fowler superheated Midland design.
Weight: 48 tons 15 cwt.
Pressure: 175 lb. Su.
Cyls.: 20″ × 26″.
Dr. Wheels: 5′ 3″.   T.E.: 24,555 lb.
P.V.

43835	43862	43889	43916
43836	43863	43890	43917
43837	43864	43891	43918
43838	43865	43892	43919
43839	43866	43893	43920
43840	43867	43894	43921
43841	43868	43895	43922
43842	43869	43896	43923
43843	43870	43897	43924
43844	43871	43898	43925
43845	43872	43899	43926
43846	43873	43900	43927
43847	43874	43901	43928
43848	43875	43902	43929
43849	43876	43903	43930
43850	43877	43904	43931
43851	43878	43905	43932
43852	43879	43906	43933
43853	43880	43907	43934
43854	43881	43908	43935
43855	43882	43909	43936
43856	43883	43910	43937
43857	43884	43911	43938
43858	43885	43912	43939
43859	43886	43913	43940
43860	43887	43914	43941
43861	43888	43915	43942

43943	43964	43985	44006
43944	43965	43986	44007
43945	43966	43987	44008
43946	43967	43988	44009
43947	43968	43989	44010
43948	43969	43990	44011
43949	43970	43991	44012
43950	43971	43992	44013
43951	43972	43993	44014
43952	43973	43994	44015
43953	43974	43995	44016
43954	43975	43996	44017
43955	43976	43997	44018
43956	43977	43998	44019
43957	43978	43999	44020
43958	43979	44000	44021
43959	43980	44001	44022
43960	43981	44002	44023
43961	43982	44003	44024
43962	43983	44004	44025
43963	43984	44005	44026

Total 192

0-6-0   4F

Introduced 1924. Post-grouping development of Midland design with reduced boiler mountings.
*Introduced 1922. Locos. built for S. & D.J.R. to M.R. design (taken into L.M.S. stock, 1930).
Weight: Loco. 48 tons 15 cwt.
Pressure: 175 lb. Su.
Cyls.: 20″ × 26″.
Dr. Wheels: 5′ 3″.   T.E.: 24,555 lb.
P.V.

44027	44039	44051	44063
44028	44040	44052	44064
44029	44041	44053	44065
44030	44042	44054	44066
44031	44043	44055	44067
44032	44044	44056	44068
44033	44045	44057	44069
44034	44046	44058	44070
44035	44047	44059	44071
44036	44048	44060	44072
44037	44049	44061	44073
44038	44050	44062	44074

44075	44121	44167	44213	44259	44305	44351	44397
44076	44122	44168	44214	44260	44306	44352	44398
44077	44123	44169	44215	44261	44307	44353	44399
44078	44124	44170	44216	44262	44308	44354	44400
44079	44125	44171	44217	44263	44309	44355	44401
44080	44126	44172	44218	44264	44310	44356	44402
44081	44127	44173	44219	44265	44311	44357	44403
44082	44128	44174	44220	44266	44312	44358	44404
44083	44129	44175	44221	44267	44313	44359	44405
44084	44130	44176	44222	44268	44314	44360	44406
44085	44131	44177	44223	44269	44315	44361	44407
44086	44132	44178	44224	44270	44316	44362	44408
44087	44133	44179	44225	44271	44317	44363	44409
44088	44134	44180	44226	44272	44318	44364	44410
44089	44135	44181	44227	44273	44319	44365	44411
44090	44136	44182	44228	44274	44320	44366	44412
44091	44137	44183	44229	44275	44321	44367	44413
44092	44138	44184	44230	44276	44322	44368	44414
44093	44139	44185	44231	44277	44323	44369	44415
44094	44140	44186	44232	44278	44324	44370	44416
44095	44141	44187	44233	44279	44325	44371	44417
44096	44142	44188	44234	44280	44326	44372	44418
44097	44143	44189	44235	44281	44327	44373	44419
44098	44144	44190	44236	44282	44328	44374	44420
44099	44145	44191	44237	44283	44329	44375	44421
44100	44146	44192	44238	44284	44330	44376	44422
44101	44147	44193	44239	44285	44331	44377	44423
44102	44148	44194	44240	44286	44332	44378	44424
44103	44149	44195	44241	44287	44333	44379	44425
44104	44150	44196	44242	44288	44334	44380	44426
44105	44151	44197	44243	44289	44335	44381	44427
44106	44152	44198	44244	44290	44336	44382	44428
44107	44153	44199	44245	44291	44337	44383	44429
44108	44154	44200	44246	44292	44338	44384	44430
44109	44155	44201	44247	44293	44339	44385	44431
44110	44156	44202	44248	44294	44340	44386	44432
44111	44157	44203	44249	44295	44341	44387	44433
44112	44158	44204	44250	44296	44342	44388	44434
44113	44159	44205	44251	44297	44343	44389	44435
44114	44160	44206	44252	44298	44344	44390	44436
44115	44161	44207	44253	44299	44345	44391	44437
44116	44162	44208	44254	44300	44346	44392	44438
44117	44163	44209	44255	44301	44347	44393	44439
44118	44164	44210	44256	44302	44348	44394	44440
44119	44165	44211	44257	44303	44349	44395	44441
44120	44166	44212	44258	44304	44350	44396	44442

44443	44484	44525	44566
44444	44485	44526	44567
44445	44486	44527	44568
44446	44487	44528	44569
44447	44488	44529	44570
44448	44489	44530	44571
44449	44490	44531	44572
44450	44491	44532	44573
44451	44492	44533	44574
44452	44493	44534	44575
44453	44494	44535	44576
44454	44495	44536	44577
44455	44496	44537	44578
44456	44497	44538	44579
44457	44498	44539	44580
44458	44499	44540	44581
44459	44500	44541	44582
44460	44501	44542	44583
44461	44502	44543	44584
44462	44503	44544	44585
44463	44504	44545	44586
44464	44505	44546	44587
44465	44506	44547	44588
44466	44507	44548	44589
44467	44508	44549	44590
44468	44509	44550	44591
44469	44510	44551	44592
44470	44511	44552	44593
44471	44512	44553	44594
44472	44513	44554	44595
44473	44514	44555	44596
44474	44515	44556	44597
44475	44516	44557*	44598
44476	44517	44558*	44599
44477	44518	44559*	44600
44478	44519	44560*	44601
44479	44520	44561*	44602
44480	44521	44562	44603
44481	44522	44563	44604
44482	44523	44564	44605
44483	44524	44565	44606

Total 580

4-6-0   5MT

Introduced 1934. Stanier L.M.S. taper boiler design.

Experimental locomotives:—
1. Introduced 1947. Stephenson link motion (outside), Timken roller bearings.
2. Introduced 1948. Caprotti Valve Gear.
3. Introduced 1948. Caprotti Valve Gear, Timken roller bearings.
4. Introduced 1948. Caprotti Valve Gear, Timken roller bearings, double chimney.
5. Introduced 1947. Timken roller bearings.
6. Introduced 1947. Timken roller bearings, double chimney.
7. Introduced 1949. Fitted with steel firebox.
8. Introduced 1950. Skefco roller bearings.
9. Introduced 1950. Timken roller bearings on driving coupled axle only.
10. Introduced 1950. Skefco roller bearings on driving coupled axle only.
11. Introduced 1951. Caprotti valve gear, Skefco roller bearings.

Weights: Loco. $\begin{cases} 72 \text{ tons 2 cwt.} \\ 75 \text{ tons 6 cwt. (1, 5, 6,} \\ \quad 8, 9, 10). \\ 74 \text{ tons 0 cwt. (2, 3, 4,} \\ \quad 11). \\ 72 \text{ tons 2 cwt. (7).} \end{cases}$

Pressure: 225 lb. Su.
Cyls.: (O) $18\frac{1}{2}'' \times 28''$.
Dr. Wheels: 6' 0".   T.E.: 25,455 lb.
Walschaerts Valve Gear, and P.V. except where otherwise shown.

44658	44671[10]	44684[8]	44697[9]
44659	44672[10]	44685[8]	44698
44660	44673[10]	44686[11]	44699
44661	44674[10]	44687[11]	44700
44662	44675[10]	44688[9]	44701
44663	44676[10]	44689[9]	44702
44664	44677[10]	44690[9]	44703
44665	44678[8]	44691[9]	44704
44666	44679[8]	44692[9]	44705
44667	44680[8]	44693[9]	44706
44668[10]	44681[8]	44694[9]	44707
44669[10]	44682[8]	44695[9]	44708
44670[10]	44683[8]	44696[9]	44709

44710	44556[4]	44802	44848	44894	44934	44974	45014
44711	44557[4]	44803	44849	44895	44935	44975	45015
44712	44558[5]	44804	44850	44896	44936	44976	45016
44713	44559[5]	44805	44851	44897	44937	44977	45017
44714	44560[5]	44806	44852	44898	44938	44978	45018
44715	44561[5]	44807	44853	44899	44939	44979	45019
44716	44562[5]	44808	44854	44900	44940	44980	45020
44717	44563[5]	44809	44855	44901	44941	44981	45021
44718[7]	44564[5]	44810	44856	44902	44942	44982	45022
44719[7]	44565[6]	44811	44857	44903	44943	44983	45023
44720[7]	44566[6]	44812	44858	44904	44944	44984	45024
44721[7]	44567[1]	44813	44859	44905	44945	44985	45025
44722[7]	44768	44814	44860	44906	44946	44986	45026
44723[7]	44769	44815	44861	44907	44947	44987	45027
44724[7]	44770	44816	44862	44908	44948	44988	45028
44725[7]	44771	44817	44863	44909	44949	44989	45029
44726[7]	44772	44818	44864	44910	44950	44990	45030
44727[7]	44773	44819	44865	44911	44951	44991	45031
44728	44774	44820	44866	44912	44952	44992	45032
44729	44775	44821	44867	44913	44953	44993	45033
44730	44776	44822	44868	44914	44954	44994	45034
44731	44777	44823	44869	44915	44955	44995	45035
44732	44778	44824	44870	44916	44956	44996	45036
44733	44779	44825	44871	44917	44957	44997	45037
44734	44780	44826	44872	44918	44958	44998	45038
44735	44781	44827	44873	44919	44959	44999	45039
44736	44782	44828	44874	44920	44960	45000	45040
44737	44783	44829	44875	44921	44961	45001	45041
44738[2]	44784	44830	44876	44922	44962	45002	45042
44739[2]	44785	44831	44877	44923	44963	45003	45043
44740[2]	44786	44832	44878	44924	44964	45004	45044
44741[2]	44787	44833	44879	44925	44965	45005	45045
44742[2]	44788	44834	44880	44926	44966	45006	45046
44743[2]	44789	44835	44881	44927	44967	45007	45047
44744[2]	44790	44836	44882	44928	44968	45008	45048
44745[2]	44791	44837	44883	44929	44969	45009	45049
44746[2]	44792	44838	44884	44930	44970	45010	45050
44747[2]	44793	44839	44885	44931	44971	45011	45051
44748[3]	44794	44840	44886	44932	44972	45012	45052
44749[3]	44795	44841	44887	44933	44973	45013	45053
44750[3]	44796	44842	44888				
44751[3]	44797	44843	44889				
44752[3]	44798	44844	44890				
44753[3]	44799	44845	44891				
44754[3]	44800	44846	44892				
44755[4]	44801	44847	44893				

NOTE

To understand the system of reference marks used in this book it is essential to read the notes on page 2.

29

45054	45095	45136	45177	45218	45264	45310	45356
45055	45096	45137	45178	45219	45265	45311	45357
45056	45097	45138	45179	45220	45266	45312	45358
45057	45098	45139	45180	45221	45267	45313	45359
45058	45099	45140	45181	45222	45268	45314	45360
45059	45100	45141	45182	45223	45269	45315	45361
45060	45101	45142	45183	45224	45270	45316	45362
45061	45102	45143	45184	45225	45271	45317	45363
45062	45103	45144	45185	45226	45272	45318	45364
45063	45104	45145	45186	45227	45273	45319	45365
45064	45105	45146	45187	45228	45274	45320	45366
45065	45106	45147	45188	45229	45275	45321	45367
45066	45107	45148	45189	45230	45276	45322	45368
45067	45108	45149	45190	45231	45277	45323	45369
45068	45109	45150	45191	45232	45278	45324	45370
45069	45110	45151	45192	45233	45279	45325	45371
45070	45111	45152	45193	45234	45280	45326	45372
45071	45112	45153	45194	45235	45281	45327	45373
45072	45113	45154*	45195	45236	45282	45328	45374
45073	45114	45155	45196	45237	45283	45329	45375
45074	45115	45156*	45197	45238	45284	45330	45376
45075	45116	45157*	45198	45239	45285	45331	45377
45076	45117	45158*	45199	45240	45286	45332	45378
45077	45118	45159	45200	45241	45287	45333	45379
45078	45119	45160	45201	45242	45288	45334	45380
45079	45120	45161	45202	45243	45289	45335	45381
45080	45121	45162	45203	45244	45290	45336	45382
45081	45122	45163	45204	45245	45291	45337	45383
45082	45123	45164	45205	45246	45292	45338	45384
45083	45124	45165	45206	45247	45293	45339	45385
45084	45125	45166	45207	45248	45294	45340	45386
45085	45126	45167	45208	45249	45295	45341	45387
45086	45127	45168	45209	45250	45296	45342	45388
45087	45128	45169	45210	45251	45297	45343	45389
45088	45129	45170	45211	45252	45298	45344	45390
45089	45130	45171	45212	45253	45299	45345	45391
45090	45131	45172	45213	45254	45300	45346	45392
45091	45132	45173	45214	45255	45301	45347	45393
45092	45133	45174	45215	45256	45302	45348	45394
45093	45134	45175	45216	45257	45303	45349	45395
45094	45135	45176	45217	45258	45304	45350	45396
				45259	45305	45351	45397
				45260	45306	45352	45398
				45261	45307	45353	45399
				45262	45308	45354	45400
				45263	45309	45355	45401

* NAMES:

45154 Lanarkshire Yeomanry.
45156 Ayrshire Yeomanry.
45157 The Glasgow Highlander.
45158 Glasgow Yeomanry.

45402	45427	45452	45476
45403	45428	45453	45477
45404	45429	45454	45478
45405	45430	45455	45479
45406	45431	45456	45480
45407	45432	45457	45481
45408	45433	45458	45482
45409	45434	45459	45483
45410	45435	45460	45484
45411	45436	45461	45485
45412	45437	45462	45486
45413	45438	45463	45487
45414	45439	45464	45488
45415	45440	45465	45489
45416	45441	45466	45490
45417	45442	45467	45491
45418	45443	45468	45492
45419	45444	45469	45493
45420	45445	45470	45494
45421	45446	45471	45495
45422	45447	45472	45496
45423	45448	45473	45497
45424	45449	45474	45498
45425	45450	45475	45499
45426	45451		

Total 842

"Patriot" Class

4-6-0　　　　　　**6P & 7P**

*6P Introduced 1930. Fowler 3-cyl. rebuild of L.N.W. "Claughton" Class (introduced 1912), retaining original wheels and other details.

Remainder. Introduced 1933. New locos. to Fowler design (45502–41 were officially considered as rebuilds).

†7P Introduced 1946. Ivatt rebuild o Fowler locos. with large taper boiler new cylinders and double chimney.

Weights: Loco. $\begin{cases} 80 \text{ tons } 15 \text{ cwt.} \\ 82 \text{ tons } 0 \text{ cwt.}† \end{cases}$

Pressure: $\begin{cases} 200 \text{ lb. Su.} \\ 250 \text{ lb. Su.}† \end{cases}$

Cyls.: $\begin{cases} (3) \ 18'' \times 26'' \\ (3) \ 17'' \times 26''† \end{cases}$

Dr. Wheels: 6' 9"

T.E.: $\begin{cases} 26,520 \text{ lb.} \\ 29,570 \text{ lb.}† \end{cases}$

Walschaerts Valve Gear. P.V.

45500*Patriot
45501*St. Dunstan's
45502 Royal Naval Division
45503 The Royal Leicestershire
　　　 Regiment
45504 Royal Signals
45505 The Royal Army
　　　 Ordnance Corps
45506 The Royal Pioneer Corps
45507 Royal Tank Corps
45508
45509 The Derbyshire
　　　 Yeomanry
45510
45511 Isle of Man
45512†Bunsen
45513
45514†Holyhead
45515 Caernarvon
45516 The Bedfordshire and
　　　 Hertfordshire Regiment
45517
45518 Bradshaw
45519 Lady Godiva
45520 Llandudno
45521†Rhyl
45522†Prestatyn
45523†Bangor
45524 Blackpool
45525†Colwyn Bay
45526†Morecambe and Heysham
45527†Southport
45528†
45529†Stephenson
45530†Sir Frank Ree
45531†Sir Frederick Harrison
45532†Illustrious
45533 Lord Rathmore
45534†E. Tootal Broadhurst
45535†Sir Herbert Walker,
　　　 K.C.B.
45536†Private W. Wood, V.C.
45537 Private E. Sykes, V.C.
45538 Giggleswick
45539 E. C. Trench
45540†Sir Robert Turnbull

45541 Duke of Sutherland
45542
45543 Home Guard
45544
45545†Planet
45546 Fleetwood
45547
45548 Lytham St. Annes
45549
45550
45551

Total 52

" Jubilee " Class

4-6-0   6P & 7P

6P Introduced 1934. Stanier L.M.S. taper boiler development of the " Patriot " class.

*Introduced 1936. Boiler fitted with double chimney ; this boiler was acquired by 45742 in 1940.

†**7P** Introduced 1942. Rebuilt with larger boiler and double chimney

Weights: Loco.: $\begin{cases} 79 \text{ tons } 11 \text{ cwt.} \\ 82 \text{ tons } 0 \text{ cwt.†} \end{cases}$

Pressure: $\begin{cases} 225 \text{ lb. Su.} \\ 250 \text{ lb. Su.†} \end{cases}$

Cyls.: (3) $17'' \times 26''$.
Dr. Wheels: 6' 9".

T.E.: $\begin{cases} 26,610 \text{ lb.} \\ 29,570 \text{ lb.†} \end{cases}$

Walschaerts Valve Gear. P.V.

45552 Silver Jubilee
45553 Canada
45554 Ontario
45555 Quebec
45556 Nova Scotia
45557 New Brunswick
45558 Manitoba
45559 British Columbia
45560 Prince Edward Island
45561 Saskatchewan
45562 Alberta
45563 Australia
45564 New South Wales
45565 Victoria
45566 Queensland
45567 South Australia
45568 Western Australia
45569 Tasmania
45570 New Zealand
45571 South Africa
45572 Eire
45573 Newfoundland
45574 India
45575 Madras
45576 Bombay
45577 Bengal
45578 United Provinces
45579 Punjab
45580 Burma
45581 Bihar and Orissa
45582 Central Provinces
45583 Assam
45584 North West Frontier
45585 Hyderabad
45586 Mysore
45587 Baroda
45588 Kashmir
45589 Gwalior
45590 Travancore
45591 Udaipur
45592 Indore
45593 Kolhapur
45594 Bhopal
45595 Southern Rhodesia
45596 Bahamas
45597 Barbados
45598 Basutoland
45599 Bechuanaland
45600 Bermuda
45601 British Guiana
45602 British Honduras
45603 Solomon Islands
45604 Ceylon
45605 Cyprus
45606 Falkland Islands
45607 Fiji
45608 Gibraltar
45609 Gilbert and Ellice Islands
45610 Gold Coast
45611 Hong Kong

Class 7F 2-8-0 No. 53803. [R. J. Buckley

Class 7F 2-8-0 No. 53806 (with larger boiler). [G. D. Bonner

Class 8F 2-8-0 No. 48761. [J. Davenport

Class 2P (Ex S. & D.J.) 4-4-0 No. 40326.

[R. K. Evans

Class 2P (Ex-L.M.S.) 4-4-0 No. 40698.

[R. J. Buckley

Class 4P 4-4-0 No. 41166.

G. D. Bonner

Class 3P (Pickersgill) 4-4-0 No. 54480. [R. K. Evans

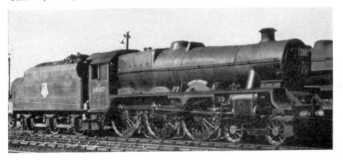

Class 6P 4-6-0 No. 45552 *Silver Jubilee*. [J. E. Wilkinson

Class 6P 4-6-0 No. 45696 *Arethusa* (with small tender). [R. J. Buckley

Class 7P 4-6-0 No. 46148 *The Manchester Regiment.*

[*K. Field*

Class 6P 4-6-0 No. 45501 *St. Dunstan's.*

[*E. Treacy*

Class 7P 4-6-0 No. 46121 *Highland Light Infantry, City of Glasgow Regiment.*
[L. A. Strudwick

Class 8P 4-6-2 No. 46209 *Princess Beatrice.*
[B. Sackville

Class 8P 4-6-2 No. 46239 *City of Chester.*
[A. R. Carpenter

Class 5MT 4-6-0 No. 44744 (with Caprotti valve gear).

[R. K. Evans

Caprotti valve gear on L.M.R. Class 5MT loco.

[C. R. L. Coles

Class 5MT 4-6-0 No. 44766 (with double chimney).

[S. D. Wainwright

Class 5MT 4-6-0 No. 44971 (with self-weighing tender). [R. J. Buckley

Class 5MT (Riddles) 4-6-0 No. 73033. [J. Robertson

Class 4MT (Riddles) 4-6-0 No. 75032. [G. Wheeler

Left: Class 4F 0-6-0 No. 44133.

[*R. J. Buckley*

Centre: Class 2F 0-6-0T No. 47169.

[*R. Broughton*

Bottom: Class 3F 0-6-0T No. 47241 (with condensing gear).

[*R. E. Vincent*

45612	Jamaica
45613	Kenya
45614	Leeward Islands
45615	Malay States
45616	Malta G.C.
45617	Mauritius
45618	New Hebrides
45619	Nigeria
45620	North Borneo
45621	Northern Rhodesia
45622	Nyasaland
45623	Palestine
45624	St. Helena
45625	Sarawak
45626	Seychelles
45627	Sierra Leone
45628	Somaliland
45629	Straits Settlements
45630	Swaziland
45631	Tanganyika
45632	Tonga
45633	Aden
45634	Trinidad
45635	Tobago
45636	Uganda
45638	Zanzibar
45639	Raleigh
45640	Frobisher
45641	Sandwich
45642	Boscawen
45643	Rodney
45644	Howe
45645	Collingwood
45646	Napier
45647	Sturdee
45648	Wemyss
45649	Hawkins
45650	Blake
45651	Shovell
45652	Hawke
45653	Barham
45654	Hood
45655	Keith
45656	Cochrane
45657	Tyrwhitt
45658	Keyes

45659	Drake
45660	Rooke
45661	Vernon
45662	Kempenfelt
45663	Jervis
45664	Nelson
45665	Lord Rutherford of Nelson
45666	Cornwallis
45667	Jellicoe
45668	Madden
45669	Fisher
45670	Howard of Effingham
45671	Prince Rupert
45672	Anson
45673	Keppel
45674	Duncan
45675	Hardy
45676	Codrington
45677	Beatty
45678	De Robeck
45679	Armada
45680	Camperdown
45681	Aboukir
45682	Trafalgar
45683	Hogue
45684	Jutland
45685	Barfleur
45686	St. Vincent
45687	Neptune
45688	Polyphemus
45689	Ajax
45690	Leander
45691	Orion
45692	Cyclops
45693	Agamemnon
45694	Bellerophon
45695	Minotaur
45696	Arethusa
45697	Achilles
45698	Mars
45699	Galatea
45700	Amethyst
45701	Conqueror
45702	Colossus
45703	Thunderer

45704 Leviathan
45705 Seahorse
45706 Express
45707 Valiant
45708 Resolution
45709 Implacable
45710 Irresistible
45711 Courageous
45712 Victory
45713 Renown
45714 Revenge
45715 Invincible
45716 Swiftsure
45717 Dauntless
45718 Dreadnought
45719 Glorious
45720 Indomitable
45721 Impregnable
45722 Defence
45723 Fearless
45724 Warspite
45725 Repulse
45726 Vindictive
45727 Inflexible
45728 Defiance
45729 Furious
45730 Ocean
45731 Perseverance
45732 Sanspareil
45733 Novelty
45734 Meteor
45735†Comet
45736†Phoenix
45737 Atlas
45738 Samson
45739 Ulster
45740 Munster
45741 Leinster
45742*Connaught

Total 190

For full details of
BRITISH RAILWAYS
DIESEL LOCOMOTIVES
see the
A.B.C. OF BRITISH RAILWAYS
LOCOMOTIVES PT. II.

"Royal Scot" Class
4-6-0   7P

*Introduced 1927. Fowler L.M.S. parallel boiler design.

†Introduced 1935. Stanier taper boiler rebuild with simple cyls. of experimental high pressure loco. No. 6399 *Fury.*

Remainder. Introduced 1943. Stanier rebuild of Fowler locos. with taper boiler, new cylinders and double chimney.

Weights: Loco.$\begin{cases} 84 \text{ tons } 18 \text{ cwt.*} \\ 84 \text{ tons } 1 \text{ cwt.†} \\ 83 \text{ tons.} \end{cases}$

Pressure: 250 lb. Su.

Cyls.: (3) 18″ × 26″.

Dr. Wheels: 6′ 9″.   T.E.: 33,150 lb.

Walschaerts Valve Gear.   P.V.

46100 Royal Scot
46101 Royal Scots Grey
46102 Black Watch
46103 Royal Scots Fusilier
46104 Scottish Borderer
46105 Cameron Highlander
46106 Gordon Highlander
46107 Argyll and Sutherland Highlander
46108 Seaforth Highlander
46109 Royal Engineer
46110 Grenadier Guardsman
46111 Royal Fusilier
46112 Sherwood Forester
46113 Cameronian
46114 Coldstream Guardsman
46115 Scots Guardsman
46116 Irish Guardsman
46117 Welsh Guardsman
46118 Royal Welch Fusilier
46119 Lancashire Fusilier
46120 Royal Inniskilling Fusilier
46121 Highland Light Infantry, City of Glasgow Regiment

46122 Royal Ulster Rifleman
46123 Royal Irish Fusilier
46124 London Scottish
46125 3rd Carabinier
46126 Royal Army Service Corps
46127 Old Contemptibles
46128 The Lovat Scouts
46129 The Scottish Horse
46130 The West Yorkshire Regiment
46131 The Royal Warwickshire Regiment
46132 The King's Regiment Liverpool
46133 The Green Howards
46134*The Cheshire Regiment
46135 The East Lancashire Regiment
46136 The Border Regiment
46137*The Prince of Wales's Volunteers (South Lancashire)
46138 The London Irish Rifleman
46139 The Welch Regiment
46140 The King's Royal Rifle Corps
46141 The North Staffordshire Regiment
46142 The York & Lancaster Regiment
46143 The South Staffordshire Regiment
46144 Honourable Artillery Company
46145 The Duke of Wellington's Regt. (West Riding)
46146 The Rifle Brigade
46147 The Northamptonshire Regiment
46148*The Manchester Regiment
46149 The Middlesex Regiment
46150 The Life Guardsman
46151 The Royal Horse Guardsman
46152 The King's Dragoon Guardsman

46153 The Royal Dragoon
46154 The Hussar
46155 The Lancer
46156*The South Wales Borderer
46157 The Royal Artilleryman
46158 The Loyal Regiment
46159 The Royal Air Force
46160 Queen Victoria's Rifleman
46161 King's Own
46162 Queen's Westminster Rifleman
46163 Civil Service Rifleman
46164 The Artists' Rifleman
46165 The Ranger (12th London Regt.)
46166 London Rifle Brigade
46167 The Hertfordshire Regiment
46168 The Girl Guide
46169 The Boy Scout
46170†British Legion

Total 71

" Princess Royal " Class
4-6-2   8P

*Introduced 1933. Stanier L.M.S. taper boiler design.

Remainder. Introduced 1935. Development of original design with alterations to valve gear, boiler and other details.

Weight : Loco.: 104 tons 10 cwt.

Pressure: 250 lb. Su.

Cyls.: (4) 16¼″ × 28″.

Dr. Wheels: 6′ 6″. T.E.: 40,285 lb.

Walschaerts Valve Gear and rocking shafts, P.V.

43

46200*The Princess Royal
46201*Princess Elizabeth
46203 Princess Margaret Rose
46204 Princess Louise
46205 Princess Victoria
46206 Princess Marie Louise
46207 Princess Arthur of
      Connaught
46208 Princess Helena Victoria
46209 Princess Beatrice
46210 Lady Patricia
46211 Queen Maud
46212 Duchess of Kent

Total 12

"Princess Coronation" Class

4-6-2   8P

Introduced 1938. Stanier L.M.S. enlargement of "Princess Royal" class. All except Nos. 46230-4/49-55 originally streamlined (introduced 1937. Streamlining removed from 1946).

*Introduced 1947. Ivatt development with roller bearings and detail alterations.

Weights: { 105 tons 5 cwt.
{ 106 tons 8 cwt.*

Pressure: 250 lb. Su.

Cyls.: (4) $16\frac{1}{2}'' \times 28''$.

Dr. Wheels: 6' 9".   T.E.: 40,000 lb.

Walschaerts Valve Gear and rocking shafts, P.V.

46220 Coronation
46221 Queen Elizabeth
46222 Queen Mary
46223 Princess Alice
46224 Princess Alexandra
46225 Duchess of Gloucester
46226 Duchess of Norfolk
46227 Duchess of Devonshire
46228 Duchess of Rutland
46229 Duchess of Hamilton
46230 Duchess of Buccleuch

46231 Duchess of Atholl
46232 Duchess of Montrose
46233 Duchess of Sutherland
46234 Duchess of Abercorn
46235 City of Birmingham
46236 City of Bradford
46237 City of Bristol
46238 City of Carlisle
46239 City of Chester
46240 City of Coventry
46241 City of Edinburgh
46242 City of Glasgow
46243 City of Lancaster
46244 King George VI
46245 City of London
46246 City of Manchester
46247 City of Liverpool
46248 City of Leeds
46249 City of Sheffield
46250 City of Lichfield
46251 City of Nottingham
46252 City of Leicester
46253 City of St. Albans
46254 City of Stoke-on-Trent
46255 City of Hereford
46256*Sir William A. Stanier,
      F.R.S.
46257*City of Salford

Total 38

2-6-0   2MT

Introduced 1946. Ivatt L.M.S. taper boiler design.
Weight: Loco. 47 tons 2 cwt.
Pressure: 200 lb. Su.
Cyls.: { (O) $16'' \times 24''$.
{ (O) $16\frac{1}{2}'' \times 24''$*
Dr. Wheels: 5' 0".   T.E.: { 17,410 lb.
{ 18,510 lb.*
Walschaerts Valve Gear, P.V.

46400	46405	46410	46415
46401	46406	46411	46416
46402	46407	46412	46417
46403	46408	46413	46418
46404	46409	46414	46419

46420	46447	46474*	46501*
46421	46448	46475*	46502*
46422	46449	46476*	46503†
46423	46450	46477*	46504*
46424	46451	46478*	46505*
46425	46452	46479*	46506*
46426	46453	46480*	46507*
46427	46454	46481*	46508*
46428	46455	46482*	46509*
46429	46456	46483*	46510*
46430	46457	46484*	46511*
46431	46458	46485*	46512*
46432	46459	46486*	46513*
46433	46460	46487*	46514*
46434	46461	46488*	46515*
46435	46462	46489*	46516*
46436	46463	46490*	46517*
46437	46464	46491*	46518*
46438	46465*	46492*	46519*
46439	46466*	46493*	46520*
46440	46467*	46494*	46521*
46441	46468*	46495*	46522*
46442	46469*	46496*	46523*
46443	46470*	46497*	46524*
46444	46471*	46498*	46525*
46445	46472*	46499*	46526*
46446	46473*	46500*	46527*

Total: 128

2-4-2T   1P

Introduced 1890. Webb L.N.W. design.
Weight : 50 tons 10 cwt.
Pressure: 150 lb.
Cyls.: 17″×24″.
Dr. Wheels: 5′ 8½″.   T.E.: 12,910 lb.
Allan straight link gear.

46604	46616	46666	46712

Total 4

NOTE
To understand the system of reference marks used in this book it is essential to read the notes on page 2.

0-4-0ST   0F

Introduced 1932. Kitson design prepared to Stanier's requirements for L.M.S.
Weight: 33 tons 0 cwt.
Pressure: 160 lb.
Cyls.: (O) 15½″×30″.
Dr. Wheels: 3′ 10″.   T.E.: 14,205 lb.

47000	47003	47006	47008
47001	47004	47007	47009
47002	47005		**Total 10**

0-6-0T   2F

Introduced 1928. Fowler L.M.S. short-wheelbase dock tanks.
Weight: 43 tons 12 cwt.
Pressure: 160 lb.
Cyls.: (O) 17″×22″.
Dr. Wheels: 3′ 11″.   T.E.: 18,400 lb.
Walschaerts Valve Gear.

47160	47163	47166	47168
47161	47164	47167	47169
47162	47165		

Total 10

0-4-0T   Sentinel

Geared Sentinel locos.
*Introduced 1929. Single-speed locos. for S. & D.J. (taken into L.M.S. stock 1930).

†Introduced 1930. Two-speed locos. for L.M.S.

‡Introduced 1932. Single-speed loco. for L.M.S.

Weight:$\begin{cases} 27 \text{ tons } 15 \text{ cwt.*} \\ 20 \text{ tons } 17 \text{ cwt.†} \\ 18 \text{ tons } 18 \text{ cwt.‡} \end{cases}$
Pressure: 275 lb. Su.

Cyls.:$\begin{cases} (4) \ 6\frac{3}{4}″\times9″.* \\ 6\frac{3}{4}″\times9″.†‡ \end{cases}$

Dr. Wheels:$\begin{cases} 3′ \ 1\frac{1}{2}″.* \\ 2′ \ 6\frac{3}{4}″.†‡ \end{cases}$

T.E.:$\begin{cases} 15,500 \text{ lb.*} \\ 11,800 \text{ lb.†‡} \end{cases}$

Poppet Valves.

47181†	47183†	47190*	47191*
47182†	47184‡		

Total 6

45

0-6-0T   3F

Introduced 1899. Johnson large Midland design, rebuilt with Belpaire boiler from 1919; fitted with condensers for London area.
*Introduced 1899. Non-condensing locos.
Weight: 48 tons 15 cwt.
Pressure: 160 lb.
Cyls.: 18″ × 26″.
Dr. Wheels: 4′ 7″.   T.E.: 20,835 lb.

47200	47215	47230*	47245
47201*	47216	47231*	47246*
47202	47217	47232*	47247
47203	47218	47233*	47248*
47204	47219	47234*	47249
47205	47220	47235*	47250*
47206	47221	47236*	47251
47207	47222	47237*	47252*
47208	47223	47238*	47253*
47209	47224	47239*	47254*
47210	47225	47240	47255*
47211	47226	47241	47256*
47212	47227	47242	47257*
47213	47228	47243	47258*
47214	47229	47244	47259*

Total 60

0-6-0T   3F

Introduced 1924. Post-grouping development of Midland design with detail alterations.
*Introduced 1929. Locos. built for S. & D.J. (taken into L.M.S. stock 1930).
†Push-and-pull fitted.
Weight: 49 tons 10 cwt.
Pressure: 160 lb.
Cyls.: 18″ × 26″.
Dr. Wheels: 4′ 7″.   T.E.: 20,835 lb.

47260	47270	47280	47290
47261	47271	47281	47291
47262	47272	47282	47292
47263	47273	47283	47293
47264	47274	47284	47294
47265	47275	47285	47295
47266	47276	47286	47296
47267	47277	47287	47297
47268	47278	47288	47298
47269	47279	47289	47299

47300	47346	47392	47438
47301	47347	47393	47439
47302	47348	47394	47440
47303	47349	47395	47441
47304	47350	47396	47442
47305	47351	47397	47443
47306	47352	47398	47444
47307	47353	47399	47445
47308	47354	47400	47446
47309	47355	47401	47447
47310*	47356	47402	47448
47311*	47357	47403	47449
47312*	47358	47404	47450
47313*	47359	47405	47451
47314*	47360	47406	47452
47315*	47361	47407	47453
47316*	47362	47408	47454
47317	47363	47409	47455
47318	47364	47410	47457
47319	47365	47411	47458
47320	47366	47412	47459
47321	47367	47413	47460
47322	47368	47414	47461
47323	47369	47415	47462
47324	47370	47416	47463
47325	47371	47417	47464
47326	47372	47418	47465
47327	47373	47419	47466
47328	47374	47420	47467
47329	47375	47421	47468
47330	47376	47422	47469
47331	47377	47423	47470
47332	47378	47424	47471
47333	47379	47425	47472
47334	47380	47426	47473
47335	47381	47427	47474
47336	47382	47428	47475
47337	47383	47429	47476
47338	47384	47430	47477†
47339	47385	47431	47478†
47340	47386	47432	47479†
47341	47387	47433	47480†
47342	47388	47434	47481†
47343	47389	47435	47482
47344	47390	47436	47483
47345	47391	47437	47484

47485	47531	47578	47626	47673	47676	47678	47680
47486	47532	47579	47627	47674	47677	47679	47681†
47487	47533	47580	47628	47675			

Total 417

47488	47534	47581	47629
47489	47535	47582	47630
47490	47536	47583	47631
47491	47537	47584	47632
47492	47538	47585	47633
47493	47539	47586	47634
47494	47540	47587	47635
47495	47541	47588	47636
47496	47542	47589	47637
47497	47543	47590	47638
47498	47544	47591	47639
47499	47545	47592	47640
47500	47546	47593	47641
47501	47547	47594	47642
47502	47548	47595	47643
47503	47549	47596	47644
47504	47550	47597	47645
47505	47551	47598	47646
47506	47552	47599	47647
47507	47554	47600	47648
47508	47555	47601	47649
47509	47556	47602	47650
47510	47557	47603	47651
47511	47558	47604	47652
47512	47559	47605	47653
47513	47560	47606	47654
47514	47561	47607	47655†
47515	47562	47608	47656
47516	47563	47609	47657
47517	47564	47610	47658
47518	47565	47611	47659
47519	47566	47612	47660
47520	47567	47614	47661
47521	47568	47615	47662
47522	47569	47616	47664
47523	47570	47618	47665
47524	47571	47619	47666
47525	47572	47620	47667
47526	47573	47621	47668
47527	47574	47622	47669
47528	47575	47623	47670
47529	47576	47624	47671
47530	47577	47625	47672

0-4-2ST   1F

Introduced 1896. Webb L.N.W. Bissel truck design.
Weight: 34 tons 17 cwt.
Pressure: 150 lb.
Cyls.: 17″ × 24″.
Dr. Wheels: 4′ 5½″.   T.E.: 16,530 lb.

47862**S**   **Total 1**

2-6-6-2T   Beyer-Garratt

*Introduced 1927. Fowler & Beyer-Peacock, L.M.S. design with fixed coal bunker.
Remainder. Introduced 1930. Development with detail alterations, later fitted with revolving coal bunkers. No. 47997 built 1927 to original design.
Weights: { 148 tons 15 cwt.*
155 tons 10 cwt.
Pressure: 190 lb. Su.
Cyls. (4) 18½″ × 26″.
Dr. Wheels: 5′ 3″.   T.E.: 45,620 lb.
Walschaerts Valve Gear. P.V.

47967	47976	47984	47992
47968	47977	47985	47993
47969	47978	47986	47994
47970	47979	47987	47995
47971	47980	47988	47996
47972	47981	47989	47997
47973	47982	47990	47998*
47974	47983	47991	47999*
47975			

Total 33

2-8-0 8F

Introduced 1935. Stanier L.M.S. taper boiler design.
Weight: Loco. 72 tons 2 cwt.
Pressure: 225 lb. Su.
Cyls.: (O) 18½″×28″.
Dr. Wheels: 4′ 8½″.   T.E.: 32,440 lb.
Walschaerts Valve Gear. P.V.

48000	48064	48109	48147	48185	48251	48297	48346
48001	48065	48110	48148	48186	48252	48301	48347
48002	48067	48111	48149	48187	48253	48302	48348
48003	48069	48112	48150	48188	48254	48303	48349
48004	48070	48113	48151	48189	48255	48304	48350
48005	48073	48114	48152	48190	48256	48305	48351
48006	48074	48115	48153	48191	48257	48306	48352
48007	48075	48116	48154	48192	48258	48307	48353
48008	48076	48117	48155	48193	48259	48308	48354
48009	48077	48118	48156	48194	48260	48309	48355
48010	48078	48119	48157	48195	48261	48310	48356
48011	48079	48120	48158	48196	48262	48311	48357
48012	48080	48121	48159	48197	48263	48312	48358
48016	48081	48122	48160	48198	48264	48313	48359
48017	48082	48123	48161	48199	48265	48314	48360
48018	48083	48124	48162	48200	48266	48315	48361
48020	48084	48125	48163	48201	48267	48316	48362
48024	48085	48126	48164	48202	48268	48317	48363
48026	48088	48127	48165	48203	48269	48318	48364
48027	48089	48128	48166	48204	48270	48319	48365
48029	48090	48129	48167	48205	48271	48320	48366
48033	48092	48130	48168	48206	48272	48321	48367
48035	48093	48131	48169	48207	48273	48322	48368
48036	48094	48132	48170	48208	48274	48323	48369
48037	48095	48133	48171	48209	48275	48324	48370
48039	48096	48134	48172	48210	48277	48325	48371
48045	48097	48135	48173	48211	48277	48326	48372
48046	48098	48136	48174	48212	48278	48327	48373
48050	48099	48137	48175	48213	48279	48328	48374
48053	48100	48138	48176	48214	48280	48329	48375
48054	48101	48139	48177	48215	48281	48330	48376
48055	48102	48140	48178	48216	48282	48331	48377
48056	48103	48141	48179	48217	48283	48332	48378
48057	48104	48142	48180	48218	48284	48333	48379
48060	48105	48143	48181	48219	48285	48334	48380
48061	48106	48144	48182	48220	48286	48335	48381
48062	48107	48145	48183	48221	48287	48336	48382
48063	48108	48146	48184	48222	48288	48337	48383
				48223	48289	48338	48384
				48224	48290	48339	48385
				48225	48291	48340	48386
				48246	48292	48341	48387
				48247	48293	48342	48388
				48248	48294	48343	48389
				48249	48295	48344	48390
				48250	48296	48345	48391

48392	48438	48494	48544	48630	48666	48702	48738
48393	48439	48495	48545	48631	48667	48703	48739
48394	48440	48500	48546	48632	48668	48704	48740
48395	48441	48501	48547	48633	48669	48705	48741
48396	48442	48502	48548	48634	48670	48706	48742
48397	48443	48503	48549	48635	48671	48707	48743
48398	48444	48504	48550	48636	48672	48708	48744
48399	48445	48505	48551	48637	48673	48709	48745
48400	48446	48506	48552	48638	48674	48710	48746
48401	48447	48507	48553	48639	48675	48711	48747
48402	48448	48508	48554	48640	48676	48712	48748
48403	48449	48509	48555	48641	48677	48713	48749
48404	48450	48510	48556	48642	48678	48714	48750
48405	48451	48511	48557	48643	48679	48715	48751
48406	48452	48512	48558	48644	48680	48716	48752
48407	48453	48513	48559	48645	48681	48717	48753
48408	48454	48514	48600	48646	48682	48718	48754
48409	48455	48515	48601	48647	48683	48719	48755
48410	48456	48516	48602	48648	48684	48720	48756
48411	48457	48517	48603	48649	48685	48721	48757
48412	48458	48518	48604	48650	48686	48722	48758
48413	48459	48519	48605	48651	48687	48723	48759
48414	48460	48520	48606	48652	48688	48724	48760
48415	48461	48521	48607	48653	48689	48725	48761
48416	48462	48522	48608	48654	48690	48726	48762
48417	48463	48523	48609	48655	48691	48727	48763
48418	48464	48524	48610	48656	48692	48728	48764
48419	48465	48525	48611	48657	48693	48729	48765
48420	48466	48526	48612	48658	48694	48730	48766
48421	48467	48527	48613	48659	48695	48731	48767
48422	48468	48528	48614	48660	48696	48732	48768
48423	48469	48529	48615	48661	48697	48733	48769
48424	48470	48530	48616	48662	48698	48734	48770
48425	48471	48531	48617	48663	48699	48735	48771
48426	48472	48532	48618	48664	48700	48736	48772
48427	48473	48533	48619	48665	48701	48737	
48428	48474	48534	48620				
48429	48475	48535	48621				
48430	48476	48536	48622				
48431	48477	48537	48623				
48432	48478	48538	48624				
48433	48479	48539	48625				
48434	48490	48540	48626				
48435	48491	48541	48627				
48436	48492	48542	48628				
48437	48493	48543	48629				

Total 663

0-8-0   6F & 7F

G1 Class 6F
*Introduced 1912. Bowen Cooke L.N.W. superheated design, developed from earlier saturated design (many rebuilt from earlier Webb, Whale and Bowen Cooke compound and simple designs introduced 1892 onwards). Many later rebuilt with Belpaire boilers.

G2 Class 7F
†Introduced 1921. Development of G1 with higher pressure boiler. Many later rebuilt with Belpaire boilers.

G2a Class 7F
Remainder. Introduced 1936. G1 locos. rebuilt with G2 Belpaire boilers.

Weights: Loco.: $\begin{cases} 60 \text{ tons } 15 \text{ cwt. (G1).} \\ 62 \text{ tons } 0 \text{ cwt. (G2, G2a).} \end{cases}$

Pressure: $\begin{cases} 160 \text{ lb. Su. (G1).} \\ 175 \text{ lb. Su. (G2, G2a).} \end{cases}$

Cyls.: $20\frac{1}{2}'' \times 24''$.
Dr. Wheels: $4' 5\frac{1}{2}''$.

T.E.: $\begin{cases} 25,640 \text{ lb. (G1).} \\ 28,045 \text{ lb. (G2, G2a).} \end{cases}$

Joy Valve Gear. P.V.

Nos. 48893–49394 CLASSES G1* AND G2a.

48893	48944	49025	49066
48895	48945	49027	49068
48898	48950	49028	49070
48899	48951	49033	49073
48905	48952	49034	49077
48907	48953	49035	49078
48914	48964	49037	49079
48915	49002	49044	49081
48917	49005	49045	49082
48921	49007	49046	49087
48922	49008	49047	49088
48926	49009	49048	49093
48927	49010	49049	49094
48930	49018	49051	49099
48932	49020	49057	49104
48940	49021	49061	49105
48942	49023	49063	49106
48943	49024	49064	49108

49109	49164	49252	49340
49112	49167	49254	49341
49113	49168	49260	49342
49114	49172	49262	49343
49115	49173	49266	49344
49116	49174	49267	49345
49117	49177	49268	49348
49119	49180	49270	49350
49120	49181	49271	49352
49121	49186	49275	49354
49122	49189	49276	49355
49125	49191	49277	49357
49126	49196	49278	49358
49129	49198	49281	49361
49130	49199	49287	49366
49132	49200	49288	49367
49134S	49202	49289	49368
49137	49203	49293	49373
49139	49209	49301	49375
49140*S	49210	49304	49376
49141	49212	49306	49377
49142	49214	49308	49378
49143	49216	49310	49381
49144	49223	49311	49382
49145	49224	49313	49385
49146	49226	49314	49386
49147	49228	49315	49387
49148	49229	49316	49389
49149	49230	49318	49390
49150	49234	49321	49391
49153	49239	49322	49392
49154	49240	49323	49393
49155	49243	49327	49394
49157	49245	49328	
49158	49246	49330	
49160	49247	49335	
49161	49249	49339S	

Nos. 49395–49454† CLASS G2.

49395	49402	49409	49416
49396	49403	49410	49417
49397	49404	49411	49418
49398	49405	49412	49419
49399	49406	49413	49420
49400	49407	49414	49421
49401	49408	49415	49422

49423	49431	49439	49447
49424	49432	49440	49448
49425	49433	49441	49449
49426	49434	49442	49450
49427	49435	49443	49451
49428	49436	49444	49452
49429	49437	49445	49453
49430	49438	49446	49454

Totals G2 60 G1 1 G2a 215

0-8-0   7F

Introduced 1929. Fowler L.M.S. design, developed from L.N.W. G2.
Weight: Loco. 60 tons 15 cwt.
Pressure: 200 lb. Su.
Cyls.: 19½" × 26".
Dr. Wheels: 4' 8½".   T.E.: 29,745 lb.
Walschaerts Valve Gear. P.V.

49503	49547	49592	49657
49505	49552	49598	49659
49508	49554	49603	49662
49509	49555	49618	49664
49511	49557	49620	49666
49515	49560	49624	49667
49532	49566	49627	49668
49536	49570	49637	49672
49538	49578	49638	49674
49544	49582	49640	
49545	49586	49648	

Total 42

2-4-2T   2P

Introduced 1889. Aspinall L. & Y. Class 5 with 2 tons coal capacity.
*Introduced 1890. Locos. built or rebuilt with smaller cylinders.
†Introduced 1898. Locos. with longer tanks and 4 tons coal capacity.
‡Introduced 1905. Hughes loco. built with Belpaire boiler and extended smokebox.
¶Introduced 1910. Locos. rebuilt with Belpaire boiler.
Weights: { 55 tons 19 cwt.
55 tons 19 cwt.*
59 tons 3 cwt.†‡¶
Pressure: 180 lb.
Cyls.: { 17½"×26".* 18"×26"   T.E.: { 18,360 lb.* 18,955 lb.
Dr. Wheels: 5' 8".   Joy Valve Gear.

50621	50653*	50731*¶	50807*
50636	50655¶	50746	50818
50643*	50656*	50752*	50829†¶
50644	50660	50757	50831†
50646	50686¶	50764	50850†¶
50647	50705	50765¶	50855*†
50648	50712	50777	50865*†
50650¶	50715*	50781	50869†
50651¶	50721	50788	50887‡
50652*¶	50725	50795*	

Total 39

0-4-0ST   0F

Introduced 1891. Aspinall L. & Y. Class 21
Weight: 21 tons 5 cwt.
Pressure: 160 lb.
Cyls.: (O) 13"×18"
Dr. Wheels: 3' 0⅜".   T.E.: 11,335 lb.

51202	51217	51230	51240
51204	51218	51231	51241
51206	51221	51232	51244
51207	51222	51234	51246
51212	51227	51235	51253
51216	51229	51237	

Total 23

0-6-0ST   2F

Introduced 1891. Aspinall rebuild of L. & Y. Barton Wright Class 23 0-6-0. Originally introduced 1877.
Weight: 43 tons 17 cwt.
Pressure: 140 lb.   Cyls.: 17½"×26".
Dr. Wheels: 4' 6".   T.E.: 17,545 lb.

51304S	51358	51412S	51446S
51305S	51361	51413	51447
51307	51368S	51415	51453
51313	51371	51419	51457
51316	51375	51423	51458
51319	51376	51424	51460
51321	51379	51425	51462
51323	51381	51429S	51464
51324S	51390	51432	51470
51336	51394S	51436	51471
51338	51396	51439	51472
51343	51397	51441	51474
51345	51404	51444S	51477
51353	51408	51445	51479

51481	51497	51506	51519
51484	51498	51510	51521
51486	51499	51511	51524
51488	51500	51512	51526
51491	51503	51513	51530
51496	51504	51516	

Total 79

0-6-0T   1F

Introduced 1897. Aspinall L. & Y.
  Class 24 dock tanks.
Weight: 50 tons 0 cwt.
Pressure: 140 lb.
Cyls.: (O) 17″×24″.
Dr. Wheels: 4′ 0″.   T.E.: 15,285 lb.
Allan straight link gear.

51535	51537	51544	51546

Total 4

0-6-0   2F

Introduced 1887. Barton Wright
  L. & Y. Class 25.
Weight: Loco. 39 tons 1 cwt.
Pressure: 140 lb.
Cyls.: 17½″×26″.
Dr. Wheels: 4′ 6″.   T.E.: 17,545 lb.

52016	52024	52044	52051
52021	52031	52045	52053

Total 8

0-6-0   3F

Introduced 1889. Aspinall L. & Y. Class
  27. Nos. 52515–29 built superheated
  with roundtop boiler and extended
  smokebox, later rebuilt with
  saturated boiler and short smokebox.
*Introduced 1911. Rebuilt with Bel-
  paire boiler and extended smokebox.
†Introduced 1913. Pettigrew Furness
  Rly. design.
‡Furness 0-6-0s rebuilt with ex-L. & Y.
  boiler.

Weights: Loco. { 42 tons 3 cwt.
                 43 tons 11 cwt.*
                 42 tons 13 cwt.†
Pressure: { 180 lb.
            170 lb.†
Cyls.: 18″×26″.
Dr. Wheels: { 5′ 1″.
              4′ 7½″ †‡
T.E.: { 21,130 lb.
        21,935 lb.†
        23,225 lb.‡
Joy Valve Gear.

52089	52186	52311	52415
52093**S**	52189	52312*	52416
52094*	52194	52317	52418
52095	52196	52319*	52427
52099	52197*	52322	52429
52104	52201*	52328	52431*
52108	52203	52331	52432
52118	52207	52334	52435
52119	52212**S**	52336	52437
52120	52215	52338	52438*
52121	52216	52341	52441**S**
52123	52217	52343	52443
52125	52218**S**	52345	52445*
52129	52220	52348	52447
52132*	52225	52349	52449
52133	52230	52350	52450
52135	52232	52351	52452
52136	52235	52355	52453
52137	52236	52356	52455
52139	52237	52358	52456
52140*	52239	52360	52458
52142	52240	52366	52459
52143	52244	52368	52461
52150	52245*	52369	52464**S**
52154*	52248	52376	52465
52159	52252	52378	52466
52160	52258	52379*	52494†
52161*	52260	52381	52499‡
52162	52268	52387	52501‡
52163	52269	52388	52509‡
52164	52270	52389	52510‡
52165	52271	52390	52515
52166	52272	52393	52517**S**
52167	52273*	52397	52521
52171	52275	52399	52522
52172	52278	52400*	52523
52174	52289	52405	52524
52175	52290	52408	52526
52177	52293	52410	52527
52179	52299	52411	52529
52182	52300	52412	
52183	52305	52413	

Totals: L. & Y. 161, F.R. 5

0-6-0   3F

*Introduced 1912. Hughes L. & Y. Class 28, superheated development of Class 27.
Remainder. Introduced 1913. Rebuilds of Class 27.
Weight: Loco. 46 tons 10 cwt
Pressure: 180 lb. Su.
Cyls.: 20½″ × 26″.
Dr. Wheels: 5′ 1″.   T.E.: 27,405 lb.
Joy Valve Gear. P.V.

52549*	52561	52576	52592
52551*	52569	52582	52608
52558	52575		**Total 10**

2-8-0   7F

Introduced 1914. Fowler design for S. & D.J. with 4′ 9″ boiler (some rebuilt from 1925 series).
*Introduced 1925. Fowler design with 5′ 3″ boiler.
(All taken into L.M.S. stock, 1930.)
Weights: Loco. { 64 tons 15 cwt.
              { 68 tons 11 cwt.*
Pressure: 190 lb. Su.
Cyls.: (O) 21″ × 28″.
Dr. Wheels: 4′ 8½″.   T.E.: 35,295 lb.
Walschaerts Valve Gear. P.V.

53800	53803	53806*	53809
53801	53804	53807*	53810
53802	53805	53808	
			Total 11

4-4-0   3P

Introduced 1910. McIntosh Caledonian " Dunalastair IV Superheater " or " 139 " class.
*Introduced 1915. Superheated re-build of McIntosh Caledonian " Dunalastair IV " or " 140 " class (originally introduced 1904).
Weight: Loco. 61 tons 5 cwt.
Pressure: 180 lb. Su.
Cyls.: 20½″ × 26″.
Dr. Wheels: 6′ 6″.   T.E.: 20,915 lb. P.V.

54438*	54446	54453	54457
54439*	54448	54454	54458
54440	54450	54455	54459
54441	54451	54456	54460
54443	54452		**Total 18**

4-4-0   3P

Introduced 1916. Pickersgill Caledonian " 113 " and " 928 " classes.
Weight: Loco. 61 tons 5 cwt.
Pressure: 180 lb. Su.   Cyls.: 20″ × 26″.
Dr. Wheels: 6′ 6″.   T.E.: 20,400 lb. P.V.

54461	54465	54469	54473
54462	54466	54470	54474
54463	54467	54471	54475
54464	54468	54472	54476
			Total 16

4-4-0   3P

Introduced 1920. Pickersgill Caledonian " 72 " class.
Weight: Loco. 61 tons 5 cwt.
Pressure: 180 lb. Su.   Cyls.: 20½″ × 26″.
Dr. Wheels: 6′ 6″.   T.E.: 21,435 lb. P.V.

54477	54486	54494	54502
54478	54487	54495	54503
54479	54488	54496	54504
54480	54489	54497	54505
54482	54490	54498	54506
54483	54491	54499	54507
54484	54492	54500	54508
54485	54493	54501	
			Total 31

0-4-4T   1P

Introduced 1905. Drummond Highland design.
Weight: 35 tons 15 cwt.
Pressure: 150 lb.   Cyls.: 14″ × 20″.
Dr. Wheels: 4′ 6″.   T.E.: 9,255 lb.

55051	55053	**Total 2**

0-4-4T   2P

*Introduced 1895. McIntosh Caledonian " 19 " class, with railed coal bunkers.
Remainder. Introduced 1897. McIntosh " 92 " class, developed from " 29 " class with larger tanks and highsided coal bunkers (both classes originally fitted for condensing on Glasgow Central Low Level lines).
Weights: { 53 tons 16 cwt.*
          { 53 tons 19 cwt.
Pressure: 180 lb.   Cyls.: 18″ × 26″.
Dr. Wheels: 5′ 9″.   T.E.: 18,680 lb.

55124*	55126	55145	55146
55125	55141		**Total 6**

0-4-4T   2P

Introduced 1900. McIntosh Caledonian " 439 " or " Standard Passenger " class.
*Introduced 1915. Pickersgill locos. with detail alterations.
Weights: $\begin{cases} 53 \text{ tons } 19 \text{ cwt.} \\ 57 \text{ tons } 12 \text{ cwt.*} \end{cases}$
Pressure: 180 lb.
Cyls.: 18″ × 26″.
Dr. Wheels: 5′ 9″.   T.E.: 18,680 lb.

55160	55189	55208	55223
55162	55193	55209	55224
55164	55194	55210	55225
55165	55195	55211	55226
55167	55196	55212	55227*
55168	55197	55213	55228*
55169	55198	55214	55229*
55173	55199	55215	55230*
55174	55200	55216	55231*
55176	55201	55217	55232*
55177	55202	55218	55233*
55178	55203	55219	55234*
55182	55204	55220	55235*
55185	55206	55221	55236*
55187	55207	55222	

Total 59

0-4-4T   2P

Introduced 1922. Pickersgill Caledonian " 431 " class (developed from " 439 " class) with cast-iron front buffer beam for banking.
Weight: 57 tons 17 cwt.
Pressure: 180 lb.
Cyls.: 18¼″ × 26″.
Dr. Wheels: 5′ 9″.   T.E.: 19,200 lb.

55237	55238	55239	55240

Total 4

0-4-4T   2P

Introduced 1925. Post-Grouping development of Caledonian " 439 " class.
Weight: 59 tons 12 cwt.
Pressure: 180 lb.
Cyls.: 18¼″ × 26″.
Dr. Wheels: 5′ 9″.   T.E.: 19,200 lb.

55260	55263	55266	55268
55261	55264	55267	55269
55262	55265		

Total 10

0-4-0ST   0F

Introduced 1885. Drummond and McIntosh Caledonian " Pugs."
Weight: 27 tons 7 cwt.
Pressure: 160 lb. Cyls: (O) 14″ × 20″.
Dr. Wheels: 3′ 8″.   T.E.: 12,115 lb.

56011	56027	56030	56035
56020	56028	56031	56038
56025**S**	56029	56032**S**	56039

Total 12

0-6-0T   2F

Introduced 1911. McIntosh Caledonian dock shunters, " 498 " class.
Weight: 47 tons 15 cwt.
Pressure: 160 lb. Cyls.: (O) 17″ × 22″
Dr. Wheels: 4′ 0″.   T.E.: 18,015 lb.

56151	56157	56163	56169
56152	56158	56164	56170
56153	56159	56165	56171
56154	56160	56166	56172
56155	56161	56167	56173
56156	56162	56168	

Total 23

0-6-0T   3F

Introduced 1895. McIntosh Caledonian " 29 " and " 782 " classes (56231-9 originally condensing).
Weight: 47 tons 15cwt.
Pressure: 160 lb.   Cyls.: 18″ × 26″.
Dr. Wheels: 4′ 6″.   T.E.: 21,215 lb.

56230	56269	56306	56341	57230	57273	57341	57411
56231	56271	56307	56342	57232	57274	57345	57412
56232	56272	56308	56343	57233	57275	57346	57413
56233	56273	56309	56344	57234	57276	57347	57414
56234	56274	56310	56345	57235	57278	57348	57416
56235	56275	56311	56346	57236	57279	57349	57417
56236	56277	56312	56347	57237	57282	57350	57418
56238	56278	56313	56348	57238	57284	57353	57419
56239	56279	56314	56349	57239	57285	57354	57424
56240	56280	56315	56350	57240	57287	57355	57426
56241	56281	56316	56352	57241	57288	57356	57429
56242	56282	56317	56353	57242	57291	57357	57430
56243	56283	56318	56354	57243	57292	57359	57431
56244	56284	56319	56355	57244	57295	57360	57432
56245	56285	56320	56356	57245	57296	57361	57434
56246	56286	56321	56357	57246	57299	57362	57435
56247	56287	56322	56358	57247	57300	57363	57436
56248	56288	56323	56359	57249	57302	57364	57437
56249	56289	56324	56360	57250	57303	57365	57441
56251	56290	56325	56361	57251	57307	57366	57443
56252	56291	56326	56362	57252	57309	57367	57444
56253	56292	56327	56363	57253	57311	57368	57445
56254	56293	56328	56364	57254	57314	57369	57446
56255	56294	56329	56365	57256	57315	57370	57447
56256	56295	56330	56366	57257	57317	57373	57448
56257	56296	56331	56367	57258	57319	57375	57451
56259	56297	56332	56368	57259	57320	57377	57456
56260	56298	56333	56369	57260	57321	57378	57457
56261	56299	56334	56370	57261	57324	57383	57459
56262	56300	56335	56371	57262	57325	57384	57460
56263	56301	56336	56372	57263	57326	57385	57461
56264	56302	56337	56373	57264	57328	57386	57462
56265	56303	56338	56374	57265	57329	57389	57463
56266	56304	56339	56375	57266	57331	57392	57465
56267	56305	56340	56376	57267	57335	57396	57470
				57268	57336	57398	57472
				57269	57338	57404	57473
				57270	57339	57405	
				57271	57340	57407	

Total 140

Total 154

0-6-0   2F

Introduced 1883. Drummond Caledonian "Standard Goods"; later additions by Lambie and McIntosh.
Some rebuilt with L.M.S. boilers *
Weight: Loco. { 41 tons 6 cwt.
{ 42 tons 4 cwt.*
Pressure: 180 lb.
Cyls.: 18″×26″.
Dr. Wheels.: 5′ 0″.   T.E.: 21,480 lb.

55

0-6-0 3F

Introduced 1899. McIntosh Caledonian "812" (Nos. 57550-57628) and "652" (remainder) classes.
Weight: Loco. 45 tons 14 cwt.
Pressure: 180 lb.
Cyls.: 18½"×26".
Dr. Wheels: 5' 0".   T.E.: 22,690 lb.

57550	57575	57599	57623
57552	57576	57600	57625
57553	57577	57601	57626
57554	57579	57602	57627
57555	57580	57603	57628
57556	57581	57604	57630
57557	57582	57605	57631
57558	57583	57607	57632
57559	57585	57608	57633
57560	57586	57609	57634
57562	57587	57611	57635
57563	57588	57612	57637
57564	57589	57613	57638
57565	57590	57614	57640
57566	57591	57615	57642
57568	57592	57617	57643
57569	57593	57618	57644
57570	57594	57619	57645
57571	57595	57620	
57572	57596	57621	
57573	57597	57622	

Total 81

0-6-0 3F

Introduced 1918. Pickersgill Caledonian "294" class (superheated) and "670" classes.
Weight: Loco. 50 tons 13 cwt.
Pressure: 180 lb. Su.
Cyls.: 18½"×26".
Dr. Wheels: 5' 0".   T.E.: 22,690 lb. P.V.

57650	57661	57670	57682
57651	57663	57671	57684
57652	57665	57672	57686
57653	57666	57673	57688
57654	57667	57674	57689
57655	57668	57679	57690
57658	57669	57681	57691
57659			

Total 29

0-4-4T IP

Introduced 1875. Johnson Midland design, later rebuilt with Belpaire boiler.
Weight: 53 tons 4 cwt.
Pressure: 140 lb.
Cyls.: 18"×24".
Dr. Wheels: 5' 7".   T.E.: 13,810 lb.

58038   **Total I**

0-4-4T IP

Introduced 1881. Johnson Midland design, rebuilt with Belpaire boiler (except 58071)
*Locos. with increased boiler pressure.
†Fitted with condensing gear.
Weight: 53 tons 4 cwt.
Pressure: $\begin{cases} 140 \text{ lb.} \\ 150 \text{ lb.}* \end{cases}$
Cyls.: 18"×24".
Dr. Wheels: 5' 4".   T.E.: $\begin{cases} 14,460 \text{ lb.} \\ 15,490 \text{ lb.}* \end{cases}$

Nos. 58040-56 LOCOS. WITH 140 lb. PRESSURE.			
58040	58051	58054	58056

*Nos. 58062-91 LOCOS. WITH 150 lb. PRESSURE.			
58062	58072†	58083	58087
58065	58073†	58084	58089
58066	58077	58085	58091
58071†	58080	58086	

Total 19

0-10-0

Introduced 1919. Fowler Midland banker for Lickey incline.
Weight: Loco. 73 tons 13 cwt.
Pressure: 180 lb. Su.
Cyls. (4): 16¾"×28".
Dr .Wheels: 4' 7½".   T.E.: 43,315 lb.
Walschaerts Valve Gear.

58100   **Total I**

Class 3F 0-6-0 No. 43218. [R. J. Buckley

Class 2F 0-6-0 No. 58135 (4' 11" driving wheels) [E. Blakey

Class 2F 0-6-0 No. 58277 (5' 3" driving wheels) [R. J. Buckley

Class 3F 0-6-0T No. 56298. [J. Robertson

Class 2P 0-4-4T No. 55210 (with an ex-L.N.E. Class J36 chimney). [C. L. Kerr

Class 2F 0-6-0 No. 57261 (with cut-down chimney) [J. L. Stevenson

Class 2F 0-6-0 No. 57360 (rebuilt with L.M.S. boiler).   [*J. Robertson*

Class 3F (McIntosh) 0-6-0 No. 57632.   [*J. Robertson*

Class 3F (Pickersgill) 0-6-0 No. 57661.   [*J. Robertson*

Class 2F 0-6-0 No. 52053. [R. J. Buckley

Class 2F 0-6-0ST No. 51516. [J. Davenport

Class 2P 2-4-2T No. 50731 (with Belpaire boiler and extended smokebox).
[H. C. Casserley

Class 2P 2-4-2T No. 50887 (with large bunker and Push-and-Pull fitted).

[H. C. Casserley

Class 3F 0-6-0 No. 52240.

[A. B. Crompton

Class 3F 0-6-0 No. 52549 (with Belpaire boiler, superheater and extended smokebox).

[C. R. L. Coles

Class 3F (ex-Furness) 0-6-0 No. 52494.   [J. E. Wilkinson

Class 3F (ex-Furness) 0-6-0 No. 52499 (rebuilt with ex-L. & Y. boiler).

[J. E. Wilkinson

Class 2F 0-6-0 No. 58375.   R. M. Casserley

Class 2F 0-6-2T No. 58903. [R. M. Casserley

Class 1P 2-4-2T No. 46604. [R. M. Casserley

Class 2F 0-6-0ST No. C.D.3 (Wolverton Carr. Wks.). [K. Robey

Left: Class 0F 0-4-0ST No. 56025.

[*K. K. MacKay*

Left: Class 1P 0-4-4T No. 58072 (fitted with condensing apparatus).

[*D. D. Clegg*

Left: 0-10-0 No. 58100.

[*R. J. Buckley*

0-6-0   2F

*Introduced 1875. Johnson Midland 4' 11" design with round top boiler.
†Introduced 1917. Rebuilt with Belpaire boiler.
§Introduced 1917. Rebuilt with Belpaire boiler.
Weight: Loco. Various.
37 tons 12 cwt. to 40 tons 3 cwt.
Pressure: 160 lb.   Cyls.: 18"×26".

Dr. Wheels: $\begin{cases} 4' 11''* \\ 4' 11''† \\ 5' 3''§ \end{cases}$ T.E.: $\begin{cases} 19,420 \text{ lb.*} \\ 19,420 \text{ lb.†} \\ 18,185 \text{ lb.§} \end{cases}$

58114†	58156†	58192§	58241†
58115†	58157†	58193§	58242†
58116†	58158†	58194§	58244†
58117†	58159†	58195§	58246*
58118†	58160†	58196§	58247†
58119†	58162†	58197§	58257§
58120†	58163†	58198§	58260§
58121†	58164†	58199§	58261§
58122†	58165†	58200§	58269§
58123†	58166†	58203§	58271§
58124†	58167†	58204§	58272§
58125†	58168†	58206§	58273§
58126†	58169†	58207§	58276§
58127†	58170†	58209§	58277§
58128†	58171†	58212§	58278§
58129†	58172†	58213§	58279§
58130†	58173†	58214§	58281§
58131†	58174†	58215§	58283§
58132†	58175†	58216§	58286§
58133†	58176†	58217§	58287§
58135†	58177†	58218§	58288§
58136†	58178†	58219§	58290§
58137†	58179†	58220§	58291§
58138†	58181†	58221§	58293§
58139†	58182†	58224§	58295§
58140†	58183†	58225§	58298§
58142†	58184†	58228§	58299§
58143†	58185†	58230†	58300§
58144†	58186†	58232†	58305§
58146†	58187†	58233†	58306§
58148†	58188§	58234†	58308§
58152†	58189§	58235†	58309§
58153†	58190§	58236*	58310§
58154†	58191§	58238†	

Total 135

0-6-0   2F

Introduced 1887. Webb L.N.W. " 18 in. Goods " (" Cauliflowers ") many later rebuilt with Belpaire boilers.
Weight: Loco. 36 tons 10 cwt.
Pressure: 150 lb.
Cyls.: 18"×24".
Dr. Wheels: 5' 2½".   T.E.: 15,865 lb
Joy Valve Gear.

58375	58394	58412	58430
58376	58409	58427	

Total 7

0-6-0T   2F

Introduced 1879. Park North London design.
Weight: 45 tons 10 cwt.
Pressure: 160 lb.
Cyls.: (O) 17"×24".
Dr. Wheels: 4' 4".   T.E.: 18,140 lb.

58850	58853	58856	58860
58851	58854	58857**S**	58862
58852	58855	58859	

Total 11

0-6-2T   2F

Introduced 1882. Webb L.N.W. " Coal Tanks."
Weight: 43 tons 15 cwt.
Pressure: 150 lb.
Cyls.: 17"×24".
Dr. Wheels: 4' 5½".   T.E.: 16,530 lb.

58887	58900	58915	58926
58888	58902	58921	
58891	58903	58924	
58899	58904	58925	

Total 13

LONDON MIDLAND SERVICE LOCOS.

0-4-0 Diesel

Introduced 1936. Fowler diesel.
Weight: 21 tons 5 cwt.

E.D.1	E.D.3	E.D.5
E.D.2	E.D.4	E.D.6
		Total 6

0-6-0ST 2F

Introduced 1870. Webb version of Ramsbottom " Special Tank."

Weight: 34 tons 10 cwt.
Pressure: 140 lb.
Cyls.: 17" × 24".
Dr. Wheels: 4' 5½". T.E.: 17,005 lb

3323 (L.N.W. No.) Crewe Loco. Works
C.D.3 Wolverton Carriage Works
C.D.6   "   "   "
C.D.7   "   "   "
C.D.8 "Earlestown" Wolverton Carriage Works

BRITISH RAILWAYS STANDARD LOCOMOTIVES
Chief Officer (Mechanical Engineering) :
R. C. BOND

4-6-2 Class 7MT

Introduced 1951. Designed at Derby.
Weights : Loco. 94 tons 0 cwt.
          Tender 47 tons 4 cwt.
Pressure : 250 lb. Su.
Cyls. : (O) 20" × 28".
Driving Wheels : 6' 2". T.E. : 32,150 lb.
Walschaerts gear. P.V.

70000	Britannia	70024	Vulcan
70001	Lord Hurcomb	70025	Western Star
70002	Geoffrey Chaucer	70026	Polar Star
70003	John Bunyan	70027	Rising Star
70004	William Shakespeare	70028	Royal Star
70005	John Milton	70029	Shooting Star
70006	Robert Burns	70030	William Wordsworth
70007	Coeur-de-Lion	70031	Byron
70008	Black Prince	70032	Tennyson
70009	Alfred the Great	70033	Charles Dickens
70010	Owen Glendower	70034	Thomas Hardy
70011	Hotspur	70035	Rudyard Kipling
70012	John of Gaunt	70036	Boadicea
70013	Oliver Cromwell	70037	Hereward the Wake
70014	Iron Duke	70038	Robin Hood
70015	Apollo	70039	Sir Christopher Wren
70016	Ariel	70040	Clive of India
70017	Arrow	70041	Sir John Moore
70018	Flying Dutchman	70042	Lord Roberts
70019	Lightning	70043	Earl Kitchener
70020	Mercury	70044	Earl Haig
70021	Morning Star	70045	
70022	Tornado	70046	
70023	Venus	70047	
		70048	
		70049	
		70050	
		70051	
		70052	
		70053	
		70054	

Engines of this class are still being delivered. The names of Nos. 70043/4 are temporarily not affixed.

4-6-2   Class 8P

Introduced 1954. Designed at Derby.
Weights : Loco. 101 tons 5 cwt.
          Tender 55 tons 10 cwt.
Pressure : 250 lb. Su.
Cyls. : (3) 18″ × 28″
Driving Wheels : 6′ 2″. T.E. : 39,080 lb.
Caprotti valve gear.

71000   Duke of Gloucester

4-6-2-   Class 6MT

Introduced 1952. Designed at Derby.
Weights : Loco. 86 tons 19 cwt.
          Tender 47 tons 4 cwt.
Pressure : 225 lb.   Su.
Cyls. : (O) 19½″ × 28″.
Driving Wheels : 6′ 2″. T.E. : 27,520 lb.
Walschaerts gear. P.V.

72000	Clan Buchanan
72001	Clan Cameron
72002	Clan Campbell
72003	Clan Fraser
72004	Clan Macdonald
72005	Clan Macgregor
72006	Clan Mackenzie
72007	Clan Mackintosh
72008	Clan Macleod
72009	Clan Stewart

Total 10

4-6-0   Class 5MT

Introduced 1951. Designed at Doncaster.
Weights : Loco. 76 tons 4 cwt.
          Tender 47 tons 4 cwt.
Pressure : 225 lb.   Su.
Cyls. : (O) 19″ × 28″.
Driving Wheels : 6′ 2″. T.E. : 26,120 lb.
Walschaerts gear. P.V.

73000	73011	73022	73033
73001	73012	73023	73034
73002	73013	73024	73035
73003	73014	73025	73036
73004	73015	73026	73037
73005	73016	73027	73038
73006	73017	73028	73039
73007	73018	73029	73040
73008	73019	73030	73041
73009	73020	73031	73042
73010	73021	73032	73043

73044	73052	73060	73068
73045	73053	73061	73069
73046	73054	73062	73070
73047	73055	73063	73071
73048	73056	73064	73072
73049	73057	73065	73073
73050	73058	73066	73074
73051	73059	73067	

Engines of this class are still being delivered.

4-6-0   Class 4MT

Introduced 1951. Designed at Brighton.
Weights : Loco. 69 tons 0 cwt.
          Tender 43 tons 3 cwt.
Pressure : 225 lb.   Su.
Cyls. : (O) 18″ × 28″.
Driving Wheels : 5′ 8″. T.E. : 25,100 lb.
Walschaerts gear. P.V.

75000	75020	75040	75060
75001	75021	75041	75061
75002	75022	75042	75062
75003	75023	75043	75063
75004	75024	75044	75064
75005	75025	75045	75065
75006	75026	75046	75066
75007	75027	75047	75067
75008	75028	75048	75068
75009	75029	75049	75069
75010	75030	75050	75070
75011	75031	75051	75071
75012	75032	75052	75072
75013	75033	75053	75073
75014	75034	75054	75074
75015	75035	75055	75075
75016	75036	75056	75076
75017	75037	75057	75077
75018	75038	75058	75078
75019	75039	75059	75079

Engines of this class are still being delivered.

2-6-0   Class 4MT

Introduced 1953. Designed at Doncaster.
Weights : Loco. 59 tons 2 cwt.
          Tender 42 tons 3 cwt.
Pressure : 225 lb.   Su.
Cyls. : (O) 17½″ × 26″.
Driving Wheels : 5′ 3″. T.E. : 24,170 lb.
Walschaerts gear. P.V.

76000	76012	76024	76036
76001	76013	76025	76037
76002	76014	76026	76038
76003	76015	76027	76039
76004	76016	76028	76040
76005	76017	76029	76041
76006	76018	76030	76042
76007	76019	76031	76043
76008	76020	76032	76044
76009	76021	76033	
76010	76022	76034	
76011	76023	76035	

Engines of this class are still being delivered.

2-6-0   Class 3MT

Introduced 1954.
Weights : Loco.   57 tons 9 cwt.
             Tender 42 tons 3 cwt.
Pressure : 200 lb.
Cyls. : (O) 17½" × 26"
Driving Wheels : 5' 3" T.E. : 21,490 lb.
Walschaerts gear. P.V.

77000	77005	77010	77015
77001	77006	77011	77016
77002	77007	77012	77017
77003	77008	77013	77018
77004	77009	77014	77019

2-6-0   Class 2MT

Introduced 1953. Designed at Derby.
Weights : Loco.   49 tons 5 cwt.
             Tender 36 tons 17 cwt.
Pressure : 200 lb.   Su.
Cyls. : (O) 16½" × 24".
Driving Wheels : 5' 0". T.E. : 15,515 lb.
Walschaerts gear. P.V.

78000	78012	78024	78036
78001	78013	78025	78037
78002	78014	78026	78038
78003	78015	78027	78039
78004	78016	78028	78040
78005	78017	78029	78041
78006	78018	78030	78042
78007	78019	78031	78043
78008	78020	78032	78044
78009	78021	78033	
78010	78022	78034	
78011	78023	78035	

Engines of this class are still being delivered.

2-6-4T   Class 4MT

Introduced 1951. Designed at Brighton.
Weight : 88 tons 10 cwt.
Pressure : 225 lb.   Su.
Cyls. : (O) 18" × 28".
Driving Wheels : 5' 8". T.E. : 25,100 lb.
Walschaerts gear. P.V.

80000	80029	80058	80087
80001	80030	80059	80088
80002	80031	80060	80089
80003	80032	80061	80090
80004	80033	80062	80091
80005	80034	80063	80092
80006	80035	80064	80093
80007	80036	80065	80094
80008	80037	80066	80095
80009	80038	80067	80096
80010	80039	80068	80097
80011	80040	80069	80098
80012	80041	80070	80099
80013	80042	80071	80100
80014	80043	80072	80101
80015	80044	80073	80102
80016	80045	80074	80103
80017	80046	80075	80104
80018	80047	80076	80105
80019	80048	80077	80106
80020	80049	80078	80107
80021	80050	80079	80108
80022	80051	80080	80109
80023	80052	80081	80110
80024	80053	80082	80111
80025	80054	80083	80112
80026	80055	80084	80113
80027	80056	80085	80114
80028	80057	80086	80115

Engines of this class are still being delivered.

2-6-2T   Class 3MT

Introduced 1952. Designed at Swindon.
Weight : 73 tons 10 cwt.
Pressure : 200 lb.   Su.
Cyls. : (O) 17½" × 26".
Driving Wheels : 5' 3". T.E. : 21,490 lb.
Walschaerts gear. P.V.

82000	82002	82004	82006
82001	82003	82005	82007

82008	82018	82028	82038
82009	82019	82029	82039
82010	82020	82030	82040
82011	82021	82031	82041
82012	82022	82032	82042
82013	82023	82033	82043
82014	82024	82034	82044
82015	82025	82035	
82016	82026	82036	
82017	82027	82037	

Engines of this class are still being delivered.

2-6-2T   Class 2MT

Introduced 1953. Designed at Derby.
Weight : 63 tons 5 cwt.
Pressure : 200 lb.
Cyls. : (O) 16½″ × 24″.
Driving Wheels : 5′ 0″. T.E. : 18,515 lb.
Walschaerts gear. P.V.

84000	84008	84016	84024
84001	84009	84017	84025
84002	84010	84018	84026
84003	84011	84019	84027
84004	84012	84020	84028
84005	84013	84021	84029
84006	84014	84022	
84007	84015	84023	

Engines of this class are still being delivered.

2-8-0   Class WD

Ministry of Supply " Austerity " 2-8-0 locomotives purchased by British Railways, 1948.
Introduced 1943. Riddles M.o.S. design.
Weights : Loco. 70 tons 5 cwt.
                    Tender 55 tons 10 cwt.
Pressure:225 lb. Su. Cyls.: (O)19″×28″.
Driving Wheels : 4′ 8½″. T.E. : 34,215 lb
Walschaerts gear. P.V.

90000	90010	90020	90030	90040	90086	90132	90178
90001	90011	90021	90031	90041	90087	90133	90179
90002	90012	90022	90032	90042	90088	90134	90180
90003	90013	90023	90033	90043	90089	90135	90181
90004	90014	90024	90034	90044	90090	90136	90182
90005	90015	90025	90035	90045	90091	90137	90183
90006	90016	90026	90036	90046	90092	90138	90184
90007	90017	90027	90037	90047	90093	90139	90185
90008	90018	90028	90038	90048	90094	90140	90186
90009	90019	90029	90039	90049	90095	90141	90187
				90050	90096	90142	90188
				90051	90097	90143	90189
				90052	90098	90144	90190
				90053	90099	90145	90191
				90054	90100	90146	90192
				90055	90101	90147	90193
				90056	90102	90148	90194
				90057	90103	90149	90195
				90058	90104	90150	90196
				90059	90105	90151	90197
				90060	90106	90152	90198
				90061	90107	90153	90199
				90062	90108	90154	90200
				90063	90109	90155	90201
				90064	90110	90156	90202
				90065	90111	90157	90203
				90066	90112	90158	90204
				90067	90113	90159	90205
				90068	90114	90160	90206
				90069	90115	90161	90207
				90070	90116	90162	90208
				90071	90117	90163	90209
				90072	90118	90164	90210
				90073	90119	90165	90211
				90074	90120	90166	90212
				90075	90121	90167	90213
				90076	90122	90168	90214
				90077	90123	90169	90215
				90078	90124	90170	90216
				90079	90125	90171	90217
				90080	90126	90172	90218
				90081	90127	90173	90219
				90082	90128	90174	90220
				90083	90129	90175	90221
				90084	90130	90176	90222
				90085	90131	90177	90223

90224	90270	90316	90362	90408	90454	90500	90546
90225	90271	90317	90363	90409	90455	90501	90547
90226	90272	90318	90364	90410	90456	90502	90548
90227	90273	90319	90365	90411	90457	90503	90549
90228	90274	90320	90366	90412	90458	90504	90550
90229	90275	90321	90367	90413	90459	90505	90551
90230	90276	90322	90368	90414	90460	90506	90552
90231	90277	90323	90369	90415	90461	90507	90553
90232	90278	90324	90370	90416	90462	90508	90554
90233	90279	90325	90371	90417	90463	90509	90555
90234	90280	90326	90372	90418	90464	90510	90556
90235	90281	90327	90373	90419	90465	90511	90557
90236	90282	90328	90374	90420	90466	90512	90558
90237	90283	90329	90375	90421	90467	90513	90559
90238	90284	90330	90376	90422	90468	90514	90560
90239	90285	90331	90377	90423	90469	90515	90561
90240	90286	90332	90378	90424	90470	90516	90562
90241	90287	90333	90379	90425	90471	90517	90563
90242	90288	90334	90380	90426	90472	90518	90564
90243	90289	90335	90381	90427	90473	90519	90565
90244	90290	90336	90382	90428	90474	90520	90566
90245	90291	90337	90383	90429	90475	90521	90567
90246	90292	90338	90384	90430	90476	90522	90568
90247	90293	90339	90385	90431	90477	90523	90569
90248	90294	90340	90386	90432	90478	90524	90570
90249	90295	90341	90387	90433	90479	90525	90571
90250	90296	90342	90388	90434	90480	90526	90572
90251	90297	90343	90389	90435	90481	90527	90573
90252	90298	90344	90390	90436	90482	90528	90574
90253	90299	90345	90391	90437	90483	90529	90575
90254	90300	90346	90392	90438	90484	90530	90576
90255	90301	90347	90393	90439	90485	90531	90577
90256	90302	90348	90394	90440	90486	90532	90578
90257	90303	90349	90395	90441	90487	90533	90579
90258	90304	90350	90396	90442	90488	90534	90580
90259	90305	90351	90397	90443	90489	90535	90581
90260	90306	90352	90398	90444	90490	90536	90582
90261	90307	90353	90399	90445	90491	90537	90583
90262	90308	90354	90400	90446	90492	90538	90584
90263	90309	90355	90401	90447	90493	90539	90585
90264	90310	90356	90402	90448	90494	90540	90586
90265	90311	90357	90403	90449	90495	90541	90587
90266	90312	90358	90404	90450	90496	90542	90588
90267	90313	90359	90405	90451	90497	90543	90589
90268	90314	90360	90406	90452	90498	90544	90590
90269	90315	90361	90407	90453	90499	90545	90591

90592	90628	90664	90700
90593	90629	90665	90701
90594	90630	90666	90702
90595	90631	90667	90703
90596	90632	90668	90704
90597	90633	90669	90705
90598	90634	90670	90706
90599	90635	90671	90707
90600	90636	90672	90708
90601	90637	90673	90709
90602	90638	90674	90710
90603	90639	90675	90711
90604	90640	90676	90712
90605	90641	90677	90713
90606	90642	90678	90714
90607	90643	90679	90715
90608	90644	90680	90716
90609	90645	90681	90717
90610	90646	90682	90718
90611	90647	90683	90719
90612	90648	90684	90720
90613	90649	90685	90721
90614	90650	90686	90722
90615	90651	90687	90723
90616	90652	90688	90724
90617	90653	90689	90725
90618	90654	90690	90726
90619	90655	90691	90727
90620	90656	90692	90728
90621	90657	90693	90729
90622	90658	90694	90730
90623	90659	90695	90731
90624	90660	90696	90732
90625	90661	90697	Vulcan
90626	90662	90698	
90627	90663	90699	

Total 733

2-10-0   8F   Class WD

Ministry of Supply "Austerity" 2-10-0 locomotives purchased by British Railways, 1948.
Introduced 1943 Riddles M.o.S. design.
Weights : Loco.   78 tons 6 cwt.
　　　　　　Tender 55 tons 10 cwt.
Pressure : 225 lb. Cyls. : (O) 19″ × 28″.
Driving Wheels : 4′ 8½″. T.E. : 34,215 lb.
Walschaerts gear. P.V.

90750	90757	90764	90771
90751	90758	90765	90772
90752	90759	90766	90773
90753	90760	90767	90774
90754	90761	90768	
90755	90762	90769	
90756	90763	90770	

Total 25

2-10-0   Class 9F

Introduced 1954. Designed at Crewe.
Weights : Loco.   86 tons 14 cwt.
　　　　　　Tender 52 tons 10 cwt.
Pressure : 250 lb.
Cyls. : (O) 20″ × 28″.
Driving Wheels : 5′ 0″. T.E. : 39,670 lb.
Walschaerts gear. P.V.

92000	92010	92020	92030
92001	92011	92021	92031
92002	92012	92022	92032
92003	92013	92023	92033
92004	92014	92024	92034
92005	92015	92025	92035
92006	92016	92026	92036
92007	92017	92027	92037
92008	92018	92028	92038
92009	92019	92029	92039

Engines of this class are still being delivered.

L.M. ELECTRIC MOTOR COACH NUMBERS
LONDON DISTRICT

OERLIKON STOCK

M28000	28231	28242	28251	28260	28270	28280	28290
28223	28232	28243	28252	28261	28271	28281	28291
28224	28233	28244	28253	28262	28272	28282	28292
28225	28234	28245	28254	28263	28273	28283	28293
28226	28235	28246	28255	28264	28274	28284	28294
28227	28237	28247	28256	28265	28275	28285	28295
28228	28238	28248	28257	28266	28276	28286	28296
28229	28239	28249	28258	28267	28277	28287	28297
28230	28240	28250	28259	28268	28278	28288	28298
	28241			28269	28279	28289	28299

COMPARTMENT STOCK

M28001	28004	28007	28010	28013	28017	28021	28025
28002	28005	28008	28011	28014	28018	28022	
28003	28006	28009	28012	28015	28019	28023	
				28016	28020	28024	

LIVERPOOL—SOUTHPORT LINE

COMPARTMENT STOCK

M28301	28304	28307	28310	28332	28342	28353	28363
28302	28305	28308		28333	28343	28354	28364
28303	28306	28309		28334	28344	28355	28365
				28335	28345	28356	28366
				28336	28347	28357	28367

FLUSH-PANELLED STOCK

M28311	28316	28322	28327	28337	28348	28358	28368
28312	28317	28323	28328	28338	28349	28359	28369
28313	28318	28324	28329	28339	28350	28360	
28314	28319	28325	28330	28340	28351	28361	
28315	28321	28326	28331	28341	28352	28362	

BAGGAGE CARS

M28496   28497

MERSEY RAILWAY

1st CLASS				3rd CLASS			
M28405	28409	28413	28417	M28419	28423	28427	28431
28406	28410	28414	28418	28420	28424	28428	28432
28407	28411	28415		28421	28425	28429	
28408	28412	28416		28422	28426	28430	

MANCHESTER—BURY

M28500	28505	28510	28515	28520	28525	28529	28533
28501	28506	28511	28516	28521	28526	28530	28534
28502	28507	28512	28517	28522	28527	28531	28535
28503	28508	28513	28518	28523	28528	28532	28537
28504	28509	28514	28519	28524			

LANCASTER—MORECAMBE—HEYSHAM

M28219 | 28220 | 28221 | 28222

WIRRAL RAILWAY

M 28672	28677	28682	28687
28673	28678	28683	28688
28674	28679	28684	28689
28675	28680	28685	28690
28676	28681	28686	

MANCHESTER, S. JUNCTION & ALTRINCHAM RAILWAY

M28571	28575	28579	28583	28587	28591
28572	28576	28580	28584	28588	28592
28573	28577	28581	28585	28589	28593
28574	28578	28582	28586	28590	28594

THE **ABC** OF
BRITISH RAILWAYS LOCOMOTIVES

PART 4 - Nos. 60000-99999
EASTERN, NORTH EASTERN
SCOTTISH REGION, EX-W.D. &
B.R. STANDARD STEAM
LOCOMOTIVES
also E. & N.E.R. Electric Units

SUMMER
1954
EDITION

LONDON :

Ian Allan Ltd

FOREWORD

THIS booklet lists all British Railways locomotives numbered between 60000 and 99999 and E. & N.E. electric *train* units. This series of numbers includes all Eastern, North Eastern and Scottish (ex-L.N.E.R.) Region steam locomotives, i.e. steam locomotives of the former L.N.E.R., new British Railways standard locomotives and ex-Ministry of Supply locos. Under the general British Railways renumbering scheme, the numbers of L.N.E.R. steam locomotives were increased by 60000, with the exception of Classes W1 and L1. A later scheme involved the renumbering of all ex-M.o.S. locomotives in the 90000 series, and there have also been minor amendments to Classes B16 to make way for new locomotives.

Former L.N.E.R. electric, diesel electric and petrol *locomotives* have been renumbered in the 20000 and 15000 series, and details of them will be found in ABC of British Railways Locomotives, Part 2 (Nos. 10000-39999).

NOTES ON THE USE OF THIS BOOK

In the list of locomotives which follow :

1. Many of the classes listed are sub-divided, the sub-divisions being denoted in some cases by " Parts " shown thus : D16/3. At the head of each class will be found a list of such sub-divisions, if any, usually arranged in order of introduction. Each part is given there a reference mark by which its relevant dimensions, if differing from those of other parts, and the locos included in this part, may be identified. Any other differences between locomotives are also indicated, with reference marks, below the details of the class's introduction.

2. The lists of dimensions at the head of each class show locomotives fitted with two inside cylinders, Stephenson gear and slide valves, unles otherwise stated, e.g. (O)=two outside cylinders, P.V.=piston valves.

3. The following method is used to denote superheated locomotives, the letters being inserted, where applicable, after the boiler pressure details : Su=All engines superheated.

SS=Some engines superheated.

4. The date on which the first locomotive of a class was built is denoted by " Introduced."

5. The numbers of locomotives in service have been checked to April 24th, 1954.

6. S denotes Service (Departmental) locomotive still carrying B.R. number (see page 43). This reference letter is introduced only for the reader's guidance and is not borne by the locomotive concerned.

BRITISH RAILWAYS
EASTERN & NORTH EASTERN REGION
Chief Mechanical Engineer
A. H. Peppercorn - - 1948-1949
(post abolished)

LOCOMOTIVE SUPERINTENDENTS AND CHIEF MECHANICAL ENGINEERS OF THE L.N.E.R.

Sir Nigel Gresley   1923—1941 | E. Thompson 1941—1946
A. H. Peppercorn 1946-1947

Great Northern Railway
A. Sturrock	..	1850—1866
P. Stirling	..	1866—1895
H. A. Ivatt	..	1896—1911
H. N. Gresley	..	1911—1922

North Eastern Railway
E. Fletcher	..	1854—1883
A. McDonnell*	..	1883—1884
T. W. Worsdell	..	1885—1890
W. Worsdell	..	1890—1910
Sir Vincent Raven		1910—1922

Great Eastern Railway
R. Sinclair	..	1862—1866
S. W. Johnson	..	1866—1873
W. Adams	..	1873—1878
M. Bromley	..	1878—1881
T. W. Worsdell	..	1881—1885
J. Holden	..	1885—1907
S. D. Holden	..	1908—1912
A. J. Hill	..	1912—1922

Lancashire, Derbyshire and East Coast Railway
R. A. Thom	..	1902—1907

Manchester, Sheffield and Lincolnshire Railway
Richard Peacock		—1854
W. G. Craig	..	1854—1859

Charles Sacré	..	1859—1886
T. Parker	..	1886—1893
H. Pollitt	..	1893—1897

Great Central Railway
H. Pollitt	..	1897—1900
J. G. Robinson	..	1900—1922

Hull and Barnsley Railway
M. Stirling	..	1885—1922

Midland and Great Northern Joint Railway
W. Marriott	..	1884—1924

North British Railway
T. Wheatley†	..	1867—1874
D. Drummond	..	1875—1882
M. Holmes	..	1882—1903
W. P. Reid	..	1903—1919
W. Chalmers	..	1919—1922

Great North of Scotland Railway
D. K. Clark	..	1853—1855
J. F. Ruthven	..	1855—1857
W. Cowan	..	1857—1883
J. Manson	..	1883—1890
J. Johnson	..	1890—1894
W. Pickersgill	..	1894—1914
T. E. Heywood	..	1914—1922

* Between McDonnell and T. W. Worsdell there was an interval during which the office was covered by a Locomotive Committee.

† Previous to whom, the records are indeterminate.

BRITISH RAILWAYS LOCOMOTIVES SHEDS AND SHED CODES

THIS LIST INCLUDES ONLY THOSE DEPOTS WHICH HAVE ENGINES ALLOCATED TO THEM. IT DOES NOT INCLUDE OVERNIGHT STABLING OR SIGNING-ON POINTS.

LONDON MIDLAND REGION

1A Willesden	**9A Longsight**	18D Staveley
1B Camden	9B Stockport (Edgeley)	Sheepbridge
1C Watford	9C Macclesfield	
1D Devons Road (Bow)	9D Buxton	**19A Sheffield**
1E Bletchley	9E Trafford Park	19B Millhouses
Leighton Buzzard	9F Heaton Mersey	19C Canklow
Newport Pagnell	9G Northwich	
		20A Leeds (Holbeck)
2A Rugby	**10A Springs Branch**	20B Stourton
Market Harborough	**(Wigan)**	20C Royston
Seaton	10B Preston	20D Normanton
2B Nuneaton	10C Patricroft	20E Manningham
2C Warwick	10D Plodder Lane (Bolton)	Ilkley
2D Coventry	10E Sutton Oak	20F Skipton
2E Northampton		Keighley
	11A Carnforth	20G Hellifield
3A Bescot	11B Barrow	
3B Bushbury	Coniston	**21A Saltley**
3C Walsall	11C Oxenholme	21B Bournville
3D Aston	11D Tebay	21C Bromsgrove
3E Monument Lane	11E Lancaster	
		22A Bristol
5A Crewe North	**12A Carlisle (Upperby)**	22B Gloucester
Whitchurch	12C Penrith	Tewkesbury
5B Crewe South	12D Workington	Dursley
Crewe (Gresty	12E Moor Row	
Lane)		**24A Accrington**
5C Stafford	**14A Cricklewood**	24B Rose Grove
5D Stoke	14B Kentish Town	24C Lostock Hall
5E Alsager	14C St. Albans	24D Lower Darwen
5F Uttoxeter		24E Blackpool
	15A Wellingborough	Blackpool North
6A Chester	15B Kettering	24F Fleetwood
6B Mold Junction	15C Leicester	
6C Birkenhead	15D Bedford	**25A Wakefield**
6D Chester (Northgate)		25B Huddersfield
6E Wrexham	**16A Nottingham**	25C Goole
6F Bidston	Southwell	25D Mirfield
6G Llandudno Junction	16C Kirkby	25E Sowerby Bridge
6H Bangor	16D Mansfield	25F Low Moor
6J Holyhead		25G Farnley Junction
6K Rhyl	**17A Derby**	
Denbigh	17B Burton	**26A Newton Heath**
	Horninglow	26B Agecroft
8A Edge Hill	Overseal	26C Bolton
8B Warrington	17C Coalville	26D Bury
Warrington	17D Rowsley	26E Bacup
(Arpley)	Cromford	26F Lees
8C Speke Junction	Middleton	26G Belle Vue
8D Widnes	Sheep Pasture	
Widnes (C.L.C.)		**27A Bank Hall**
8E Brunswick (Liverpool)	**18A Toton**	27B Aintree
8F Warrington (C.L.C.)	18B Westhouses	27C Southport
	18C Hasland	27D Wigan (ex-L. & Y.)
		27E Walton

4

EASTERN REGION

30A Stratford	**32A Norwich**	35B Grantham
Ilford	Cromer	35C Peterborough (Spital)
Brentford	Wells-on-Sea	
Chelmsford	Dereham	**36A Doncaster**
Epping	Swaffham	36B Mexborough
Wood St.	Wymondham	Wath
(Walthamstow)	**32B Ipswich**	36C Frodingham
Palace Gates	Felixstowe Beach	36D Barnsley
Enfield Town	Aldeburgh	36E Retford
30B Hertford East	Stowmarket	Newark
Ware	**32C Lowestoft**	
Buntingford	**32D Yarmouth (South**	**37A Ardsley**
30C Bishops Stortford	Town)	37B Copley Hill
30D Southend (Victoria)	**32E Yarmouth (Vauxhall)**	37C Bradford
Southminster	**32F Yarmouth Beach**	
30E Colchester	**32G Melton Constable**	**38A Colwick**
Clacton	Norwich City	Derby (Friargate)
Walton-on-Naze	Cromer Beach	Leicester (ex-G.N.)
Maldon		38B Annesley
Braintree	**33A Plaistow**	38C Leicester (ex-G.C.)
30F Parkeston	Upminster	38D Staveley
	33B Tilbury	38E Woodford Halse
	33C Shoeburyness	
31A Cambridge		**39A Gorton**
Ely	**34A Kings Cross**	Dinting
Huntingdon East	34B Hornsey	Hayfield
Saffron Walden	34C Hatfield	39B Sheffield (Darnall)
31B March	34D Hitchin	
Wisbech	34E Neasden	**40A Lincoln**
31C Kings Lynn	Aylesbury	Lincoln (St. Marks)
Hunstanton	Chesham	40B Immingham
31D South Lynn		40C Louth
31E Bury St. Edmunds	**35A New England**	40D Tuxford
Sudbury (Suffolk)	Spalding	40E Langwith Junction
	Stamford	40F Boston

NORTH EASTERN REGION

50A York	51F West Auckland	52F North Blyth
50B Leeds (Neville Hill)	51G Haverton Hill	South Blyth
50C Selby	51H Kirkby Stephen	
50D Starbeck	51J Northallerton	**53A Hull (Dairycoates)**
50E Scarborough	Leyburn	53B Hull (Botanic
50F Malton	51K Saltburn	Gardens)
Pickering		53C Hull (Springhead)
50G Whitby	**52A Gateshead**	Alexandra Dock
	Bowes Bridge	53D Bridlington
	52B Heaton	
51A Darlington	52C Blaydon	**54A Sunderland**
Middleton-in-	Hexham	Durham
Teesdale	Alston	54B Tyne Dock
51B Newport	52D Tweedmouth	Pelton Level
51C West Hartlepool	Alnmouth	54C Borough Gardens
51D Middlesbrough	52E Percy Main	54D Consett
Guisborough		
51E Stockton		

5

SCOTTISH REGION

60A Inverness
  Dingwall
  Kyle of Lochalsh
60B Aviemore
  Boat of Garten
60C Helmsdale
  Dornoch
  Tain
60D Wick
  Thurso
60E Forres

61A Kittybrewster
  Ballater
  Fraserburgh
  Peterhead
61B Aberdeen (Ferryhill)
61C Keith
  Banff
  Elgin

62A Thornton
  Anstruther
  Burntisland
  Ladybank
  Methil
62B Dundee (Tay Bridge)
  Arbroath
  Montrose
  St. Andrews
62C Dunfermline (Upper)
  Alloa
  Inverkeithing
  Kelty

63A Perth South
  Aberfeldy
  Blair Atholl
  Crieff
63B Stirling
  Killin
  Stirling (Shore Road)
63C Forfar
63D Fort William
  Mallaig
63E Oban
  Ballachulish

64A St. Margarets (Edinburgh)
  Dunbar
  Galashiels
  Longniddry
  North Berwick
  Peebles
  Seafield
  South Leith
64B Haymarket
64C Dalry Road
64D Carstairs
64E Polmont
64F Bathgate
64G Hawick
  Kelso
  Riccarton

65A Eastfield (Glasgow)
65B St. Rollox

65C Parkhead
65D Dawsholm
  Dumbarton
65E Kipps
65F Grangemouth
65G Yoker
65H Helensburgh
  Arrochar
65I Balloch

66A Polmadie (Glasgow)
66B Motherwell
  Morningside
66C Hamilton
66D Greenock (Ladyburn)
  Greenock (Princes Pier)

67A Corkerhill (Glasgow)
67B Hurlford
  Beith
  Muirkirk
67C Ayr
67D Ardrossan

68A Carlisle (Kingmoor)
68B Dumfries
  Kirkcudbright
68C Stranraer
  Newton Stewart
68D Beattock
68E Carlisle Canal
  Silloth

SOUTHERN REGION

70A Nine Elms
70B Feltham
70C Guildford
70D Basingstoke
70E Reading

71A Eastleigh
  Winchester
  Lymington
  Andover Junction
71B Bournemouth
  Swanage
  Hamworthy Junction
  Branksome
71C Dorchester
71D Fratton
  Midhurst
71E Newport (I.O.W.)

71F Ryde (I.O.W.)
71G Bath (S. & D.)
  Radstock
71H Templecombe
71I Southampton Docks
71J Highbridge

72A Exmouth Junction
  Seaton
  Lyme Regis
  Exmouth
  Okehampton
  Bude
72B Salisbury
72C Yeovil
72D Plymouth
  Callington
72E Barnstaple Junction
  Torrington
  Ilfracombe
72F Wadebridge

73A Stewarts Lane
73B Bricklayers Arms
73C Hither Green
73D Gillingham (Kent)
73E Faversham

74A Ashford (Kent)
  Canterbury West
74B Ramsgate
74C Dover
  Folkestone
74D Tonbridge
74E St. Leonards

75A Brighton
  Newhaven
75B Redhill
75C Norwood Junction
75D Horsham
75E Three Bridges
75F Tunbridge Wells West

6

81A	**Old Oak Common**
81B	Slough
	Marlow
	Watlington
81C	Southall
81D	Reading
	Henley-on-Thames
81E	Didcot
	Newbury
	Wallingford
81F	Oxford
	Fairford
82A	**Bristol (Bath Road)**
	Bath
	Wells
	Weston-super-Mare
	Yatton
82B	St Philip's Marsh
82C	Swindon
	Chippenham
82D	Westbury
	Frome
82E	Yeovil
82F	Weymouth
	Bridport
83A	**Newton Abbot**
	Ashburton
	Kingsbridge
83B	Taunton
	Bridgwater
	Minehead
83C	Exeter
	Tiverton Junction
83D	Laira (Plymouth)
	Princetown
	Launceston
83E	St. Blazey
	Bodmin
	Moorswater
83F	Truro
83G	Penzance
	Helston
	St. Ives

84A	**Wolverhampton**
	(Stafford Road)
84B	Oxley
84C	Banbury
84D	Leamington Spa
84E	Tyseley
	Stratford-on-Avon
84F	Stourbridge
84G	Shrewsbury
	Clee Hill
	Craven Arms
	Knighton
	Builth Road
84H	Wellington (Salop)
84J	Croes Newydd
	Bala
	Trawsfynydd
	Penmaenpool
84K	Chester
85A	**Worcester**
	Evesham
	Kingham
85B	Gloucester
	Cheltenham
	Brimscombe
	Cirencester
	Lydney
	Tetbury
85C	Hereford
	Ledbury
	Leominster
	Ross
85D	Kidderminster
86A	**Newport (Ebbw**
	Junction)
86B	Newport (Pill)
86C	Cardiff (Canton)
86D	Llantrisant
86E	Severn Tunnel
	Junction
86F	Tondu
86G	Pontypool Road
86H	Aberbeeg
86J	Aberdare
86K	Abergavenny
	Tredegar

87A	**Neath**
	Glyn Neath
	Neath (N. & B.)
87B	Duffryn Yard
87C	Danygraig
87D	Swansea East Dock
87E	Landore
87F	Llanelly
	Burry Port
	Pantyfynnon
87G	Carmarthen
87H	Neyland
	Cardigan
	Milford Haven
	Pembroke Dock
	Whitland
87J	Goodwick
87K	Swansea (Victoria)
	Upper Bank
	Gurnos
	Llandovery
88A	**Cardiff (Cathays)**
	Radyr
88B	Cardiff East Dock
88C	Barry
88D	Merthyr
	Cae Harris
	Dowlais Central
	Rhymney
88E	Abercynon
88F	Treherbert
	Ferndale
89A	**Oswestry**
	Llanidloes
	Moat Lane
	Welshpool
	(W. & L.)
89B	Brecon
	Builth Wells
89C	Machynlleth
	Aberayron
	Aberystwyth
	Aberystwyth
	(V. of R.)
	Portmadoc
	Pwllheli

4-6-2   8P6F   **Class A4**

Introduced 1935. Gresley streamlined
design with corridor tender
(except those marked †).
*Inside cylinder reduced to 17".
†Non-corridor tender (remainder
corridor).
‡Kylchap blast pipe and double
chimney.

Weights : Loco. 102 tons 19 cwt.
Tender $\begin{cases} 64 \text{ tons } 19 \text{ cwt.} \\ 60 \text{ tons } 7 \text{ cwt.†} \end{cases}$

Pressure : 250 lb. Su.
Cyls. : $\begin{cases} (3) \ 18\frac{1}{2} \times 26". \\ (2) \ 18\frac{1}{2} \times 26". \ (1) \ 17" \times 26"* \end{cases}$
Driving Wheels : 6' 8".
T.E. : $\begin{cases} 35,455 \text{ lb.} \\ 33,616 \text{ lb.*} \end{cases}$
Walschaerts gear and derived motion
P.V.

60001†	Sir Ronald Matthews
60002†	Sir Murrough Wilson
60003*	Andrew K. McCosh
60004	William Whitelaw
60005†‡	Sir Charles Newton
60006	Sir Ralph Wedgwood
60007	Sir Nigel Gresley
60008	Dwight D. Eisenhower
60009	Union of South Africa
60010	Dominion of Canada
60011	Empire of India
60012*	Commonwealth of Australia
60013	Dominion of New Zealand
60014	Silver Link
60015	Quicksilver
60016	Silver King
60017	Silver Fox
60018†	Sparrow Hawk
60019†	Bittern
60020*†	Guillemot
60021†	Wild Swan
60022‡	Mallard
60023†	Golden Eagle
60024	Kingfisher
60025	Falcon
60026†	Miles Beevor
60027	Merlin
60028	Walter K. Whigham

60029	Woodcock
60030	Golden Fleece
60031*	Golden Plover
60032	Gannet
60033‡	Seagull
60034‡	Lord Faringdon

Total 34

4-6-2   7P6F   **Class A3**

A3 Introduced 1927. Development
of Gresley G.N. 180 lb. Pacific (introduced 1922, L.N.E.R. A1, later A10)
with 220 lb. pressure (prototype and
others rebuilt from A10). Some have
G.N.-type tender† with coal rails,
remainder L.N.E.R. pattern.
*Kylchap blast pipe and double chimney.

Weights : Loco. 96 tons 5 cwt.
Tender $\begin{cases} 56 \text{ tons } 6 \text{ cwt.†} \\ 57 \text{ tons } 18 \text{ cwt.} \end{cases}$

Pressure : 220 lb. Su. Cyls. : (3) 19" × 26"
Driving Wheels : 6' 8". T.E. : 32,910 lb.
Walschaerts gear and derived motion.
P.V.

60035	Windsor Lad
60036	Colombo
60037	Hyperion
60038	Firdaussi
60039	Sandwich
60040	Cameronian
60041	Salmon Trout
60042	Singapore
60043	Brown Jack
60044	Melton
60045	Lemberg
60046	Diamond Jubilee
60047	Donovan
60048	Doncaster
60049	Galtee More
60050	Persimmon
60051	Blink Bonny
60052	Prince Palatine
60053	Sansovino
60054	Prince of Wales
60055	Woolwinder
60056	Centenary
60057	Ormonde
60058	Blair Athol

Class V2 2-6-2 No. 60872 *King's Own Yorkshire Light Infantry*   [T. K. Widd

Class B16/1 4-6-0 No. 61441   [J. Robertson

Class B16/3 4-6-0 No. 61464   [J. Cupit

Top : Class AI 4-6-2
No. 60156 Great Central
[P. Ransome-Wallis

Centre : Class A2 4-6-2
No. 60525 A. H. Pepper-
corn   [P. H. Wells

Left : Class A2/I 4-6-2
No. 60507 Highland
Chieftain [P. H. Wells

Top : Class A3 4-6-2
No. 60084 *Trigo*
[R. K. Evans

Centre : Class A4
4-6-2 No. 60004
William Whitelaw
[E. Treacy

Right : Class A2/3
4-6-2 No. 60518
Tehran [J. P. Wilson

Class B1 4-6-0 No. 61026 *Ourebi*   [*P. H. Wells*

Class B12/3 4-6-0 No. 61545   [*R. S. Potts*

Class B17/6 4-6-0 No. 61623 *Lambton Castle*   [*R. J. Buckley*

Class K1 2-6-0 No. 62031 [*P. W. Haynes*

Class K2 2-6-0 No. 61734 [*B. E. Morrison*

Class K3 2-6-0 No. 61919 [*G. D. Bonner*

Class D40 4-4-0 No. 62269

[J. L. Stevenson

Class D40 4-4-0 No. 62262 (with extended smokebox)

[J. L. Stevenson

Class D20/1 4-4-0 No. 62386 (with J39-type tender)

[P. J. Lynch

Class D16/3 4-4-0 No. 62546 *Claud Hamilton* [*R. S. Potts*

Class D16/3 4-4-0 No. 62558 (with original footplating) [*T. K. Widd*

Class D11 4-4-0 No. 62666 *Zeebrugge* [*R. K. Evans*

Above : Class D34
4-4-0 No. 62483 *Glen
Garry* [P. J Lynch

Left : Class D30
4-4-0 No. 62420
Dominie Sampson
[N. Fields

Below : Class D49/1
4-4-0 No. 62722
Huntingdonshire
[G. H. Robin

16

60059	Tracery
60060	The Tetrarch
60061	Pretty Polly
60062	Minoru
60063	Isinglass
60064	Tagalie
60065	Knight of Thistle
60066	Merry Hampton
60067	Ladas
60068	Sir Visto
60069	Sceptre
60070	Gladiateur
60071	Tranquil
60072	Sunstar
60073	St. Gatien
60074	Harvester
60075	St. Frusquin
60076	Galopin
60077	The White Knight
60078	Night Hawk
60079	Bayardo
60080	Dick Turpin
60081	Shotover
60082	Neil Gow
60083	Sir Hugo
60084	Trigo
60085	Manna
60086	Gainsborough
60087	Blenheim
60088	Book Law
60089	Felstead
60090	Grand Parade
60091	Captain Cuttle
60092	Fairway
60093	Coronach
60094	Colorado
60095	Flamingo
60096	Papyrus
60097*	Humorist
60098	Spion Kop
60099	Call Boy
60100	Spearmint
60101	Cicero
60102	Sir Frederick Banbury
60103	Flying Scotsman
60104	Solario
60105	Victor Wild
60106	Flying Fox

60107	Royal Lancer
60108	Gay Crusader
60109	Hermit
60110	Robert the Devil
60111	Enterprise
60112	St. Simon

Total 78

4-6-2 8P6F Class A1

A1/1* Introduced 1945. Thompson rebuild of A10.

A1 Peppercorn development of A1/1 for new construction.

A1† Fitted with roller bearings.

Weights : Loco. { 101 tons.*
104 tons 2 cwt.

Tender : 60 tons 7 cwt.

Pressure : 250 lb. Su.

Cyls : (3) 19″ × 26″.

Driving Wheels : 6′ 8″. T.E. : 37,400 lb.

Walschaerts gear. P.V.

60113*	Great Northern
60114	W. P. Allen
60115	Meg Merrilies
60116	Hal o' the Wynd
60117	Bois Roussel
60118	Archibald Sturrock
60119	Patrick Stirling
60120	Kittiwake
60121	Silurian
60122	Curlew
60123	H. A. Ivatt
60124	Kenilworth
60125	Scottish Union
60126	Sir Vincent Raven
60127	Wilson Worsdell
60128	Bongrace
60129	Guy Mannering
60130	Kestrel
60131	Osprey
60132	Marmion
60133	Pommern
60134	Foxhunter
60135	Madge Wildfire
60136	Alcazar
60137	Redgauntlet
60138	Boswell

17

60139	Sea Eagle
60140	Balmoral
60141	Abbotsford
60142	Edward Fletcher
60143	Sir Walter Scott
60144	King's Courier
60145	Saint Mungo
60146	Peregrine
60147	North Eastern
60148	Aboyeur
60149	Amadis
60150	Willbrook
60151	Midlothian
60152	Holyrood
60153†	Flamboyant
60154†	Bon Accord
60155†	Borderer
60156†	Great Central
60157†	Great Eastern
60158	Aberdonian
60159	Bonnie Dundee
60160	Auld Reekie
60161	North British
60162	Saint Johnstoun

Total 50

4-6-2 $\frac{8P7F}{(A2/I : 7P6F)}$ Class A2

A2/2* Introduced 1943. Original Thompson Pacific, rebuilt from Gresley Class P2 2-8-2 (introduced 1934).
Weight : Loco. 101 tons 10 cwt.
Pressure : 225 lb. Su.
Cyls. : (3) 20″ × 26″.
Driving Wheels : 6′ 2″. T.E. : 40,320 lb.

A2/I† Introduced 1944. Development of Class A2/2, incorporating Class V2 2-6-2 boiler.
Weight : Loco. 98 tons.
Pressure : 225 lb. Su.
Cyls. : (3) 19″ × 26″.
Driving Wheels : 6′ 2″. T.E. : 36,385 lb.

A2/3‡ Introduced 1946. Development of Class A2/2 for new construction.
Weight : Loco. 101 tons 10 cwt.
Pressure : 250 lb. Su.
Cyls. : (3) 19″ × 26″.
Driving Wheels : 6′ 2″. T.E. : 40,430 lb.

A2§ Introduced 1947. Peppercorn development of Class A2/2 with shorter wheelbase. (No. 60539 built with double blast pipe.)

A2** Rebuilt with double blast pipe and multiple valve regulator.
Weight : Loco. 101 tons.
Pressure : 250 lb. Su.
Cyls. : (3) 19″ × 26″.
Driving Wheels : 6′ 2″. T.E. : 40,430 lb.
Tender weight (all parts): 60 tons 7 cwt. (except Nos. 60509/10, 52 tons).
Walschaerts gear, P.V.

60500‡	Edward Thompson
60501*	Cock o' the North
60502*	Earl Marischal
60503*	Lord President
60504*	Mons Meg
60505*	Thane of Fife
60506*	Wolf of Badenoch
60507†	Highland Chieftain
60508†	Duke of Rothesay
60509†	Waverley
60510†	Robert the Bruce
60511‡	Airborne
60512‡	Steady Aim
60513‡	Dante
60514‡	Chamossaire
60515‡	Sun Stream
60516‡	Hycilla
60517‡	Ocean Swell
60518‡	Tehran
60519‡	Honeyway
60520‡	Owen Tudor
60521‡	Watling Street
60522‡	Straight Deal
60523‡	Sun Castle
60524‡	Herringbone
60525§	A. H. Peppercorn
60526**	Sugar Palm
60527§	Sun Chariot
60528§	Tudor Minstrel
60529**	Pearl Diver
60530§	Sayajirao
60531§	Bahram
60532**	Blue Peter
60533**	Happy Knight
60534§	Irish Elegance
60535§	Hornet's Beauty
60536§	Trimbush

18

60537§ Bachelor's Button
60538**Velocity
60539§ Bronzino

Totals : Class A2 15
Class A2/1 4
Class A2/2 6
Class A2/3 15

———

4-6-4   8P7F   Class W1

Introduced 1937. Rebuilt from Gresley
experimental high-pressure 4-cyl.
compound with water-tube boiler,
introduced 1929.
Weights : Loco. 107 tons 17 cwt.
          Tender 60 tons 7 cwt.
Pressure : 250 lb. Su.
Cyls. : (3) 20″ × 26″.
Driving Wheels : 6′ 8″. T.E. : 41,435 lb.
Walschaerts gear and derived motion.
    P.V.

60700   Total 1

———

2-6-2   7P6F   Class V2

Introduced 1936. Gresley design.
Weights : Loco.   93 tons 2 cwt.
          Tender 52 tons.
Pressure : 220 lb. Su.
Cyls. : (3) 18½ × 26″.
Driving Wheels : 6′ 2″. T.E. : 33,730 lb.
Walschaerts gear and derived motion.
    P.V.

60800 Green Arrow
60801
60802
60803
60804
60805
60806
60807
60808
60809 The Snapper, The East
       Yorkshire Regiment,
       The Duke of York's
       Own
60810
60811

60812
60813
60814
60815
60816
60817
60818
60819
60820
60821
60822
60823
60824
60825
60826
60827
60828
60829
60830
60831
60832
60833
60834
60835 The Green Howard,
       Alexandra, Princess of
       Wales's Own York-
       shire Regiment
60836
60837
60838
60839
60840
60841
60842
60843
60844
60845
60846
60847 St. Peter's School, York,
       A.D. 627
60848
60849
60850
60851
60852
60853
60854
60855

60856			
60857			
60858			
60859			
60860 Durham School			
60861			
60862			
60863			
60864			
60865			
60866			
60867			
60868			
60869			
60870			
60871			
60872 King's Own Yorkshire Light Infantry			
60873 Coldstreamer			
60874	60902	60930	60958
60875	60903	60931	60959
60876	60904	60932	60960
60877	60905	60933	60961
60878	60906	60934	60962
60879	60907	60935	60963
60880	60908	60936	60964
60881	60909	60937	60965
60882	60910	60938	60966
60883	60911	60939	60967
60884	60912	60940	60968
60885	60913	60941	60969
60886	60914	60942	60970
60887	60915	60943	60971
60888	60916	60944	60972
60889	60917	60945	60973
60890	60918	60946	60974
60891	60919	60947	60975
60892	60920	60948	60976
60893	60921	60949	60977
60894	60922	60950	60978
60895	60923	60951	60979
60896	60924	60952	60980
60897	60925	60953	60981
60898	60926	60954	60982
60899	60927	60955	60983
60900	60928	60956	
60901	60929	60957	

Total 184

4-6-0   5MT   Class B1

Introduced 1942. Thompson design.
Weights : Loco.   71 tons 3 cwt.
            Tender 52 tons.
Pressure : 225 lb. Su.
Cyls. : (O) 20″ × 26″.
Driving Wheels : 6′ 2″. T.E. : 26,880 lb.
Walschaerts gear. P.V.

61000	Springbok
61001	Eland
61002	Impala
61003	Gazelle
61004	Oryx
61005	Bongo
61006	Blackbuck
61007	Klipspringer
61008	Kudu
61009	Hartebeeste
61010	Wildebeeste
61011	Waterbuck
61012	Puku
61013	Topi
61014	Oribi
61015	Duiker
61016	Inyala
61017	Bushbuck
61018	Gnu
61019	Nilghai
61020	Gemsbok
61021	Reitbok
61022	Sassaby
61023	Hirola
61024	Addax
61025	Pallah
61026	Ourebi
61027	Madoqua
61028	Umseke
61029	Chamois
61030	Nyala
61031	Reedbuck
61032	Stembok
61033	Dibatag
61034	Chiru
61035	Pronghorn
61036	Ralph Assheton
61037	Jairou
61038	Blacktail
61039	Steinbok
61040	Roedeer

61041	61079	61116	61153	61200	
61042	61080	61117	61154	61201	
61043	61081	61118	61155	61202	
61044	61082	61119	61156	61203	
61045	61083	61120	61157	61204	
61046	61084	61121	61158	61205	
61047	61085	61122	61159	61206	
61048	61086	61123	61160	61207	
61049	61087	61124	61161	61208	
61050	61088	61125	61162	61209	
61051	61089	61126	61163	61210	
61052	61090	61127	61164	61211	
61053	61091	61128	61165	61212	
61054	61092	61129	61166	61213	
61055	61093	61130	61167	61214	
61056	61094	61131	61168	61215	William Henton Carver
61058	61095	61132	61169	61216	
61059	61096	61133	61170	61217	
61060	61097	61134	61171	61218	
61061	61098	61135	61172	61219	
61062	61099	61136	61173	61220	
61063	61100	61137	61174	61221	Sir Alexander Erskine-Hill
61064	61101	61138	61175		
61065	61102	61139	61176	61222	
61066	61103	61140	61177	61223	
61067	61104	61141	61178	61224	
61068	61105	61142	61179	61225	
61069	61106	61143	61180	61226	
61070	61107	61144	61181	61227	
61071	61108	61145	61182	61228	
61072	61109	61146	61183	61229	
61073	61110	61147	61184	61230	
61074	61111	61148	61185	61231	
61075	61112	61149	61186	61232	
61076	61113	61150	61187	61233	
61077	61114	61151	61188	61234	
61078	61115	61152		61235	
61189 Sir William Gray				61236	
61190				61237	Geoffrey H. Kitson
61191				61238	Leslie Runciman
61192				61239	
61193				61240	Harry Hinchliffe
61194				61241	Viscount Ridley
61195				61242	Alexander Reith Gray
61196				61243	Sir Harold Mitchell
61197				61244	Strang Steel
61198				61245	Murray of Elibank
61199				61246	Lord Balfour of Burleigh

21

61247	Lord Burghley		
61248	Geoffrey Gibbs		
61249	FitzHerbert Wright		
61250	A. Harold Bibby		
61251	Oliver Bury		

61252	61284	61316	61348
61253	61285	61317	61349
61254	61286	61318	61350
61255	61287	61319	61351
61256	61288	61320	61352
61257	61289	61321	61353
61258	61290	61322	61354
61259	61291	61323	61355
61260	61292	61324	61356
61261	61293	61325	61357
61262	61294	61326	61358
61263	61295	61327	61359
61264	61296	61328	61360
61265	61297	61329	61361
61266	61298	61330	61362
61267	61299	61331	61363
61268	61300	61332	61364
61269	61301	61333	61365
61270	61302	61334	61366
61271	61303	61335	61367
61272	61304	61336	61368
61273	61305	61337	61369
61274	61306	61338	61370
61275	61307	61339	61371
61276	61308	61340	61372
61277	61309	61341	61373
61278	61310	61342	61374
61279	61311	61343	61375
61280	61312	61344	61376
61281	61313	61345	61377
61282	61314	61346	61378
61283	61315	61347	

61379	Mayflower		

61380	61388	61396	61404
61381	61389	61397	61405
61382	61390	61398	61406
61383	61391	61399	61407
61384	61392	61400	61408
61385	61393	61401	61409
61386	61394	61402	
61387	61395	61403	

Total 409

4-6-0   5MT   Class B16

B16/1 Introduced 1920. Raven N.E. design with inside Stephenson gear.
B16/2* Introduced 1937. Gresley rebuild of B16/1 with double Walschaerts gear and derived motion for inside cylinder.
B16/3† Introduced 1944. Thompson rebuild of B16/1 with three Walschaerts gears.

Weights : Loco. { 77 tons 14 cwt.
79 tons 4 cwt.*
78 tons 19 cwt.†
Tender 46 tons 12 cwt.
Pressure : 180 lb. Su.
Cyls. : (3) 18½" × 26".
Driving Wheels : 5' 8". T.E. : 30,030 lb. P.V.

61410	61428	61446	61464†
61411	61429	61447	61465
61412	61430	61448†	61466
61413	61431	61449†	61467†
61414	61432	61450	61468†
61415	61433	61451	61469
61416	61434†	61452	61470
61417†	61435*	61453†	61471
61418†	61436	61454†	61472†
61419	61437*	61455*	61473
61420†	61438*	61456	61474
61421*	61439†	61457*	61475*
61422	61440	61458	61476†
61423	61441	61459	61477
61424	61442	61460	61478
61425	61443	61461†	
61426	61444†	61462	
61427	61445	61463†	

Totals : **Class B16/1 45**
Class B16/2 7
Class B16/3 17

For full details of
ELECTRIC AND DIESEL LOCOS
on the E., N.E. & Scottish Regions
see the
ABC OF B.R. LOCOMOTIVES
Part II, Nos. 10000-39999

For full details of
CLASS "4MT" AND "2MT" 2-6-0s
Nos. 43000-43161 & 46400-46527
on the E., N.E. & Scottish Regions
see the
ABC OF B.R. LOCOMOTIVES
Part III, Nos. 40000-59999

Class B12

4-6-0 4P3F

B12/1* Introduced 1911. S. D. Holden G.E. design with small Belpaire boiler.

B12/3 Introduced 1932. Gresley rebuild of B12/1 with large round-topped boiler and long-travel valves. (B12/2 was a development of B12/1 with Lentz valves, since rebuilt to B12/3.)

Weights : Loco. $\begin{cases} 63 \text{ tons.*} \\ 69 \text{ tons } 10 \text{ cwt.} \end{cases}$

Tender 39 tons 6 cwt.

Pressure : 180 lb. Su. Cyls. : 20″ × 28″.

Driving Wheels : 6′ 6″. T.E. : 21,970 lb.

P.V.

61502*	61539*	61556	61571
61512	61540	61557	61572
61514	61541	61558	61573
61516	61542	61561	61574
61519	61545	61562	61575
61520	61546	61564	61576
61523	61547	61565	61577
61530	61549	61566	61578
61533	61550	61567	61579
61535	61553	61568	61580
61537	61554	61569	
61538	61555	61570	

Totals : Class B12/1 2

Class B12/3 44

Classes B2 & B17

4-6-0 4MT (B2 and B17/6 : 5P4F)

B17/1 Introduced 1928. Gresley design for G.E. section with G.E.-type tenders.

B17/6² Introduced 1947. B17/1 fitted with 100A (B1 type) boiler.

B17/4³ Introduced 1936. Locos with L.N.E.R. 4,200-gallon tenders.

B17/6⁴ Introduced 1943. B17/4 fitted with 100A (B1 type) boiler.

B17/6⁵ Rebuild of streamlined B17/5 introduced in 1937. Rebuilt with 100A boiler and de-streamlined in 1951.

Weights : Loco. 77 tons 5 cwt.

Tender $\begin{cases} 39 \text{ tons } 6 \text{ cwt. }^{1 \, 2} \\ 52 \text{ tons. }^{3 \, 4 \, 5} \end{cases}$

Pressure : $\begin{cases} 180 \text{ lb.}^1 \\ 225 \text{ lb.}^2 \\ 180 \text{ lb.}^3 \\ 225 \text{ lb.}^{4 \, 5} \end{cases}$ Su.

Cyls. : (3) $17\frac{1}{2}″ × 26″$.

Driving Wheels : 6′ 8″.

T.E. : $\begin{cases} 22,485 \text{ lb.}^1 \\ 28,555 \text{ lb.}^2 \\ 22,485 \text{ lb.}^3 \\ 28,555 \text{ lb.}^{4 \, 5} \end{cases}$

Walschaerts gear and derived motion. P.V.

B2⁶ Introduced 1945. Thompson 2-cyl. rebuild of B17, with 100A boiler and N.E. tender.

B2⁷ Introduced 1945, with L.N.E.R. tender.

Weights : Loco. 73 tons 10 cwt.

Tender $\begin{cases} 46 \text{ tons } 12 \text{ cwt.}^6 \\ 52 \text{ tons.}^7 \end{cases}$

Pressure : 225 lb. Su.

Cyls. : (O) 20″ × 26″.

Driving Wheels : 6′ 8″. T.E. : 24,865 lb.

Walschaerts gear and derived motion. P.V.

61600²	Sandringham
61601¹	Holkham
61602²	Walsingham
61603⁶	Framlingham
61605²	Lincolnshire Regiment
61606²	Audley End
61607⁶	Blickling
61608²	Gunton
61609²	Quidenham
61610¹	Honingham Hall
61611¹	Raynham Hall
61612²	Houghton Hall
61613²	Woodbastwick Hall
61614⁶	Castle Hedingham
61615⁷	Culford Hall
61616⁶	Fallodon
61617⁶	Ford Castle
61618¹	Wynyard Park
61619¹	Welbeck Abbey
61620²	Clumber
61621¹	Hatfield House
61622²	Alnwick Castle
61623²	Lambton Castle
61625¹	Raby Castle
61626¹	Brancepeth Castle
61627²	Aske Hall

61629[1]	Naworth Castle
61630[2]	Tottenham Hotspur
61631[1]	Serlby Hall
61632[7]	Belvoir Castle
61633[2]	Kimbolton Castle
61634[1]	Hinchingbrooke
61635[2]	Milton
61636[2]	Harlaxton Manor
61637[1]	Thorpe Hall
61638[2]	Melton Hall
61639[6]	Norwich City
61640[1]	Somerleyton Hall
61641[2]	Gayton Hall
61642[2]	Kilverstone Hall
61643[1]	Champion Lodge
61644[6]	Earlham Hall
61645[2]	The Suffolk Regiment
61646[2]	Gilwell Park
61647[1]	Helmingham Hall
61648[2]	Arsenal
61649[3]	Sheffield United
61650[3]	Grimsby Town
61651[3]	Derby County
61652[3]	Darlington
61653[3]	Huddersfield Town
61654[4]	Sunderland
61655[4]	Middlesbrough
61656[3]	Leeds United
61657[4]	Doncaster Rovers
61658[4]	The Essex Regiment
61659[5]	East Anglian
61660[3]	Hull City
61661[3]	Sheffield Wednesday
61662[3]	Manchester United
61663[4]	Everton
61664[4]	Liverpool
61665[4]	Leicester City
61666[4]	Nottingham Forest
61667[3]	Bradford
61668[4]	Bradford City
61669[4]	Barnsley
61670[5]	City of London
61671[7]	Royal Sovereign
61672[4]	West Ham United

Totals : Class B2   10
Class B17/1   15
Class B17/4   10
Class B17/6   35

2-6-2   4MT   Class V4

Introduced 1941. Gresley design.
Weights : Loco.   70 tons 8 cwt.
            Tender 42 tons 15 cwt.
Pressure : 250 lb. Su.
Cyls. (3) 15″ × 26″.
Driving Wheels : 5′ 8″. T.E. : 27,420 lb.
Walschaerts gear and derived motion.
   P.V.

61700   Bantam Cock
61701   **Total 2**

2-6-0   4MT   Class K2

K2/2 Introduced 1914. Gresley G.N. design.
† K2/2 fitted with side-window cab in Scottish Region.
K2/1* Introduced 1931. Rebuilt from small-boilered K1 (introduced 1912).
‡ K2/1 with side-window cab.
Weights : Loco.   64 tons 8 cwt.
            Tender 43 tons 2 cwt.
Pressure : 180 lb. Su.
Cyls. : (O) 20″ × 26″.
Driving Wheels : 5′ 8″. T.E. : 23,400 lb.
   Walschaerts gear. P.V.

61720*	61731	61742	61753
61721‡	61732	61743	61754
61722‡	61733†	61744	61755†
61723*	61734†	61745	61756
61724*	61735†	61746	61757
61725*	61736	61747	61758†
61726*	61737	61748	61759
61727*	61738	61749	61760
61728*	61739	61750	61761
61729‡	61740	61751	61762
61730	61741†	61752	61763

61764† Loch Arkaig

61765	61767	61769†	61771
61766	61768	61770†	

61772† Loch Lochy
61773
61774† Loch Garry
61775† Loch Treig

61776†	61778	61780
61777	61779†	

61781† Loch Morar
61782† Loch Eil
61783† Loch Sheil

61784†	61785†	61786†

24

61787† Loch Quoich
61788† Loch Rannoch
61789† Loch Laidon
61790† Loch Lomond
61791† Loch Laggan
61792† | 61793†
61794† Loch Oich

Totals : Class K2/1 10
Class K2/2 65

Classes
2-6-0 5P6F K3 & K5

K3/2 Introduced 1924. Development of Gresley G.N. design, built to L.N.E.R. loading gauge.
K3/3* Introduced 1929. Differ in details only, such as springs, from K3/2.
‡ K3/2 fitted with G.N. tender.
(K3/1 were G.N. locos (introduced 1920), with G.N. cabs, and K3/4, K3/5 and K3/6 were variations of K3/2 differing in weight and details. These locos have now been modified to K3/2.)
Weights : Loco. 72 tons 12 cwt.
Tender { 52 tons.
43 tons 2 cwt.‡
Pressure : 180 lb. Su.
Cyls. : (3) 18½″ × 26″.
Driving Wheels : 5′ 8″. T.E. : 30,030 lb.
Walschaerts gear and derived motion. P.V.
K5† Introduced 1945. Thompson 2-cyl. rebuild of K3.
Weights : Loco. 71 tons 5 cwt.
Tender 52 tons.
Pressure : 225 lb. Su.
Cyls. : (O) 20″ × 26″.
Driving Wheels : 5′ 8″. T.E. : 29,250 lb.
Walschaerts gear. P.V.

61800	61813	61826	61839
61801	61814	61827	61840
61802	61815	61828	61841‡
61803	61816	61829	61842
61804	61817	61830	61843
61805	61818	61831	61844
61806	61819	61832	61845
61807	61820	61833	61846
61808	61821	61834	61847
61809	61822	61835	61848
61810	61823	61836	61849
61811	61824	61837	61850
61812‡	61825	61838	61851

61852	61888*	61924	61960
61853	61889*	61925	61961
61854‡	61890	61926	61962
61855‡	61891	61927	61963
61856‡	61892	61928	61964
61857‡	61893	61929	61965
61858‡	61894	61930	61966
61859‡	61895	61931	61967
61860	61896	61932	61968
61861	61897	61933	61969
61862	61898	61934	61970
61863†	61899	61935	61971
61864	61900	61936	61972
61865	61901	61937	61973
61866	61902	61938	61974
61867	61903	61939	61975
61868	61904	61940	61976
61869	61905	61941	61977
61870*	61906	61942	61978
61871*	61907	61943	61979
61872*	61908	61944	61980
61873*	61909	61945	61981
61874*	61910	61946	61982
61875*	61911	61947	61983
61876*	61912	61948	61984
61877*	61913	61949	61985
61878*	61914	61950	61986
61879*	61915	61951	61987
61880*	61916	61952	61988
61881*	61917	61953	61989
61882*	61918	61954	61990
61883*	61919	61955	61991
61884*	61920	61956	61992
61885*	61921	61957	
61886*	61922	61958	
61887*	61923	61959	

Totals : Class K3/2 172
Class K3/3 20
Class K5 1

IMPORTANT NOTE
A careful reading of the notes on page 2 is essential to understand the use of reference marks in this book.

Classes

2-6-0   5P6F   KI & K4

K4* Introduced 1937. Gresley loco for West Highland line.
Weights : Loco.   68 tons 8 cwt.
           Tender 44 tons 4 cwt.
Pressure : 200 lb. Su.
Cyls. : (3) $18\frac{1}{2}'' \times 26''$.
Driving Wheels : 5′ 2″. T.E. : 36,600 lb.
P.V.
KI/I† Introduced 1945.   Thompson 2-cyl. loco. Rebuilt from K4.
KI Introduced 1949. Peppercorn development of Thompson KI/I (No. 61991) for new construction, with increased length.
Weights : Loco.   66 tons 17 cwt.
           Tender 44 tons 4 cwt.
Pressure : 225 lb. Su.
Cyls. : (O) 20″ × 26″.
Driving Wheels : 5′ 2″. T.E. : 32,080 lb.
Walschaerts gear. P.V.

61993* Loch Long
61994* The Great Marquess
61995* Cameron of Lochiel
61996* Lord of the Isles
61997† MacCailin Mor
61998* Macleod of Macleod

62001	62019	62037	62055
62002	62020	62038	62056
62003	62021	62039	62057
62004	62022	62040	62058
62005	62023	62041	62059
62006	62024	62042	62060
62007	62025	62043	62061
62008	62026	62044	62062
62009	62027	62045	62063
62010	62028	62046	62064
62011	62029	62047	62065
62012	62030	62048	62066
62013	62031	62049	62067
62014	62032	62050	62068
62015	62033	62051	62069
62016	62034	62052	62070
62017	62035	62053	
62018	62036	62054	

Totals : Class KI   70
          Class KI/I   I
          Class K4   5

4-4-0   IP   Class D40

Introduced 1899. Pickersgill G.N.of.S. design.
* Introduced 1920. Heywood superheated locos.
Weights : Loco. $\begin{cases} 46 \text{ tons } 7 \text{ cwt.} \\ 48 \text{ tons } 13 \text{ cwt.*} \end{cases}$
           Tender 37 tons 8 cwt.
Pressure : 165 lb. SS. Cyls. : 18″ × 26″
Driving Wheels : 6′ I″ T.E. : 16,185 lb.

62262	62267	62271
62264	62268	62272
62265	62269	

62273* George Davidson
62274* Benachie
62275* Sir David Stewart
62276* Andrew Bain
62277* Gordon Highlander
62278* Hatton Castle
62279* Glen Grant

Total 15

4-4-0   2P   Class D20

D20/I Introduced 1899. W. Worsdell N.E. design. Since superheated.
D20/2* Introduced 1936. D20/I rebuilt with long-travel valves.
† Locos with tender rebuilt with J39-type tank.
Weights : Loco. $\begin{cases} 54 \text{ tons } 2 \text{ cwt.} \\ 55 \text{ tons } 9 \text{ cwt.*} \end{cases}$
           Tender $\begin{cases} 41 \text{ tons } 4 \text{ cwt.} \\ 43 \text{ tons.*} \end{cases}$
Pressure : 175 lb. Su. Cyls. : 19″ × 26″
Driving Wheels : 6′ 10″ T.E. : 17,025 lb.
P.V.

62343	62358†	62378	62388
62345	62359	62380	62389
62347	62360*	62381	62392
62349*	62371*	62383	62395
62351	62372	62384	62396
62352	62374	62386†	62397†
62355	62375*	62387	

Totals : Class D20/I 23
          Class D20/2   4

4-4-0   3P   Class D30

D30/2 Introduced 1914. Development of D30/1, introduced 1912 (Reid N.B. "Scott" class) with detail differences.

Weights : Loco.   57 tons 16 cwt.
               Tender 46 tons 13 cwt.

Pressure : 165 lb. Su. Cyls. : 20″ × 26″.

Driving Wheels : 6′ 6″. T.E. : 18,700 lb. P.V.

62418	The Pirate
62419	Meg Dods
62420	Dominie Sampson
62421	Laird o' Monkbarns
62422	Caleb Balderstone
62423	Dugald Dalgetty
62424	Claverhouse
62425	Ellangowan
62426	Cuddie Headrigg
62427	Dumbledykes
62428	The Talisman
62429	The Abbot
62430	Jingling Geordie
62431	Kenilworth
62432	Quentin Durward
62434	Kettledrummle
62435	Norna
62436	Lord Glenvarloch
62437	Adam Woodcock
62438	Peter Poundtext
62439	Father Ambrose
62440	Wandering Willie
62441	Black Duncan
62442	Simon Glover

Total 24

For full details of
CLASS "4MT" AND "2MT" 2-6-0s
Nos. 43000-43161 & 46400-46527
on the E., N.E. & Scottish Regions
see the
ABC OF B.R. LOCOMOTIVES
Part III, Nos. 40000-59999

4-4-0   3P   Class D34

Introduced 1913. Reid N.B. "Glen" class.

Weights : Loco.   57 tons   4 cwt.
               Tender 46 tons 13 cwt.

Pressure : 165 lb. Su. Cyls. : 20″ × 26″.

Driving Wheels : 6′ 0″. T.E. : 20,260 lb. P.V.

62467	Glenfinnan
62468	Glen Orchy
62469	Glen Douglas
62470	Glen Roy
62471	Glen Falloch
62472	Glen Nevis
62474	Glen Croe
62475	Glen Beasdale
62477	Glen Dochart
62478	Glen Quoich
62479	Glen Sheil
62480	Glen Fruin
62482	Glen Mamie
62483	Glen Garry
62484	Glen Lyon
62485	Glen Murran
62487	Glen Arklet
62488	Glen Aladale
62489	Glen Dessary
62490	Glen Fintaig
62492	Glen Garvin
62493	Glen Gloy
62494	Glen Gour
62495	Glen Luss
62496	Glen Loy
62497	Glen Mallie
62498	Glen Moidart

Total 27

4-4-0   3P1F   Class D16

D16/3[1] Introduced 1933. Gresley rebuild of D15 with larger round-topped boiler and modified footplating. D15 was Belpaire boiler development of original J. Holden (G.E.) "Claud Hamilton" Class.

D16/3[2] Introduced 1933. Rebuild of D15 with larger round-topped boiler, modified footplating and 8″ piston valves.

D16/3³ Introduced 1936. Rebuild of D15 with larger round-topped boiler, modified footplating and 9½" piston valves.

D16/3⁴ Introduced 1938. Rebuild of D16/2 with round-topped boiler, but retaining original footplating and slide valves.

D16/3⁵ Introduced 1939. Rebuild of D16/2 with round-topped boiler and modified footplating, retaining slide valves.

(At grouping the remaining locos of the " Claud Hamilton " class retaining small round-topped boilers were classified D14. Saturated locos of D15 were originally classified D15, superheated locos with short smokeboxes D15/1 and superheated locos with extended smokeboxes D15/2. All the remaining locos were converted to D15/2 and then known simply as D15. D16/1 were the original D16 locos with short smokeboxes.)

Weights : Loco. 55 tons 18 cwt.
　　　　　　Tender 39 tons 5 cwt.
Pressure : 180 lb. Su. Cyls. : 19″ × 26″.
Driving Wheels : 7′ 0″. T.E. : 17,095 lb.

62510¹	62539¹	62566¹	62593¹
62511¹	62540¹	62567¹	62596⁴
62513¹	62541¹	62568²	62597¹
62514¹	62542⁴	62569⁴	62599³
62515¹	62543⁴	62570⁴	62601⁴
62516¹	62544⁴	62571¹	62604¹
62517¹	62545¹	62572¹	62605⁴
62518¹	62546³*	62573⁴	62606⁴
62519¹	62548¹	62574¹	62607⁴
62521¹	62549¹	62575¹	62608¹
62522¹	62551¹	62576³	62609²
62523¹	62552⁴	62577⁴	62610¹
62524¹	62553⁴	62578⁴	62611⁴
62525¹	62554⁴	62579¹	62612⁴
62526¹	62555¹	62580⁴	62613⁴
62529¹	62556⁴	62582¹	62614⁵
62530¹	62557⁴	62584⁴	62615⁴
62531¹	62558⁴	62585¹	62617⁴
62532³	62559¹	62586¹	62618⁴
62533¹	62561¹	62587²	62619⁴
62534¹	62562⁴	62588²	62620⁴
62535³	62564⁴	62589⁴	
62536³	62565⁴	62592⁴	

Total 90

* Named *Claud Hamilton*.

4-4-0　　3P　　Class D10

Introduced 1913. Robinson G.C. " Director " class.
Weights : Loco. 61 tons
　　　　　　Tender 48 tons 6 cwt.
Pressure : 180 lb. Su. Cyls. : 20″ × 26″.
Driving Wheels : 6′ 9″. T.E. : 19,645 lb. P.V.

62652	Edwin A. Beazley
62653	Sir Edward Fraser
62656	Sir Clement Royds
62658	Prince George
62659	Worsley-Taylor

Total 5

4-4-0　　3P2F　　Class D11

D11/1* Introduced 1920. Robinson G.C. " Large Director," development of D10.

D11/2 Introduced 1924. Post-grouping locos built to Scottish loading gauge. From 1938 the class has been rebuilt with long-travel valves.
Weights : Loco. 61 tons 3 cwt.
　　　　　　Tender 48 tons 6 cwt.
Pressure : 180 lb. Su. Cyls. : 20″ × 26″.
Driving Wheels : 6′ 9″. T.E. : 19,645 lb. P.V.

62660*	Butler-Henderson
62661*	Gerard Powys Dewhurst
62662*	Prince of Wales
62663*	Prince Albert
62664*	Princess Mary
62665*	Mons
62666*	Zeebrugge
62667*	Somme
62668*	Jutland
62669*	Ypres
62670*	Marne
62671	Bailie MacWheeble
62672	Baron of Bradwardine
62673	Evan Dhu
62674	Flora MacIvor
62675	Colonel Gardiner
62676	Jonathan Oldbuck
62677	Edie Ochiltree
62678	Luckie Mucklebackit
62679	Lord Glenallan

62680	Lucy Ashton
62681	Captain Craigengelt
62682	Haystoun of Bucklaw
62683	Hobbie Elliott
62684	Wizard of the Moor
62685	Malcolm Graeme
62686	The Fiery Cross
62687	Lord James of Douglas
62688	Ellen Douglas
62689	Maid of Lorn
62690	The Lady of the Lake
62691	Laird of Balmawhapple
62692	Allan-Bane
62693	Roderick Dhu
62694	James Fitzjames

Totals : **Class D11/1 11**
Class D11/2 24

4-4-0   4P   Class D49

D49/1* Introduced 1927. Gresley design with piston valves. Walschaerts gear and derived motion.
D49/2† Introduced 1928. Development of D49/1 with Lentz Rotary Cam poppet valves.
D49/2‡ Introduced 1949. Fitted with Reideger R.R. Rotary valve gear. (D49/3 comprised locos 62720-4 as built with Lentz Oscillating Cam poppet valves. From 1938 these locos were converted to D49/1. 62751-75 have larger valves than the earlier D49/2, and were at first classified D49/4).
[1]Fitted with G.C. tender.
[2]Fitted with N.E. tender.
[3]The remainder have L N.E.R. tenders.

Weights : Loco. { 66 tons.*†
{ 64 tons 10 cwt.‡
{ 48 tons 6 cwt.[1]
Tender{ 44 tons 2 cwt.[2]
{ 52 tons.[3]

Pressure : 180 lb. Su.
Cyls. : (3) 17″ × 26″
Driving Wheels : 6′ 8″. T.E. : 21,555 lb.

62700*[1]	Yorkshire
62701*[1]	Derbyshire
62702*[1]	Oxfordshire
62703*[2]	Hertfordshire
62704*[1]	Stirlingshire
62705*[1]	Lanarkshire
62706*[1]	Forfarshire
62707*[1]	Lancashire
62708*[1]	Argyllshire
62709*[1]	Berwickshire
62710*[1]	Lincolnshire
62711*[1]	Dumbartonshire
62712*[1]	Morayshire
62713*[1]	Aberdeenshire
62714*[2]	Perthshire
62715*[1]	Roxburghshire
62716*[1]	Kincardineshire
62717*[1]	Banffshire
62718*[1]	Kinross-shire
62719*[2]	Peebles-shire
62720*[1]	Cambridgeshire
62721*[1]	Warwickshire
62722*[2]	Huntingdonshire
62723*[2]	Nottinghamshire
62724*[2]	Bedfordshire
62725*[1]	Inverness-shire
62726†[3]	The Meynell
62727†[2]	The Quorn
62728*[1]	Cheshire
62729*[1]	Rutlandshire
62730*[1]	Berkshire
62731*[1]	Selkirkshire
62732*[1]	Dumfries-shire
62733*[1]	Northumberland
62734*[2]	Cumberland
62735*[1]	Westmorland
62736†[3]	The Bramham Moor
62737†[3]	The York and Ainsty
62738†[3]	The Zetland
62739†[3]	The Badsworth
62740†[3]	The Bedale
62741†[3]	The Blankney
62742†[3]	The Braes of Derwent
62743†[3]	The Cleveland
62744†[3]	The Holderness
62745†[3]	The Hurworth
62746†[3]	The Middleton
62747†[3]	The Percy
62748†[3]	The Southwold
62749†[3]	The Cottesmore
62750†[3]	The Pytchley
62751†[3]	The Albrighton
62752†[3]	The Atherstone
62753†[3]	The Belvoir
62754†[3]	The Berkeley

62755†³ The Bilsdale
62756†² The Brocklesby
62757†³ The Burton
62758†³ The Cattistock
62759†³ The Craven
62760†³ The Cotswold
62761†³ The Derwent
62762†³ The Fernie
62763‡³ The Fitzwilliam
62764‡³ The Garth
62765†³ The Goathland
62766†³ The Grafton
62767†³ The Grove
62769†³ The Oakley
62770†³ The Puckeridge
62771†³ The Rufford
62772†³ The Sinnington
62773†³ The South Durham
62774†³ The Staintondale
62775†³ The Tynedale

Totals : Class D49/1 34
Class D49/2 41

2-4-0   1MT   Class E4

Introduced 1891. J. Holden G.E. design.
* Fitted with side-window cab.
Weights : Loco.   40 tons 6 cwt.
Tender 30 tons 13 cwt.
Pressure : 160 lb. Cyls. : 17½″ × 24″.
Driving Wheels : 5′ 8″. T.E. : 14,700 lb.

62780	62785	62790	62795*
62781*	62786	62791	62796
62782	62787	62792	62797*
62783	62788*	62793*	
62784*	62789	62794	

Total 18

0-8-0   6F   Class Q6

Introduced 1913. Raven N.E. design.
* Some locos are fitted with tenders from withdrawn B15 locos.
Weights : Loco.   65 tons 18 cwt.
Tender { 44 tons 2 cwt.
44 tons.*
Pressure 180 lb. Su.
Cyls. ı (O) 20″ × 26″.
Driving Wheels : 4′ 7¼″. T.E. : 28,800 lb.
P.V.

63340	63341	63342	63343

63344	63373	63402	63431
63345	63374	63403	63432
63346	63375	63404	63433
63347	63376	63405	63434
63348	63377	63406	63435
63349	63378	63407	63436
63350	63379	63408	63437
63351	63380	63409	63438
63352	63381	63410	63439
63353	63382	63411	63440
63354	63383	63412	63441
63355	63384	63413	63442
63356	63385	63414	63443
63357	63386	63415	63444
63358	63387	63416	63445
63359	63388	63417	63446
63360	63389	63418	63447
63361	63390	63419	63448
63362	63391	63420	63449
63363	63392	63421	63450
63364	63393	63422	63451
63365	63394	63423	63452
63366	63395	63424	63453
63367	63396	63425	63454
63368	63397	63426	63455
63369	63398	63427	63456
63370	63399	63428	63457
63371	63400	63429	63458
63372	63401	63430	63459

Total 120

0-8-0   8F   Class Q7

Introduced 1919   Raven N.E. design.
Weights : Loco.   71 tons 12 cwt.
Tender 44 tons 2 cwt.
Pressure : 180 lb. Su.
Cyls. : (3) 18½″ × 26″.
Driving Wheels: 4′ 7¼″. T.E.: 36,965 lb.
P.V.

63460	63464	63468	63472
63461	63465	63469	63473
63462	63466	63470	63474
63463	63467	63471	

Total 15

Classes
O1 & O4

2-8-0 **8F (O1)**
7F (O4)

O4/1[1] Introduced 1911. Robinson G.C. design with small Belpaire boiler, steam and vacuum brakes and water scoop.

O4/3[2] Introduced 1917. R.O.D. locos. with steam brake only and no scoop Taken into L.N.E.R. stock from 1924.

O4/2[3] Introduced 1925. O4/3 with cab and boiler mountings reduced to Scottish loading gauge.

O4/5[4] Introduced 1932. Rebuilt with shortened O2-type boiler and separate smokebox saddle.

O4/6[5] Introduced 1924. Rebuilt from O5, retaining higher cab (63913-20 with side-windows).

O4/7[6] Introduced 1939. Rebuilt with shortened O2-type boiler, retaining G.C. smokebox.

O4/8[7] Introduced 1944. Rebuilt with 100A(B1) boiler, retaining original cylinders.
(O4/4 were rebuilds with O2 boilers, since rebuilt again ; O5 was a G.C. development of O4 with larger Belpaire boilers.)

Weights : Loco.
73 tons 4 cwt.[1]
73 tons 4 cwt.[2]
73 tons 4 cwt.[3]
74 tons 13 cwt.[4]
73 tons 4 cwt.[5]
73 tons 17 cwt.[6]
72 tons 10 cwt.[7]

Tender
48 tons 6 cwt. (with scoop)
47 tons 6 cwt. (without scoop)

Pressure : 180 lb. Su.
Cyls. : (O) 21″ × 26″.
Driving Wheels : 4′ 8″. T.E. : 31,325 lb. P.V.

O1[8] Introduced 1944. Thompson rebuild with 100A boiler, Walschaerts valve gear and new cylinders.
Weights : Loco. 73 tons 6 cwt.
Tender as O4.
Pressure : 225 lb. Su.
Cyls. : (O) 20″ × 26″.
Driving Wheels : 4′ 8″. T.E. : 35,520 lb. Walschaerts gear. P.V.

63570[6]	63579[8]	63589[8]	63598[1]
63571[8]	63581[1]	63590[8]	63599[1]
63572[1]	63582[6]	63591[8]	63600[6]
63573[1]	63583[1]	63592[8]	63601[1]
63574[1]	63584[1]	63593[1]	63602[1]
63575[7]	63585[1]	63594[8]	63603[6]
63576[1]	63586[1]	63595[6]	63604[1]
63577[1]	63587[1]	63596[8]	63605[1]
63578[8]	63588[6]	63597[1]	63606[1]

63607[7]	63656[2]	63704[3]	63752[8]
63608[1]	63657[2]	63705[6]	63753[2]
63609[1]	63658[1]	63706[6]	63754[2]
63610[8]	63659[2]	63707[1]	63755[8]
63611[2]	63660[1]	63708[6]	63756[2]
63612[1]	63661[6]	63709[3]	63757[1]
63613[7]	63662[6]	63710[1]	63758[8]
63614[1]	63663[8]	63711[8]	63759[2]
63615[6]	63664[1]	63712[8]	63760[8]
63616[6]	63665[2]	63713[2]	63761[6]
63617[1]	63666[2]	63714[2]	63762[1]
63618[1]	63667[2]	63715[2]	63763[2]
63619[8]	63668[2]	63716[2]	63764[2]
63620[1]	63669[6]	63717[2]	63765[2]
63621[1]	63670[8]	63718[2]	63766[2]
63622[1]	63671[1]	63719[1]	63767[2]
63623[1]	63672[2]	63720[2]	63768[8]
63624[1]	63673[6]	63721[2]	63769[2]
63625[1]	63674[3]	63722[1]	63770[6]
63626[1]	63675[6]	63723[1]	63771[2]
63628[4]	63676[8]	63724[2]	63772[6]
63629[2]	63677[1]	63725[8]	63773[8]
63630[8]	63678[8]	63726[4]	63774[2]
63631[1]	63679[2]	63727[1]	63775[6]
63632[1]	63680[3]	63728[2]	63776[2]
63633[7]	63681[2]	63729[2]	63777[8]
63634[6]	63682[3]	63730[3]	63779[2]
63635[1]	63683[1]	63731[2]	63780[8]
63636[2]	63684[1]	63732[2]	63781[2]
63637[2]	63685[2]	63733[2]	63782[2]
63638[2]	63686[2]	63734[2]	63783[2]
63639[2]	63687[8]	63735[2]	63784[8]
63640[1]	63688[2]	63736[1]	63785[7]
63641[2]	63689[8]	63737[2]	63786[8]
63642[2]	63690[3]	63738[7]	63787[2]
63643[6]	63691[2]	63739[2]	63788[4]
63644[2]	63692[1]	63740[8]	63789[8]
63645[2]	63693[1]	63741[2]	63790[2]
63646[8]	63694[2]	63742[2]	63791[2]
63647[3]	63695[2]	63743[1]	63792[8]
63648[3]	63696[2]	63744[2]	63793[2]
63649[2]	63697[2]	63745[4]	63794[6]
63650[8]	63698[1]	63746[8]	63795[8]
63651[7]	63699[6]	63747[6]	63796[8]
63652[8]	63700[1]	63748[6]	63797[1]
63653[7]	63701[2]	63749[6]	63798[2]
63654[1]	63702[2]	63750[7]	63799[1]
63655[6]	63703[2]	63751[2]	63800[2]

63801[2]	63836[7]	63862[2]	63889[2]
63802[7]	63837[8]	63863[8]	63890[8]
63803[8]	63838[8]	63864[2]	63891[6]
63804[2]	63839[7]	63865[8]	63893[7]
63805[1]	63840[2]	63867[8]	63894[6]
63806[8]	63841[2]	63868[8]	63895[2]
63807[7]	63842[2]	63869[8]	63897[2]
63808[8]	63843[8]	63870[2]	63898[2]
63812[2]	63845[2]	63872[8]	63899[2]
63813[2]	63846[2]	63873[2]	63900[2]
63816[4]	63847[6]	63874[8]	63901[8]
63817[8]	63848[6]	63876[8]	63902[5]
63818[7]	63850[2]	63877[2]	63904[5]
63819[7]	63851[4]	63878[2]	63905[5]
63821[2]	63852[2]	63879[8]	63906[5]
63822[2]	63853[7]	63880[7]	63907[5]
63823[2]	63854[8]	63881[2]	63908[5]
63824[6]	63855[2]	63882[7]	63911[5]
63827[7]	63856[8]	63883[2]	63912[5]
63828[7]	63857[6]	63884[6]	63913[5]
63829[6]	63858[8]	63885[2]	63914[5]
63832[2]	63859[2]	63886[8]	63915[5]
63833[2]	63860[6]	63887[8]	63917[5]
63835[2]	63861[2]	63888[2]	63920[5]

Totals : Class O1   58
Class O4/1   65
Class O4/2   11
Class O4/3   113
Class O4/5   6
Class O4/6   13
Class O4/7   40
Class O4/8   18

For full details of
ELECTRIC AND DIESEL LOCOS
on the E., N.E. & Scottish Regions
see the
ABC OF B.R. LOCOMOTIVES
Part II, Nos. 10000-39999

For full details of
CLASS "4MT" AND "2MT" 2-6-0s
Nos. 43000-43161 & 46400-46527
on the E., N.E. & Scottish Regions
see the
ABC OF B.R. LOCOMOTIVES
Part III, Nos. 40000-59999

IMPORTANT NOTE

A careful reading of the notes on page 2 is essential to understand the use of reference marks in this book.

2-8-0   8F   Class O2

O2/1* Introduced 1921. Development of experimental Gresley G.N. 3-cyl. loco (L.N.E.R. 3921). Subsequently rebuilt with side-window cab, and reduced boiler mountings.

O2/2† Introduced 1924 Development of O2/1 with detail differences.

O2/3 Introduced 1932. Development of O2/2 with side-window cab and reduced boiler mountings

O2/4‡ Introduced 1943. Rebuilt with 100A (B1 type) boiler and smokebox extended backwards (63924 retaining G.N. tender).

Weights : Loco. { 75 tons 16 cwt.*†
78 tons 13 cwt.‡
74 tons 2 cwt.‡

Tender { 43 tons 2 cwt. (63922-46)
52 tons (63947-87)

Pressure : 180 lb. Su.
Cyls. : (3) $18\frac{1}{2}'' \times 26''$.
Driving Wheels : 4' 8". T.E. : 36,470 lb.
Walschaerts gear and derived motion. P.V.

63922*	63939†	63956	63973
63923*	63940†	63957	63974
63924‡	63941†	63958	63975
63925*	63942†	63959	63976
63926*	63943†	63960	63977
63927*	63944†	63961	63978
63928*	63945†	63962‡	63979
63929*	63946†	63963	63980
63930*	63947	63964	63981
63931*	63948	63965	63982
63932‡	63949	63966	63983
63933†	63950‡	63967	63984
63934†	63951	63968	63985
63935†	63952	63969	63986
63936†	63953	63970	63987
63937†	63954	63971	
63938†	63955	63972	

Totals : Class O2/1   9
Class O2/2   14
Class O2/3   39
Class O2/4   4

Class Q6 0-8-0 No. 63431

Class O4/6 2-8-0 No. 63912

Class O2/3 2-8-0 No. 63981

Left : Class J1 0-6-0
No. 65013 *[P. J. Lynch*

Below : Class J5 0-6-0
No. 65498 *[J. F. Aylard*

Left : Class J2 0-6-0
No. 65020 *[P. H. Wells*

Class J6 0-6-0 No. 64214   [T. K. Widd

Class J15 0-6-0 No. 65438   [A. R. Carpenter

Class J11 0-6-0 No. 64306   [M. J. Ecclestone

Class J17 0-6-0 No. 65538

[H. C. Casserley

Class J19 0-6-0 No. 64640

[B. E. Morrison

Class J20/I 0-6-0 No. 64684

[A. R. Carpenter

0-6-0　　2F　　Class J3

Introduced 1912. Larger-boilered re-build of J4.
Weights : Loco.　42 tons 12 cwt.
　　　　　Tender 38 tons 10 cwt.
Pressure : 175 lb. Cyls. : 17½″ × 26″.
Driving Wheels : 5′ 2″. T.E. : 19,105 lb.

64131	64132	64140

Total 3

0-6-0　　2P3F　　Class J6

Introduced 1911. Gresley G.N. design.
Weights : Loco.　50 tons 10 cwt.
　　　　　Tender 43 tons 2 cwt.
Pressure : 170 lb. Su. Cyls. : 19″ × 26″.
Driving Wheels : 5′ 2″. T.E. : 21,875 lb.
P.V.

64170	64198	64226	64254
64171	64199	64227	64255
64172	64200	64228	64256
64173	64201	64229	64257
64174	64202	64230	64258
64175	64203	64231	64259
64176	64204	64232	64260
64177	64205	64233	64261
64178	64206	64234	64262
64179	64207	64235	64263
64180	64208	64236	64264
64181	64209	64237	64265
64182	64210	64238	64266
64183	64211	64239	64267
64184	64212	64240	64268
64185	64213	64241	64269
64186	64214	64242	64270
64187	64215	64243	64271
64188	64216	64244	64272
64189	64217	64245	64273
64190	64218	64246	64274
64191	64219	64247	64275
64192	64220	64248	64276
64193	64221	64249	64277
64194	64222	64250	64278
64195	64223	64251	64279
64196	64224	64252	
64197	64225	64253	

Total 110

0-6-0　　2P3F　　Class J11

Introduced 1901. Robinson G.C. design
Parts 1 and 4 have 3,250 gallon
tenders : Parts 2 and 5, 4,000 gallon.
Parts 1 and 2 have higher boiler
mountings ; Parts 4 and 5 low. All
Parts 4 and 5 are superheated, and
some of Parts 1 and 2. There are
frequent changes between these parts.

J11/3* Introduced 1942. Rebuilt with
long-travel piston valves and boiler
higher pitched.

Weights : Loco.
{ 51 tons 19 cwt. (Sat.)
52 tons 2 cwt. (Su.)
53 tons 6 cwt.* }

Tender
{ 44 tons 3 cwt. (3,250 gall.)
48 tons 6 cwt. (4,000 gall.) }

Pressure : 180 lb. SS. Cyls. : 18½″ × 26″.
Driving Wheels : 5′ 2″. T.E. : 21,960 lb.

64280	64312	64344	64377
64281	64313	64345	64378
64282	64314*	64346*	64379*
64283*	64315	64347	64380
64284*	64316*	64348	64381
64285	64317*	64349	64382
64286	64318*	64350	64383
64287	64319	64351	64384
64288	64320	64352*	64385
64289	64321	64353	64386*
64290	64322	64354*	64387
64291	64323	64355	64388
64292	64324*	64356	64389
64293	64325	64357	64390
64294	64326	64358	64391
64295	64327	64359*	64392
64296	64328	64360	64393*
64297	64329	64361	64394
64298	64330	64362*	64395
64299	64331	64363	64396
64300	64332*	64364*	64397
64301	64333*	64365	64398
64302	64334	64366	64399
64303	64335	64368	64400
64304*	64336	64369	64401
64305	64337	64370	64402*
64306	64338	64371	64403
64307	64339	64372	64404
64308	64340	64373*	64405
64309	64341	64374	64406*
64310	64342	64375*	64407
64311	64343	64376	64408

64409	64421	64433	64445
64410	64422	64434	64446
64411	64423	64435	64447
64412	64424	64436	64448
64413	64425	64437	64449
64414	64426	64438	64450*
64415	64427*	64439*	64451
64416	64428	64440	64452
64417*	64429	64441*	64453
64418*	64430	64442*	
64419	64431	64443	
64420*	64432	64444	

Totals : Class J11/3 31
Class J11 (other parts) 142

0-6-0   3F   Class J35

J35/5* Introduced 1906. Reid N.B.
    design with piston valves.
J35/4 Introduced 1908. Slide valves.
    (Parts 1, 2 and 3 were variations of
    Parts 4 and 5 before superheating.)
Weights : Loco. $\begin{cases} 51 \text{ tons.*} \\ 50 \text{ tons 15 cwt.} \end{cases}$
        Tender $\begin{cases} 38 \text{ tons 1 cwt.*} \\ 37 \text{ tons 15 cwt.} \end{cases}$
Pressure : 180 lb. Su. Cyls. : $18\frac{1}{4}'' \times 26''$.
Driving Wheels : 5′ 0″. T.E. : 22,080 lb.

64460*	64482	64500	64520
64461*	64483	64501	64521
64462*	64484	64502	64522
64463*	64485	64504	64523
64464*	64486	64505	64524
64466*	64487	64506	64525
64468*	64488	64507	64526
64470*	64489	64509	64527
64471*	64490	64510	64528
64472*	64491	64511	64529
64473*	64492	64512	64530
64474*	64493	64513	64531
64475*	64494	64514	64532
64476*	64495	64515	64533
64477*	64496	64516	64534
64478	64497	64517	64535
64479	64498	64518	
64480	64499	64519	

Totals : Class J35/4 55
Class J35/5 15

0-6-0   5F   Class J37

Introduced 1914. Reid N.B. design.
    Superheated development of J35.
Weights : Loco.   54 tons 14 cwt
        Tender 40 tons 19 cwt
Pressure : 180 lb. Su. Cyls. : $19\frac{1}{4}'' \times 26''$.
Driving Wheels : 5′ 0″. T.E. : 25,210 lb.
P.V.

64536	64562	64588	64614
64537	64563	64589	64615
64538	64564	64590	64616
64539	64565	64591	64617
64540	64566	64592	64618
64541	64567	64593	64619
64542	64568	64594	64620
64543	64569	64595	64621
64544	64570	64596	64622
64545	64571	64597	64623
64546	64572	64598	64624
64547	64573	64599	64625
64548	64574	64600	64626
64549	64575	64601	64627
64550	64576	64602	64628
64551	64577	64603	64629
64552	64578	64604	64630
64553	64579	64605	64631
64554	64580	64606	64632
64555	64581	64607	64633
64556	64582	64608	64634
64557	64583	64609	64635
64558	64584	64610	64636
64559	64585	64611	64637
64560	64586	64612	64638
64561	64587	64613	64639

Total 104

0-6-0   3P5F   Class J19

Introduced 1912. S. Holden G.E.
    design rebuilt with round-topped
    boiler from 1934
* Rebuilt with 19″ cyls. and 180 lb.
    pressure.
† Rebuilt with 19″ cyls. and 160 lb.
    pressure.
Weights : Loco.   50 tons 7 cwt.
        Tender 38 tons 5 cwt.
Pressure $\begin{cases} 170 \text{ lb. Su.} \\ 180 \text{ lb. Su.*} \\ 160 \text{ lb. Su.†} \end{cases}$

Cyls. : $\begin{cases} 20'' \times 26''. \\ 19'' \times 26''.*† \end{cases}$
Driving Wheels : 4' 11".
T.E. : $\begin{cases} 27,430 \text{ lb.} \\ 26,215 \text{ lb.*} \\ 23,300 \text{ lb.†} \end{cases}$
P.V.

64640	64649	64658	64667
64641	64650	64659	64668
64642	64651	64660	64669
64643	64652	64661	64670
64644	64653	64662	64671*
64645	64654	64663	64672†
64646	64655	64664*	64673
64647	64656	64665	64674
64648	64657	64666	

Total 35

0-6-0   5F   Class J20

J20* Introduced 1920. Hill G.E. design with Belpaire boiler.
J20/1 Introduced 1943. Rebuilt with B12/1 type round-topped boiler.
Weights : Loco.   54 tons 15 cwt.
        Tender 38 tons 5 cwt.
Pressure : 180 lb. Su. Cyls. : 20" × 28".
Driving Wheels : 4' 11". T.E. : 29,045 lb.
P.V.

64675	64682	64688	64694
64676*	64683	64689	64695
64677	64684	64690	64696*
64678	64685	64691	64697
64679	64686	64692	64698*
64680	64687*	64693	64699
64681			

Totals : Class J20   4
        Class J20/1 21

0-6-0   4P5F   Class J39

Introduced 1926. Gresley design.
J39/1 Standard 3,500 gallon tender.
J39/2* Standard 4,200 gallon tender.
J39/3† Various N.E. tenders (3,940 gallon on 64843-5, 4,125 gallon on 64855-9).
Weights : Loco.   57 tons 17 cwt.
Tender $\begin{cases} 44 \text{ tons } 4 \text{ cwt.} \\ 52 \text{ tons } 13 \text{ cwt.*} \end{cases}$ and others
Pressure : 180 lb. Su. Cyls. : 20" × 26".
Driving Wheels : 5' 2". T.E. : 25,665 lb.
P.V.

64700	64703	64706	64709
64701	64704	64707	64710
64702	64705	64708	64711

64712	64760	64808	64856†
64713	64761	64809	64857†
64714	64762	64810	64858†
64715	64763	64811	64859†
64716	64764	64812	64860
64717	64765	64813	64861
64718	64766	64814	64862
64719	64767	64815	64863
64720	64768	64816	64864
64721	64769	64817	64865
64722	64770	64818	64866
64723	64771	64819	64867
64724	64772	64820*	64868
64725	64773	64821*	64869
64726	64774	64822*	64870
64727	64775	64823	64871
64728	64776	64824	64872*
64729	64777	64825	64873*
64730	64778	64826	64874*
64731	64779	64827	64875*
64732	64780	64828	64876*
64733	64781	64829	64877*
64734	64782	64830	64878*
64735	64783	64831	64879*
64736	64784*	64832	64880*
64737	64785*	64833	64881*
64738	64786*	64834	64882*
64739	64787*	64835	64883*
64740	64788*	64836	64884*
64741	64789*	64837	64885*
64742	64790*	64838*	64886*
64743	64791*	64839*	64887*
64744	64792*	64840*	64888*
64745	64793*	64841*	64889*
64746	64794*	64842*	64890*
64747	64795*	64843†	64891*
64748	64796	64844†	64892*
64749	64797	64845†	64893*
64750	64798	64846	64894*
64751	64799	64847	64895*
64752	64800	64848	64896*
64753	64801	64849	64897*
64754	64802	64850	64898*
64755	64803	64851	64899*
64756	64804	64852	64900*
64757	64805	64853	64901*
64758	64806	64854	64902*
64759	64807	64855†	64903*

64904*	64926*	64948*	64970*
64905*	64927*	64949*	64971†
64906*	64928*	64950*	64972†
64907*	64929*	64951*	64973†
64908*	64930*	64952*	64974†
64909*	64931*	64953*	64975†
64910*	64932*	64954*	64976†
64911*	64933	64955*	64977†
64912*	64934	64956*	64978†
64913*	64935	64957*	64979†
64914*	64936	64958*	64980†
64915*	64937	64959*	64981†
64916*	64938	64960*	64982†
64917*	64939	64961*	64983†
64918*	64940	64962*	64984†
64919*	64941	64963*	64985†
64920*	64942	64964*	64986†
64921*	64943	64965*	64987†
64922*	64944	64966*	64988†
64923*	64945*	64967*	
64924*	64946*	64968*	
64925*	64947*	64969*	

Totals : **Class J39/1 156**
Class J39/2 106
Class J39/3 27

0-6-0   **2MT**   **Class J1**

Introduced 1908. Ivatt G.N. design.
Weights : Loco.   46 tons 14 cwt.
Tender 43 tons 2 cwt.
Pressure : 175 lb.   Cyls. : 18″ × 26″.
Driving Wheels : 5′ 8″. T.E. : 18,430 lb.

65002	65013

Total 2

0-6-0   **2MT**   **Class J2**

Introduced 1912. Ivatt/Gresley G.N. design.
Weights : Loco.   50 tons 10 cwt.
Tender 43 tons 2 cwt.
Pressure : 170 lb. Su. Cyls. : 19″ × 26″.
Driving Wheels : 5′ 8″. T.E. : 19,945 lb.
P.V.

65020   **Total 1**

0-6-0   **2F**   **Class J21**

Introduced 1886. T. W. Worsdell N.E. design.   Majority built as 2-cyl. compounds and later rebuilt as simple locos.
* Rebuilt with superheater, Stephenson gear and piston valves.
† Rebuilt with piston valves, superheater removed.
Weights : Loco. $\begin{cases} 43 \text{ tons } 15 \text{ cwt.*} \\ 42 \text{ tons } 9 \text{ cwt.†} \end{cases}$
Tender   36 tons 19 cwt.
Pressure : 160 lb. SS.
Cyls. : 19″ × 24″.
T.E. : 19,240 lb.
Driving Wheels : 5′ 1¼″.

65033*	65062*	65088*	65099†
65035†	65064*	65089*	65100†
65038*	65068*	65090*	65103*
65039†	65070†	65091*	65110*
65042†	65075*	65092*	65117†
65047*	65078*	65097*	65119*
65061*	65082*	65098*	

Total 27

0-6-0   **2F**   **Class J10**

J10/4* Introduced 1896. Pollitt development of J10/2 with larger bearings and larger tenders.
J10/6 Introduced 1901. Robinson locos with larger bearings and small tenders.
Weights : Loco.   41 tons 6 cwt.
Tender $\begin{cases} 37 \text{ tons } 6 \text{ cwt.} \\ 43 \text{ tons.*} \end{cases}$
Pressure : 160 lb. Cyls. : 18″ × 26″.
Driving Wheels : 5′ 1″. T.E. : 18,780 lb.

65131	65143*	65158*	65170*
65132*	65144*	65159*	65171*
65133*	65145*	65160*	65173
65134*	65146*	65162	65175
65135*	65147*	65164*	65176
65138*	65148*	65165*	65177
65139	65153*	65166*	65178*
65140*	65156*	65167*	65180
65142*	65157*	65169*	65181

65182	65191	65198	65205
65184	65192	65199	65208
65185	65194	65200	65209
65186	65196	65202	
65187	65197	65203	

Totals : Class J10/4 27
Class J10/6 27

0-6-0   2F   Class J36

Introduced 1888. Holmes N.B. design.
Weights : Loco.   41 tons 19 cwt.
          Tender 33 tons 9 cwt.
Pressure : 165 lb. Cyls. : 18½″ × 26″.
Driving Wheels : 5′ 0″. T.E. : 19,690 lb.

65210	65211	65213	65214
65216 Byng			
65217 French			
65218	65221		
65222 Somme			
65224 Mons			
65225	65228	65230	65232
65227	65229		
65233 Plumer			
65234			
65235 Gough			
65236 Horne			
65237	65239	65241	65242
65243 Maude			
65244	65247	65249	65251
65246	65248	65250	65252
65253 Joffre			
65257	65259	65261	65266
65258	65260	65265	65267
65268 Allenby			
65270	65288	65306	65317
65273	65290	65307	65318
65275	65293	65309	65319
65276	65295	65310	65320
65277	65296	65311	65321
65280	65297	65312	65323
65281	65300	65313	65324
65282	65303	65314	65325
65285	65304	65315	65327
65287	65305	65316	65329

65330	65335	65342	65346
65331	65338	65343	
65333	65339	65344	
65334	65341	65345	

Total 96

0-6-0   1P2F   Class J15

Introduced 1883. Worsdell G.E. design,
  modified by J. Holden.
* Fitted with side-window cab for
  Colne Valley line.
Weights : Loco.   37 tons 2 cwt.
          Tender 30 tons 13 cwt.
Pressure : 160 lb. Cyls. : 17½″ × 24″.
Driving Wheels: 4′ 11″. T.E.: 16,940 lb.

65356	65430	65450	65466
65359	65432*	65451	65467
65361	65433	65452	65468
65370	65434	65453	65469
65384	65435	65454	65470
65388	65438*	65455	65471
65389	65440	65456	65472
65390	65441	65457	65473
65391*	65442	65458	65474
65404	65443	65459	65475
65405*	65444	65460	65476
65417	65445	65461	65477
65420	65446	65462	65478
65422	65447	65463	65479
65424*	65448	65464	
65425	65449	65465	

Total 62

0-6-0   3F   Class J5

Introduced 1909. Ivatt G.N. design
* Rebuilt with superheater.
Weights : Loco.   47 tons 6 cwt.
          Tender 43 tons 2 cwt.
Pressure : { 175 lb.
            170 lb. Su.*
Cyls. : 18″ × 26″.
Driving Wheels : 5′ 2″.
T.E. : { 20,210 lb.
         19,630 lb.*

65480*	65486	65493	65495
65483	65490	65494	65498
65485			

Total 9

41

0-6-0 2P4F Class J17

Introduced 1901. J. Holden G.E. design. Many rebuilt from round-top boiler J16, introduced 1900.
* Fitted with small tender.

Weights : Loco.   45 tons 8 cwt.
Tender { 30 tons 12 cwt.*
38 tons 5 cwt.

Pressure : 180 lb. Su. Cyls. : 19" × 26".
Driving Wheels : 4' 11". T.E. : 24,340 lb.

65500*	65523	65545	65568
65501*	65524	65546	65569
65502*	65525	65547	65570
65503*	65526	65548	65571*
65504*	65527	65549	65572
65505*	65528*	65551	65573
65506*	65529	65552	65574
65507*	65530	65553	65575
65508*	65531	65554	65576
65509	65532	65555	65577
65510*	65533	65556	65578
65511*	65534	65557	65579
65512*	65535	65558	65580
65513*	65536	65559	65581
65514*	65537	65560	65582
65515*	65538	65561	65583
65516*	65539	65562	65584
65517*	65540	65563	65585
65518*	65541	65564	65586
65519*	65542	65565	65587
65520	65543	65566	65588
65521	65544	65567	65589
65522			**Total 89**

0-6-0 3F Class J25

Introduced 1898. W. Worsdell N.E. design.
• Original design, saturated, with slide valves.
† Rebuilt with superheater and piston valves.
‡ Rebuilt with piston valves, superheater removed.

Weights : Loco. { 39 tons 11 cwt.*
41 tons 14 cwt.†
40 tons 17 cwt.‡
Tender 36 tons 19 cwt.

Pressure : 160 lb. SS. Cyls. : 18½" × 26".
Driving Wheels : 4' 7¼". T.E. : 21,905 lb.

65645†	65650*	65656*	65662†
65647*	65654‡	65657*	65663*
65648*	65655*	65661*	65666*

65667*	65687*	65698*	65714*
65670*	65688*	65699*	65716*
65671*	65689*	65700*	65717†
65673‡	65690*	65702‡	65720*
65675*	65691*	65705*	65723*
65677‡	65693*	65706†	65726*
65680*	65694*	65708*	65727*
65683‡	65695*	65710*	65728*
65685*	65696*	65712*	
65686*	65697*	65713*	

Total 50

0-6-0 5F Class J26

Introduced 1904. W Worsdell N.E. design.

Weights : Loco. 46 tons 16 cwt.
Tender 36 tons 19 cwt.

Pressure : 180 lb. Cyls. : 18½" × 26".
Driving Wheels : 4' 7¼". T.E. : 24,640 lb.

65730	65743	65756	65769
65731	65744	65757	65770
65732	65745	65758	65771
65733	65746	65759	65772
65734	65747	65760	65773
65735	65748	65761	65774
65736	65749	65762	65775
65737	65750	65763	65776
65738	65751	65764	65777
65739	65752	65765	65778
65740	65753	65766	65779
65741	65754	65767	
65742	65755	65768	

Total 50

0-6-0 5F Class J27

Introduced 1906. W. Worsdell N.E design developed from J26.
* Introduced 1921. Raven locos. Superheated, with piston valves.
† Introduced 1943. Piston valves, superheater removed.

Weights : Loco. { 47 tons Sat.
49 tons 10 cwt. Su.
Tender 36 tons 19 cwt.

Pressure : 180 lb. SS. Cyls. : 18½" × 26"
Driving Wheels : 4' 7¼". T.E. : 24,640 lb.

65780	65782	65784	65786
65781	65783	65785	65787

65788	65815	65842	65869*
65789	65816	65843	65870†
65790	65817	65844	65871*
65791	65818	65845	65872*
65792	65819	65846	65873†
65793	65820	65847	65874*
65794	65821	65848	65875†
65795	65822	65849	65876†
65796	65823	65850	65877†
65797	65824	65851	65878*
65798	65825	65852	65879†
65799	65826	65853	65880*
65800	65827	65854	65881*
65801	65828	65855	65882†
65802	65829	65856	65883*
65803	65830	65857	65884†
65804	65831	65858	65885*
65805	65832	65859	65886*
65806	65833	65860†	65887*
65807	65834	65861†	65888†
65808	65835	65862†	65889*
65809	65836	65863*	65890*
65810	65837	65864†	65891†
65811	65838	65865†	65892*
65812	65839	65866*	65893*
65813	65840	65867†	65894*
65814	65841	65868†	

Total 115

0-6-0   6F   Class J38

Introduced 1926. Gresley design. Predecessor of J39, with 4' 8" wheels, boiler 6" longer than J39 and smokebox 6" shorter.
* Rebuilt with J39 boiler.
Weights : Loco. 58 tons 19 cwt.
          Tender 44 tons 4 cwt.
Pressure : 180 lb. Su. Cyls.: 20" × 26".
Driving Wheels : 4' 8" T.E. : 28,415 lb. P.V.

65900	65909	65918*	65927*
65901	65910	65919	65928
65902	65911	65920	65929
65903*	65912	65921	65930
65904	65913	65922	65931
65905	65914	65923	65932
65906*	65915	65924	65933
65907	65916	65925	65934
65908*	65916*	65926*	

Total 35

2-4-2T   IMT   Class F4

Introduced 1884. Worsdell G.E. design, modified by J. Holden.
Weight : 53 tons 19 cwt.
Pressure : 160 lb. Cyls. : 17½" × 24".
Driving Wheels : 5' 4". T.E. : 15,620 lb.

67157	67162	67174	67187

Total 4

2-4-2T   IMT   Class F5

Introduced 1911. S. D. Holden design. (Rebuilt from F4.)
* Introduced 1949. Push-and-pull fitted.
Weight : 53 tons 19 cwt.
Pressure : 180 lb. Cyls. : 17½" × 24".
Driving Wheels : 5' 4". T.E.: 17,570 lb.

67188	67196	67204	67212
67189	67197	67205	67213
67190	67198	67206	67214
67191	67199	67207	67215
67192	67200*	67208	67216
67193*	67201	67209	67217
67194	67202*	67210	67218
67195	67203*	67211	67219

Total 32

2-4-2T   IMT   Class F6

Introduced 1911. S. D. Holden design, development of F4 with higher pressure and larger tanks.
Weight : 56 tons 9 cwt.
Pressure : 180 lb. Cyls. : 17½" × 24".
Driving Wheels : 5' 4". T.E. : 17,570 lb.

67220	67225	67230	67235
67221	67226	67231	67236
67222	67227	67232	67237
67223	67228	67233	67238
67224	67229	67234	67239

Total 20

IMPORTANT NOTE

A careful reading of the notes on page 2 is essential to understand the use of reference marks in this book.

0-4-4T IMT Class G5

Introduced 1894. W. Worsdell N.E. design.
* Push-and-pull fitted.
† Push-and-pull fitted and rebuilt with larger tanks.
Weight : 54 tons 4 cwt.
Pressure : 160 lb. Cyls. : 18″ × 24″.
Driving Wheels : 5′ 1¼″. T.E. : 17,265 lb.

67240	67270	67300	67326
67241	67271	67301	67327
67243	67272	67302	67328
67246	67273*	67304	67329
67247	67274	67305*	67332
67248	67277*	67307	67333
67249	67278	67308	67334
67250*	67279*	67309	67336
67251	67280*	67310	67337*
67253*	67281*	67311*	67338
67254	67282*	67312	67339*
67256	67283	67314	67340†
67258	67284	67315	67341
67259	67286*	67316	67342
67261*	67288	67318	67343
67262	67289	67319	67344
67263	67290	67320	67345
67265	67293	67321	67346
67266	67294	67322*	67347
67267	67296	67323*	67349
67268	67297*	67324	
67269*	67298	67325	

Total 86

4-4-2T IMT Class C12

Introduced 1898. Ivatt G N. design.
*†Boiler pressure reduced to 170 lb.
†‡Push-and-pull fitted.
Weight : 62 tons 6 cwt.
Pressure : { 175 lb.
              170 lb.*†
Cyls. : 18″ × 26″.
Driving Wheels : 5′ 8″.
T.E. : { 18,425 lb.
         17,900 lb.*†

67350	67357	67362	67365
67352	67360	67363†	67366
67353	67361	67364	67367

67368	67379	67386‡	67395
67369	67380	67387‡	67397
67371	67382	67389	67398*
67374†	67383	67391	
67375	67384	67392	
67376	67385	67394	

Total 33

4-4-2T 2P1F Class C13

Introduced 1903. Robinson G.C design, later rebuilt with superheater.
* Push-and-pull fitted.
Weight : 66 tons 13 cwt.
Pressure : 160 lb. Su. Cyls. : 18″ × 26″
Driving Wheels : 5′ 7″. T.E. : 17,100 lb.

67400	67412	67421*	67430
67401	67413	67422	67431
67402	67414	67423	67432
67403	67415	67424	67433*
67405	67416*	67425	67434
67407	67417*	67426	67436*
67408	67418*	67427	67437
67409	67419	67428	67438*
67411	67420*	67429	67439

Total 36

4-4-2T 2P1F Class C14

Introduced 1907. Robinson G.C. design, later superheated, development of C13. With detail differences.
Weight : 71 tons.
Pressure : 160 lb. Su. Cyls. : 18″ × 26″.
Driving Wheels : 5′ 7″. T.E. : 17,100 lb.

67440	67443	67446	67449
67441	67444	67447	67450
67442	67445	67448	67451

Total 12

4-4-2T 2P Class C15

Introduced 1911. Reid N.B. design.
* Push-and-pull fitted.
Weight : 68 tons 15 cwt.
Pressure : 175 lb. Cyls. : 18″ × 26″
Driving Wheels : 5′ 9″. T.E. : 18,160 lb.

67452	67456	67459	67462
67454	67457	67460*	67463
67455	67458	67461	67465

Class J36 0-6-0 No. 65243 *Maude* [W. J. V. Anderson

Class J35 0-6-0 No. 64501 [B. R. Goodland

Class J37 0-6-0 No. 64580 [B. E. Morrison

Class J25 0-6-0 No. 65702

[R. E. Vincent

Class J26 0-6-0 No. 65773

[M. J. Ecclestone

Class J27 0-6-0 No. 65866

[J. F. Aylard

Top : Class F5 2-4-2T
No. 67209
  [*A. R. Carpenter*

Centre : Class F6 2-4-2T
No. 67238
  [*G. K. Anderson*

Right : Class C13 4-4-2T
No. 67436 [*D. Cartmel*

47

Left : Class Y3
Sentinel No. 41
(Ex-68177)
[*A. B. Crompton*

Below : Class V1
2-6-2T No. 67674
[*T. K. Widd*

Left : Class J70
Tram Loco No. 68225
[*P. H. Wells*

67466	67472	67476	67481
67467	67473	67477	
67469	67474	67478	
67470	67475*	67480	

Total 25

4-4-2T   2P   Class C16

Introduced 1915. Reid N.B. design, superheated development of C15.
* Superheater removed.
Weight : 72 tons 10 cwt.
Pressure : 165 lb. SS. Cyls. : 19″ × 26″.
Driving Wheels : 5′ 9″. T.E. : 19,080 lb.
P.V.

67482	67488	67493	67498
67483*	67489	67494	67499
67484	67490	67495	67500
67485	67491	67496	67501
67486	67492	67497	67502
67487			

Total 21

2-6-2T   V1 (3MT)   Classes   V1 & V3   V3 (4MT)

V1 Introduced 1930. Gresley design.
V3* Introduced 1939. Development of V1 with higher pressure (locos numbered below 67682 rebuilt from V1).
Weights : { 84 tons.
{ 86 tons 16 cwt.*
Pressure : { 180 lb. Su.
{ 200 lb. Su.*
Cyls. : (3) 16″ × 26″.
Driving Wheels : 5′ 8″.
T.E. : { 22,465 lb.
{ 24,960 lb.*
Walschaerts gear, derived motion. P.V.

67600	67613	67626*	67639
67601	67614	67627*	67640
67602	67615*	67628	67641
67603	67616	67629	67642
67604*	67617	67630	67643
67605*	67618	67631	67644
67606*	67619	67632	67645
67607	67620*	67633	67646
67608	67621	67634*	67647
67609*	67622	67635	67648
67610	67623	67636*	67649
67611*	67624*	67637	67650
67612*	67625*	67638	67651

67652*	67662	67672*	67682*
67653	67663	67673	67683*
67654	67664	67674	67684*
67655	67665	67675*	67685*
67656*	67666	67676	67686*
67657	67667	67677	67687*
67658	67668	67678	67688*
67659	67669*	67679*	67689*
67660	67670	67680	67690*
67661	67671	67681	67691*

Totals : Class V1   62
Class V3   30

2-6-4T   4MT   Class L1

Introduced 1945. Thompson design.
* Introduced 1954. Boiler pressure reduced to 200 lb.
Weight : 89 tons 9 cwt.
Pressure : { 225 lb.
{ 200 lb.*
Cyls. : (O) 20″ × 26″.
Driving Wheels : 5′ 2″. T.E. : { 32,080 lb.
Walschaerts gear.   P.V. { 28,515 lb.*

67701	67726	67751	67776
67702	67727	67752	67777
67703	67728	67753	67778
67704	67729	67754	67779
67705	67730	67755	67780
67706	67731	67756	67781
67707	67732	67757	67782
67708	67733	67758	67783
67709	67734	67759	67784
67710	67735	67760	67785
67711	67736	67761	67786
67712	67737	67762	67787
67713	67738	67763	67788
67714	67739	67764	67789
67715	67740	67765	67790
67716	67741	67766	67791
67717	67742	67767	67792
67718	67743	67768	67793
67719	67744	67769	67794
67720	67745	67770	67795
67721	67746	67771	67796
67722	67747	67772	67797
67723	67748	67773	67798*
67724	67749	67774	67799
67725	67750	67775	67800

Total 100

0-6-0ST 4F Class J94

Introduced 1943. Riddles M.o.S. design.
(Bought from M.o.S. 1946).
Weight : 48 tons 5 cwt.
Pressure : 170 lb. Cyls. : 18″ × 26″.
Driving Wheels : 4′ 3″. T.E. : 23,870 lb.

68006	68025	68044	68063
68007	68026	68045	68064
68008	68027	68046	68065
68009	68028	68047	68066
68010	68029	68048	68067
68011	68030	68049	68068
68012	68031	68050	68069
68013	68032	68051	68070
68014	68033	68052	68071
68015	68034	68053	68072
68016	68035	68054	68073
68017	68036	68055	68074
68018	68037	68056	68075
68019	68038	68057	68076
68020	68039	68058	68077
68021	68040	68059	68078
68022	68041	68060	68079
68023	68042	68061	68080
68024	68043	68062	

Total 75

0-4-0T Dock Tank Class Y8

Introduced 1890. T. W. Worsdell N.E.
design.
Weight : 15 tons 10 cwt.
Pressure : 140 lb. Cyls. : 11″ × 15″.
Driving Wheels : 3′ 0″. T.E. : 6,000 lb.

68091　　　　　　　　Total 1

0-4-0ST 0F Class Y9

Introduced 1882. Holmes N.B. design.
* Locos running permanently attached
to wooden tenders.
Weights : Loco.　27 tons 16 cwt.
　　　　　　Tender　6 tons.*
Pressure : 130 lb. Cyls. : (O) 14″ × 20″.
Driving Wheels : 3′ 8″. T.E. 9,845 lb.

68093*	68098*	68103*	68109*
68094*	68099*	68104	68110
68095	68100	68105	68112*
68096	68101	68106*	68113
68097	68102	68108*	68114*

68115	68118*	68121*	68124
68116*	68119*	68122*	
68117*	68120*	68123	

Total 30

0-4-0T Dock Tank Class Y4

Introduced 1913. Hill G.E. design.
Weight : 38 tons 1 cwt.
Pressure : 180 lb. Cyls. : (O) 17″ × 20″.
Driving Wheels : 3′ 10″. T.E. : 19,225 lb.
Walschaerts gear.
(See also page 51)

68125　|　68126　|　68127　|　68128

Total 5

0-4-0T Unclass Class Y1

Sentinel Wagon Works design. Single-
speed Geared Sentinel Locomotives.
The parts of this class differ in details.
including size of boiler and fuel
capacity.
Y1/1* Introduced 1925.
Y1/2† Introduced 1927.
§ Sprocket gear ratio 9 : 25 (remainder
11 : 25).
Weights : $\begin{cases} 20 \text{ tons } 17 \text{ cwt.*} \\ 19 \text{ tons } 16 \text{ cwt.†} \end{cases}$
Pressure : 275 lb. Su. Cyls. : 6¾″ × 9″.
Driving Wheels : 2′ 6″.
T.E. : $\begin{cases} 7,260 \text{ lb.} \\ 8,870 \text{ lb.§} \end{cases}$
Poppet valves.
(See also page 51)

68138†	68144†§	68150†§
68140†	68145†§	68151†§
68142†	68148†§	68152S*
68143†§	68149†§	68153S†

Totals :　Class Y1/1　5
　　　　　　Class Y1/2　12

0-4-0T Unclass Class Y3

Sentinel Wagon Works design. Two-
speed Geared Sentinel Locos.
Introduced 1927.
* Sprocket gear ratio 15 : 19 (re-
mainder 19 : 19).
Weight : 20 tons 16 cwt.
Pressure : 275 lb. Su. Cyls. : 6¾″ × 9″.
Driving Wheels : 2′ 6″.
T.E. : $\begin{cases} \text{Low Gear : 12,600 lb.} \\ \text{High Gear : 4,705 lb.} \\ \text{Low Gear : 15,960 lb.*} \\ \text{High Gear : 5,960 lb.*} \end{cases}$
Poppet valves.
(See also page 51)

68155	68160	68180*	68185
68156	68162	68182*	
68158	68164	68183*	
68159	68169	68184	

Total 20

0-4-2T oF Class Z4

Introduced 1915. Manning-Wardle design for G.N. of S.
Weight : 25 tons 17 cwt.
Pressure : 160 lb. Cyls. : (O) 13″ × 20″.
Driving Wheels : 3′ 6″. T.E. : 10,945 lb.

68190	68191	**Total 2**

DEPARTMENTAL LOCOMOTIVES

In addition to service locomotives (denoted by a bold " S " in these pages) that are still shown with numbers in the British Railways series, a number of E. & N.E. Region departmental locomotives have been renumbered between I and 100. These are shown below, with their former B.R. numbers in brackets.

0-6-0ST 3F Class J52/2
(For dimensions see page 54)

1 (68845)	2 (68816)

0-4-0T Unclass Class Y3
(For dimensions—15:19 gear ratio—see page 50).

3 (68181)	40 (68173)
5 (68165)	41 (68177)
7 (68166)	42 (68178)
38 (68168)	

0-4-0T Unclass Class Y1/1
(For dimensions see page 50)

4 (68132)	37 (68130)
6 (68133)	39 (68131)

0-6-0T 2F Class J66
(For dimensions see page 53)

31 (68382)	32 (68370)
36 (68378)	

0-4-0T Dock Tank Class Y4
(For dimensions see page 50)

33 (68129)

0-4-0T Unclass Class Y1/4

Sentinel Wagon Works design. (This part introduced 1927). Single-speed Geared Sentinel Locomotives. The three parts of this class differ in details, including size of boiler and fuel capacity.
Sprocket gear ratio 11: 25.
Weight : 19 tons 7 cwt.
Pressure : 275 lb. Su.
Cyls.: 6¾″ × 9″.
Driving Wheels : 2′ 6″.
T.E.: 7,260 lb.   Poppet valves.

51 (68136)	**Total 1**

0-4-0 Diesel Mechanical

Introduced 1950 : Hibberd & Co. for North Eastern Region.
Weight : 11 tons.
Engine : English National Gas type DA 4, 4-cyls., 52 h.p. at 1,250 r.p.m. Transmission spur type gear box with roller chains : three forward and three reverse gears

52 (11104)	**Total 1**

0-4-2T 0F Class Z5

Introduced 1915. Manning-Wardle design for G.N. of S.
Weight : 30 tons 18 cwt.
Pressure : 160 lb. Cyls.: (O) 14″ × 20″.
Driving Wheels : 4′ 0″. T.E. : 11,105 lb.

| 68192 | 68193 | | **Total 2** |

0-6-0T Dock Tank Class J63

Introduced 1906. Robinson G.C. design.
Weight : 37 tons 9 cwt.
Pressure : 160 lb. Cyls.: (O) 13″ × 20″.
Driving Wheels : 3′ 6″. T.E. : 10,260 lb.

| 68204 | 68206 | 68209 | 68210 |
| 68205 | 68207 | | |

Total 6

0-6-0T Unclass Class J65

Introduced 1889. J. Holden G.E. design.
Weight : 36 tons 11 cwt.
Pressure : 160 lb. Cyls. : 14″ × 20″.
Driving Wheels : 4′ 0″. T.E. : 11,105 lb.

| 68214 | | **Total 1** |

0-6-0T (Tram Locos)
Dock Tank Class J70

Introduced 1903. J. Holden G.E. design.
Weight : 27 tons 1 cwt.
Pressure : 180 lb. Cyls.: (O) 12″ × 15″.
Driving Wheels : 3′ 1″. T.E. : 8,930 lb.
Walschaerts gear.

| 68222 | 68223 | 68225 | 68226 |

Total 4

0-6-0T Unclass Class J71

Introduced 1886. T. W. Worsdell N.E. design.
*†Altered cylinder dimensions.
Weight : 37 tons 12 cwt.
Pressure : 140 lb. Dr. Wheels : 4′ 7½″

Cyls.: $\begin{cases} 16″ × 22″ \\ 16\frac{1}{2}″ × 22″* \\ 18″ × 22″† \end{cases}$ T.E.: $\begin{cases} 12,130 \text{ lb.} \\ 13,300 \text{ lb.}* \\ 15,355 \text{ lb.}† \end{cases}$

68230*	68253*	68273	68296
68232	68254	68275	68297
68233	68256	68276	68298
68234*	68258*	68278	68300
68235	68259*	68279	68301
68236	68260	68280*	68303*
68238	68262	68283	68304*
68239	68263	68284	68305*
68240	68264	68287*	68306*
68242	68265	68289*	68307*
68244	68266	68290	68308*
68245	68267	68291	68309*
68246*	68269	68292	68312†
68250*	68270	68293*	68313*
68251	68271	68294	68314
68252*	68272	68295	68316*

Total 64

0-6-0T 0F Class J88

Introduced 1904. Reid N.B. design with short wheelbase.
Weight : 38 tons 14 cwt.
Pressure : 130 lb. Cyls.: (O) 15″ × 22″.
Driving Wheels : 3′ 9″. T.E. : 12,155 lb.

68320	68329	68338	68347
68321	68330	68339	68348
68322	68331	68340	68349
68323	68332	68341	68350
68324	68333	68342	68351
68325	68334	68343	68352
68326	68335	68344	68353
68327	68336	68345	68354
68328	68337	68346	

Total 35

0-6-0T 3F Class J73

Introduced 1891. W. Worsdell N.E. design.
Weight : 46 tons 15 cwt.
Pressure : 160 lb. Cyls. : 19″ × 24″.
Driving Wheels : 4′ 7¼″. T.E. : 21,320 lb.

68355	68358	68361	68363
68356	68359	68362	68364
68357	68360		

Total 10

0-6-0T 2F Class J66

Introduced 1886. J. Holden G.E. design.
Weight : 40 tons 6 cwt.
Pressure : 160 lb. Cyls. : 16½″ × 22″.
Driving Wheels : 4′ 0″. T.E. 16,970 lb.
(See also page 51)

68374 | 68383

Total 5

0-6-0T 2F Class J77

Introduced 1899. W. Worsdell N.E.
rebuild of Fletcher 0-4-4T originally
built 1874-84.
* Darlington rebuilds with square-
cornered cab roof (remainder York
rebuilds with rounded cab).
Weight : 43 tons.
Pressure : 160 lb. Cyls. : 17″ × 22″.
Driving Wheels : 4′ 1¼″. T.E. : 17,560 lb.

68391	68407	68422	68432*
68392*	68408	68423	68434
68393*	68409	68424	68435
68395*	68410	68425	68436
68397*	68412*	68426	68437
68399	68413	68427	68438
68401	68414	68428	68440*
68402	68417	68429	
68405*	68420*	68430	
68406	68421	68431	

Total 37

0-6-0T 2F Class J83

Introduced 1900. Holmes N.B. design.
Weight : 45 tons 5 cwt.
Pressure : 150 lb. Cyls. : 17″ × 26″.
Driving Wheels : 4′ 6″. T.E. : 17,745 lb.

68442	68452	68463	68473
68443	68453	68464	68474
68444	68454	68465	68475
68445	68455	68466	68476
68446	68456	68467	68477
68447	68457	68468	68478
68448	68458	68469	68479
68449	68459	68470	68480
68450	68460	68471	68481
68451	68461	68472	

Total 39

Classes

0-6-0T 2F J67 & J69

J67/1* Introduced 1890. J. Holden
G.E. design with 160 lb. pressure.

J69/1† Introduced 1902. Development
of J67 with 180 lb. pressure, larger
tanks and larger firebox (some
rebuilt from J67).

J67/2‡ Introduced 1937. Rebuild of
J69 with 160 lb. boiler and small
firebox.

J69/2§ Introduced 1950. J67/1 rebuilt
with 180 lb. boiler and large firebox.

Weights : $\begin{cases} 40 \text{ tons.*‡} \\ 40 \text{ tons 9 cwt.†§} \end{cases}$
Pressure : $\begin{cases} 160 \text{ lb.*‡} \\ 180 \text{ lb.†§} \end{cases}$
Cyls. : 16½″ × 22″.
Driving Wheels : 4′ 0″.
T.E. : $\begin{cases} 16,970 \text{ lb.*‡} \\ 19,090 \text{ lb.†§} \end{cases}$

68490§	68522§	68555†	68587†
68491†	68523*	68556†	68588†
68492*	68524†	68557†	68589*
68493*	68526†	68558†	68590*
68494†	68527†	68559†	68591†
68495†	68528†	68560†	68592*
68496*	68529‡	68561†	68593†
68497†	68530†	68562†	68594*
68498§	68531‡	68563†	68595*
68499†	68532†	68565†	68596†
68500†	68534†	68566†	68597‡
68501†	68535†	68567†	68598†
68502†	68536‡	68568†	68599†
68503†	68537†	68569†	68600†
68504†	68538†	68570†	68601†
68507†	68540‡	68571†	68602†
68508†	68541†	68572‡	68603†
68510§	68542†	68573†	68605†
68511*	68543†	68574†	68606*
68512§	68544†	68575†	68607†
68513§	68545†	68576†	68608*
68514*	68546†	68577†	68609†
68515*	68547‡	68578†	68610‡
68516*	68549†	68579†	68611†
68517*	68550†	68581†	68612†
68518*	68551†	68583*	68613†
68519§	68552†	68584*	68616†
68520§	68553†	68585†	68617†
68521*	68554†	68586*	68618†

68619†	68626†	68631†	68636†
68621†	68628‡	68632†	
68623†	68629†	68633†	
68625†	68630†	68635†	

Totals : **Class J67/1 24**

Class J67/2 9

Class J69/1 88

Class J69/2 8

0-6-0T 2F Class J68

Introduced 1912. Hill G.E. development of J69 with side-window cab.
Weight : 42 tons 9 cwt.
Pressure : 180 lb. Cyls. : 16½″ × 22″.
Driving Wheels : 4′ 0″. T.E. : 19,090 lb.

68638	68646	68654	68662
68639	68647	68655	68663
68640	68648	68656	68664
68641	68649	68657	68665
68642	68650	68658	68666
68643	68651	68659	
68644	68652	68660	
68645	68653	68661	

Total 29

0-6-0T 2F Class J72

Introduced 1898. W. Worsdell N.E. design.
* Altered cylinder dimensions.
Weight : 38 tons 12 cwt.
Pressure : 140 lb. Cyls. : $\begin{cases} 17″ \times 24″ \\ 18″ \times 24″* \end{cases}$
Driving Wheels : 4′ 1¼″.
T.E. : $\begin{cases} 16,760 \text{ lb.} \\ 18,790 \text{ lb.}* \end{cases}$

68670	68675	68680	68685*
68671	68676	68681	68686
68672	68677	68682	68687
68673	68678	68683	68688
68674	68679	68684	68689

IMPORTANT NOTE

A careful reading of the notes on page 2 is essential to understand the use of reference marks in this book.

68690	68707	68723	68739
68691	68708	68724	68740
68692	68709	68725	68741
68693	68710	68726	68742
68694	68711	68727	68743
68695	68712	68728	68744
68696	68713	68729	68745
68697	68714	68730	68746
68698	68715	68731	68747
68699	68716	68732	68748
68700	68717	68733	68749
68701	68718	68734	68750
68702	68719	68735	68751
68703	68720	68736	68752
68704	68721	68737	68753
68705	68722	68738	68754
68706			

(Class continued with No. 69001)

0-6-0ST 3F Class J52

J52/2 Introduced 1897. Ivatt standard G.N. saddletank with domed boiler.
J52/1* Introduced 1922. Rebuild of Stirling domeless saddletank (introduced 1892)—non-condensing.
J52/1† Introduced 1922. Condensing rebuild of Stirling locos.
‡ J52/2 with boiler pressure raised to 175 lb.
Weight : 51 tons 14 cwt.
Pressure : $\begin{cases} 170 \text{ lb.} \text{Cyls. : } 18″ \times 26″*. \\ 175 \text{ lb.}‡ \end{cases}$
Driving Wheels: 4′ 8″. T.E.: $\begin{cases} 21,735 \text{ lb.} \\ 22,370 \text{ lb.}‡ \end{cases}$
(See also page 51)

68757†	68783†	68802*	68818
68758†	68784†	68804*	68819
68759†	68785†	68805	68820
68760†	68787†	68806	68821
68761†	68788†	68807	68822
68764*	68790*	68808	68823
68765*	68791†	68809	68824
68768*	68793†	68810	68826
68769*	68795*	68811	68827
68771*	68796†	68812	68828
68772*	68797*	68813	68829
68777†	68798*	68814	68830
68778†	68799*	68815	68831
68781†	68800*	68817	68832

68833	68848	68862	68876‡	68954†	68964†	68974†	68984§
68834	68849	68863	68877	68955†	68965†	68975†	68985§
68835	68850	68864	68878	68956†	68966†	68976†	68986§
68836	68851	68865	68879	68957†	68967†	68977†	68987§
68837	68852	68866	68880	68958†	68968†	68978§	68988§
68838	68853	68867	68881	68959†	68969†	68979§	68989§
68839	68854	68868	68882	68960†	68970†	68980§	68990§
68840‡	68855	68869	68883	68961†	68971†	68981§	68991§
68841	68856	68870	68884	68962†	68972†	68982§	
68842	68857	68871	68885	68963†	68973†	68983§	
68843	68858	68872	68886				
68844	68859	68873	68887				
68846	68860‡	68874	68888				
68847	68861	68875	68889				

Totals : Class J52/1 30
Class J52/2 84

Totals : Class J50/1 10
Class J50/2 40
Class J50/3 38
Class J50/4 14

0-6-0T   4F   Class J50

J50/2* Introduced 1922. Gresley G.N. design (68900-19 rebuilt from smaller J51, built 1915-22).
J50/3† Introduced 1926. Post-grouping development with detail differences.
J50/1‡ Introduced 1929. Rebuilt from smaller J51, built 1913-4.
J50/4§ Introduced 1937. Development of J50/3 with larger bunker.
Weights : { 56 tons 6 cwt.‡
{ 58 tons 3 cwt.†§
{ 57 tons.*
Pressure : 175 lb. Cyls. : 18½″ × 26″.
Driving Wheels : 4′ 8″. T.E. : 23,635 lb.

68890‡	68906*	68922*	68938*
68891‡	68907*	68923*	68939*
68892‡	68908*	68924*	68940*
68893‡	68909*	68925*	68941†
68894‡	68910*	68926*	68942†
68895‡	68911*	68927*	68943†
68896‡	68912*	68928*	68944†
68897‡	68913*	68929*	68945†
68898‡	68914*	68930*	68946†
68899‡	68915*	68931*	68947†
68900*	68916*	68932*	68948†
68901*	68917*	68933*	68949†
68902*	68918*	68934*	68950†
68903*	68919*	68935*	68951†
68904*	68920*	68936*	68952†
68905*	68921*	68937*	68953†

0-6-0T   2F   Class J72

(Continued from 68754)

69001	69008	69015	69022
69002	69009	69016	69023
69003	69010	69017	69024
69004	69011	69018	69025
69005	69012	69019	69026
69006	69013	69020	69027
69007	69014	69021	69028

Total 113

2-6-4T   5F   Class L3

Introduced 1914. Robinson G.C. design.
Weight : 97 tons 9 cwt.
Pressure : 180 lb. Su. Cyls. : 21″ × 26″.
Driving Wheels : 5′ 1″. T.E. : 28,760 lb.

69050	69060	69065	69069
69052	69064		

Total 6

0-6-2T   3F   Class N10

Introduced 1902. W. Worsdell N.E. design.
Weight : 57 tons 14 cwt.
Pressure : 160 lb. Cyls. : 18½″ × 26″.
Driving Wheels: 4′ 7¼″. T.E.: 21,905 lb.

55

69090	69095	69100	69106
69091	69096	69101	69107
69092	69097	69102	69108
69093	69098	69104	69109
69094	69099	69105	

Total 19

69210	69214	69218	69222
69211	69215	69219	69223
69212	69216	69220	69224
69213	69217	69221	

Totals : Class N15/2 93
Class N15/2 6

0-6-2T 3F Class N13

Introduced 1913. Stirling H. & B. design.
Weight : 61 tons 9 cwt.
Pressure : 175 lb. Cyls. : 18″ × 26″.
Driving Wheels : 4′ 6″. T.E. : 23,197 lb.

69114	69116	69117	69119
69115			

Total 5

0-6-2T 3MT Class N15

N15/2* Introduced 1910. Reid N.B.
design developed from N14. Cowlairs
incline banking locos.
N15/1 Introduced 1910. Development
of N15/2 with smaller bunker for
normal duties.
Weights : $\begin{cases} 62 \text{ tons } 1 \text{ cwt.*} \\ 60 \text{ tons } 18 \text{ cwt.} \end{cases}$
Pressure : 175 lb. Cyls. : 18″ × 26″.
Driving Wheels : 4′ 6″. T.E. : 23,205 lb.

69126*	69147	69168	69189
69127*	69148	69169	69190
69128*	69149	69170	69191
69129*	69150	69171	69192
69130*	69151	69172	69193
69131*	69152	69173	69194
69132	69153	69174	69195
69133	69154	69175	69196
69134	69155	69176	69197
69135	69156	69177	69198
69136	69157	69178	69199
69137	69158	69179	69200
69138	69159	69180	69201
69139	69160	69181	69202
69140	69161	69182	69203
69141	69162	69183	69204
69142	69163	69184	69205
69143	69164	69185	69206
69144	69165	69186	69207
69145	69166	69187	69208
69146	69167	69188	69209

0-6-2T 1P2F Class N4

N4/2 Introduced 1889. Parker M.S.
& L. design.
(N4/1 was N4/2 with longer chimney.)
Weight : 61 tons 10 cwt.
Pressure : 160 lb. Cyls. 18″ × 26″.
Driving Wheels : 5′ 1″. T.E. : 18,780 lb.
Joy gear.

69225	69230	69232	69235
69228	69231	69233	69236

Total 8

0-6-2T 2MT Class N5

N5/2 Introduced 1891. Parker M.S.
& L. design developed from N4.
Weight : 62 tons 7 cwt.
Pressure : 160 lb. Cyls. : 18″ × 26″.
Driving Wheels : 5′ 1″. T.E. : 18,780 lb.

69250	69270	69288	69307
69253	69271	69290	69308
69254	69272	69291	69309
69255	69273	69292	69310
69256	69274	69293	69312
69257	69275	69294	69313
69258	69276	69295	69314
69259	69277	69296	69315
69260	69278	69297	69316
69261	69279	69298	69317
69262	69280	69299	69318
69263	69281	69300	69319
69264	69282	69301	69320
69265	69283	69302	69321
69266	69284	69303	69322
69267	69285	69304	69323
69268	69286	69305	69324
69269	69287	69306	69325

69326	69338	69350	69362
69327	69339	69351	69363
69328	69340	69352	69364
69329	69341	69353	69365
69330	69342	69354	69366
69331	69343	69355	69367
69332	69344	69356	69368
69333	69345	69357	69369
69334	69346	69358	69370
69335	69347	69359	
69336	69348	69360	
69337	69349	69361	

Total 117

0-6-2T   2MT   Class N8

* Introduced 1886. T. W. Worsdell
N.E. design, saturated, with Joy's gear
and slide valves (majority rebuilt
from compounds).
† Rebuilt with superheater, Stephenson
gear and piston valves, 24″ piston
stroke.
‡ As † but with 26″ stroke.
§ Rebuilt with Stephenson gear and
piston valves, superheater removed,
24″ stroke.
¶ As § but with 26″ piston stroke.
Weights : { 56 tons 5 cwt.*§¶
{ 58 tons 14 cwt.†‡
Pressure : 160 lb. SS.
Cyls. : { 18″ × 24″.*
{ 19″ × 24″.†§
{ 19″ × 26″.‡¶
Driving Wheels : 5′ 1¼″.
T.E. : { 17,265 lb.*
{ 19,235 lb.†§
{ 20,840 lb.‡¶

69377†	69381¶	69386‡	69392*
69378§	69385†	69390†	69394†

Total 8

0-6-2T   3MT   Class N9

Introduced 1893. T. W. Worsdell N.E.
design.
Weight : 56 tons 10 cwt.
Pressure : 160 lb.   Cyls. : 19″ × 26″.
Driving Wheels : 5′ 1¼″. T.E. : 20,840 lb.

69424	69427	69429

Total 3

0-6-2T   2MT   Class N1

* Introduced 1907. Ivatt G.N. design,
prototype of class.
†‡§¶ Introduced 1907. Standard design
with shorter tanks and detail differ-
ences.
§¶Rebuilt with superheater and reduced
pressure.
‡¶Fitted with condensing gear.
Weights : { 64 tons 14 cwt.*
{ 65 tons 17 cwt.
Pressure : { 175 lb.
{ 170 lb. Su.§¶
Cyls. : 18″ × 16″.
Driving Wheels : 5′ 8″.
T.E. : { 18,430 lb.
{ 17,900 lb.§¶

69430*	69444†	69458‡	69471‡
69431‡	69445‡	69459†	69472§
69432‡	69447†	69460‡	69474†
69433‡	69449†	69461‡	69475‡
69434‡	69450†	69462‡	69476‡
69435¶	69451‡	69463‡	69477‡
69436§	69452§	69464¶	69478¶
69437‡	69453‡	69465‡	69481¶
69439¶	69454†	69466‡	69482¶
69440†	69455‡	69467‡	69483§
69441‡	69456‡	69469‡	69484‡
69443†	69457‡	69470‡	69485‡

Total 48

For full details of
ELECTRIC AND DIESEL LOCOS
on the E., N.E. & Scottish Regions
see the
ABC OF B.R. LOCOMOTIVES
Part II, Nos. 10000-39999

For full details of
CLASS "4MT" AND "2MT" 2-6-0s
Nos. 43000-43161 & 46400-46527
on the E., N.E. & Scottish Regions
see the
ABC OF B.R. LOCOMOTIVES
Part III, Nos. 40000-59999

0-6-2T 3P2F Class N2

N2/2* Introduced 1925. Post-grouping development of Gresley G.N. N2/1, introduced 1920, which class is now included in N2/2. Condensing gear and small chimney.

N2/2† Condensing gear removed.

N2/3‡ Introduced 1925. Locos built non-condensing, originally fitted with large chimney. Some now with small chimney.

N2/4§ Introduced 1928. Development of N2/2, slightly heavier. Condensing gear and small chimney.
(The small chimneys are to suit the Metropolitan loading gauge, for working to Moorgate St. Condensing gear has been removed from or added to certain locos transferred from or to the London area).

Weights : $\begin{cases} 70 \text{ tons } 5 \text{ cwt.} \text{*†} \\ 70 \text{ tons } 8 \text{ cwt.} \text{‡} \\ 71 \text{ tons } 9 \text{ cwt.} \text{§} \end{cases}$

Pressure : 170 lb. Su. Cyls. : 19″ × 26″.
Driving Wheels : 5′ 8″. T.E. : 19,945 lb.
P.V.

69490*	69515†	69540*	69565‡
69491*	69516†	69541*	69566‡
69492*	69517†	69542*	69567‡
69493*	69518†	69543*	69568§
69494*	69519†	69544*	69569§
69495*	69520*	69545*	69570§
69496*	69521*	69546*	69571§
69497*	69522*	69547*	69572§
69498*	69523*	69548*	69573§
69499*	69524*	69549*	69574§
69500*	69525*	69550†	69575§
69501†	69526*	69551†	69576§
69502†	69527*	69552†	69577§
69503†	69528*	69553†	69578§
69504*	69529*	69554†	69579§
69505†	69530*	69555†	69580§
69506*	69531*	69556§	69581§
69507†	69532*	69557†	69582§
69508†	69533*	69558†	69583§
69509†	69534*	69559†	69584§
69510†	69535*	69560†	69585§
69511†	69536*	69561†	69586§
69512*	69537*	69562‡	69587§
69513*	69538*	69563‡	69588§
69514†	69539*	69564‡	69589§

69590§	69592§	69594‡	69596‡
69591§	69593§	69595‡	

Totals : Class N2/2 **70**
Class N2/3 **9**
Class N2/4 **28**

0-6-2T 3MT Class N7

N7/1¹ Introduced 1925. Post-grouping development of Hill G.E. design with detail differences.

N7/2² Introduced 1926. Development of N7/1 with long-travel valves.

N7/3³ Introduced 1927. Doncaster-built version of N7/2 with round-topped boiler.

N7/4⁴ Introduced 1940. Pre-grouping N7 (G.E.) rebuilt with round-topped boiler, retaining short-travel valves.

N7/5⁵ Introduced 1943. N7/1 rebuilt with round-topped boiler, retaining short-travel valves.

N7/3⁶ Introduced 1943. N7/2 rebuilt with round-topped boiler.

Weights : $\begin{cases} 63 \text{ tons } 13 \text{ cwt.}^1 \\ 64 \text{ tons } 17 \text{ cwt.}^2 \\ 64 \text{ tons.}^3 \\ 61 \text{ tons } 16 \text{ cwt.}^4 \\ 64 \text{ tons.}^5 \\ 64 \text{ tons.}^6 \end{cases}$

Pressure : 180 lb. Su. Cyls. : 18″ × 24″.
Driving Wheels : 4′ 10″. T.E. : 20,515 lb.
Walschaerts gear, P.V.

69600⁴	69618⁴	69636⁵	69654⁵
69601⁴	69619⁴	69637¹	69655¹
69602⁴	69620⁴	69638⁵	69656⁵
69603³	69621⁴	69639⁵	69657⁵
69604⁴	69622⁵	69640⁵	69658⁵
69605⁴	69623⁵	69641⁵	69659⁵
69606⁴	69624¹	69642⁵	69660⁵
69607⁴	69625⁵	69643⁵	69661⁵
69608⁴	69626⁵	69644⁵	69662⁵
69609⁴	69627¹	69645¹	69663⁵
69610⁴	69628⁵	69646¹	69664⁵
69611⁴	69629¹	69647⁵	69665⁵
69612⁴	69630⁵	69648⁵	69666⁵
69613⁴	69631¹	69649⁵	69667⁵
69614⁴	69632⁵	69650⁵	69668⁵
69615⁴	69633⁵	69651⁵	69669⁵
69616⁴	69634⁵	69652⁵	69670⁵
69617⁴	69635⁵	69653⁵	69671⁵

69672[6]	69688[6]	69704[3]	69720[3]
69673[6]	69689[2]	69705[3]	69721[3]
69674[6]	69690[2]	69706[3]	69722[3]
69675[6]	69691[6]	69707[3]	69723[3]
69676[6]	69692[6]	69708[3]	69724[3]
69677[6]	69693[6]	69709[3]	69725[3]
69678[6]	69694[2]	69710[3]	69726[3]
69679[6]	69695[2]	69711[3]	69727[3]
69680[6]	69696[6]	69712[3]	69728[3]
69681[6]	69697[6]	69713[3]	69729[3]
69682[6]	69698[6]	69714[3]	69730[3]
69683[2]	69699[6]	69715[3]	69731[3]
69684[6]	69700[6]	69716[3]	69732[3]
69685[6]	69701[6]	69717[3]	69733[3]
69686[6]	69702[3]	69718[3]	
69687[6]	69703[3]	69719[3]	

Totals : Class N7/1 8
Class N7/2 5
Class N7/3 57
Class N7/4 22
Class N7/5 42

4-6-2T 3F Class A7

Introduced 1910. Raven N.E. design, later rebuilt with superheater and reduced pressure.
* Saturated.
Weight : 87 tons 10 cwt.
Pressure : { 160 lb. Su. / 180 lb.*
Cyls. : (3) 16½″ × 26″.
Driving Wheels : 4′ 7¼″.
T.E. : { 26,140 lb. / 29,405 lb.*
P.V.

69770	69776	69782	69787*
69771	69778*	69783	69788
69772	69779	69784	
69773	69780	69785	
69774	69781	69786	

Total 17

IMPORTANT NOTE

A careful reading of the notes on page 2 is essential to understand the use of reference marks in this book.

4-6-2T 3MT Class A5

A5/1 Introduced 1911. Robinson G.C. design.
A5/2* Introduced 1925. Post-grouping development of A5/1 with reduced boiler mountings and detail differences.
Weights : { 85 tons 18 cwt. / 90 tons 11 cwt.*
Pressure : 180 lb. Su. Cyls. : 20″ × 26″.
Driving Wheels : 5′ 7″. T.E. : 23,750 lb. P.V.

69800	69811	69822	69833*
69801	69812	69823	69834*
69802	69813	69824	69835*
69803	69814	69825	69836*
69804	69815	69826	69837*
69805	69816	69827	69838*
69806	69817	69828	69839*
69807	69818	69829	69840*
69808	69819	69830*	69841*
69809	69820	69831*	69842*
69810	69821	69832*	

Totals : Class A5/1 30
Class A5/2 13

4-6-2T 3MT Class A8

Introduced 1931. Gresley rebuild of Raven Class "D" 4-4-4T (introduced 1913).
Weight : 86 tons 18 cwt.
Pressure : 175 lb. Su.
Cyls. : (3) 16½″ × 26″.
Driving Wheels : 5′ 9″. T.E. : 22,940 lb. P.V.

69850	69862	69874	69886
69851	69863	69875	69887
69852	69864	69876	69888
69853	69865	69877	69889
69854	69866	69878	69890
69855	69867	69879	69891
69856	69868	69880	69892
69857	69869	69881	69893
69858	69870	69882	69894
69859	69871	69883	
69860	69872	69884	
69861	69873	69885	

Total 45

0-8-4T 6F Class S1

S1/1* Introduced 1907. Robinson G.C. design, since rebuilt with superheater.

S1/2† Introduced 1932. S1/1 rebuilt with booster and superheater, booster since removed.

S1/3‡ Introduced 1932. New locos built with booster, booster later removed.

Weights : { 99 tons 6 cwt.*
99 tons 2 cwt.†
99 tons 1 cwt.‡

Pressure : 180 lb. Su.
Cyls. : (3) 18″ × 26″.
Driving Wheels : 4′ 8″. T.E. : 34,525 lb.

| 69900* | 69902* | 69904‡ | 69905‡ |
| 69901† | | | |

Totals : Class S1/1 2
Class S1/2 1
Class S1/3 2

4-8-0T 5F Class T1

Introduced 1909. W. Worsdell N.E. design.
* Rebuilt with superheater.
Weight : 85 tons 8 cwt.
Pressure : 175 lb. SS.
Cyls. : (3) 18″ × 26″.
Driving Wheels : 4′ 7¼″. T.E. : 34,080 lb. P.V.

| 69910 | 69912 | 69914* | 69916 |
| 69911 | 69913 | 69915 | 69917 |

| 69918 | 69920 | 69921 | 69922 |
| 69919 | | | Total 13 |

0-8-0T 5F Class Q1

Thompson rebuild of Robinson G.C. Q4 0-8-0, introduced 1902.

Q1/1* Introduced 1942. 1,500 gallon tanks.

Q1/2 Introduced 1943. 2,000 gallon tanks.

Weights : { 69 tons 18 cwt.*
73 tons 13 cwt.

Pressure : 180 lb. Cyls. : (O) 19″ × 26″.
Driving Wheels : 4′ 8″. T.E. : 25,645 lb.

69925*	69929	69932	69935
69926*	69930	69933	69936
69927*	69931	69934	69937
69928*			

Total 13

2-8-8-2T Unclass Class U1 (Beyer-Garratt loco)

Introduced 1925. Gresley/Beyer Peacock design.
Weight : 178 tons 1 cwt.
Pressure : 180 lb. Su.
Cyls. : (6) 18½″ × 26″.
Driving Wheels : 4′ 8″. T.E. : 72,940 lb.
Walschaerts gear, derived motion. P.V.

69999 Total 1

BRITISH RAILWAYS STANDARD LOCOMOTIVES

Chief Officer (Mechanical Engineering) :

R. C. BOND

4-6-2 Class 7MT

Introduced 1951. Designed at Derby.
Weights : Loco. 94 tons 0 cwt.
Tender 47 tons 4 cwt.
Pressure : 250 lb. Su.
Cyls. : (O) 20″ × 28″.
Driving Wheels : 6′ 2″. T.E. : 32,150 lb.
Walschaerts gear. P.V.

70000	Britannia
70001	Lord Hurcomb
70002	Geoffrey Chaucer
70003	John Bunyan
70004	William Shakespeare
70005	John Milton
70006	Robert Burns
70007	Coeur-de-Lion
70008	Black Prince
70009	Alfred the Great
70010	Owen Glendower
70011	Hotspur
70012	John of Gaunt
70013	Oliver Cromwell
70014	Iron Duke
70015	Apollo
70016	Ariel
70017	Arrow
70018	Flying Dutchman

70019	Lightning
70020	Mercury
70021	Morning Star
70022	Tornado
70023	Venus
70024	Vulcan
70025	Western Star
70026	Polar Star
70027	Rising Star
70028	Royal Star
70029	Shooting Star
70030	William Wordsworth
70031	Byron
70032	Tennyson
70033	Charles Dickens
70034	Thomas Hardy
70035	Rudyard Kipling
70036	Boadicea
70037	Hereward the Wake
70038	Robin Hood
70039	Sir Christopher Wren
70040	Clive of India
70041	Sir John Moore
70042	Lord Roberts
70043	Earl Kitchener
70044	Earl Haig
70045	
70046	
70047	
70048	
70049	
70050	
70051	
70052	
70053	
70054	

Engines of this class are still being delivered. The names of Nos. 70043/4 are temporarily not affixed.

4-6-2   Class 8P

Introduced 1954. Designed at Crewe.
Weights : Loco. 00 tons 00 cwt.
           Tender 00 tons 00 cwt.
Pressure : 000 lb.
Cyls. : (3)00″ × 00″.
Driving Wheels : 0′ 0″. T.E.: 00,000 lb.
Caprotti valve gear.

71000   Duke of Gloucester

4-6-2   Class 6MT

Introduced 1952. Designed at Derby.
Weights : Loco. 86 tons 19 cwt.
           Tender 47 tons 4 cwt.
Pressure : 225 lb. Su.
Cyls. : (O) 19½″ × 28″.
Driving Wheels : 6′ 2″. T.E. : 27,520 lb.
Walschaerts gear. P.V.

72000	Clan Buchanan
72001	Clan Cameron
72002	Clan Campbell
72003	Clan Fraser
72004	Clan Macdonald
72005	Clan Macgregor
72006	Clan Mackenzie
72007	Clan Mackintosh
72008	Clan Macleod
72009	Clan Stewart

Total 10

4-6-0   Class 5MT

Introduced 1951. Designed at Doncaster.
Weights : Loco. 76 tons 4 cwt.
           Tender 47 tons 4 cwt.
Pressure : 225 lb. Su.
Cyls. : (O) 19″ × 28″.
Driving Wheels : 6′ 2″. T.E. : 26,120 lb.
Walschaerts gear. P.V.

73000	73019	73038	73057
73001	73020	73039	73058
73002	73021	73040	73059
73003	73022	73041	73060
73004	73023	73042	73061
73005	73024	73043	73062
73006	73025	73044	73063
73007	73026	73045	73064
73008	73027	73046	73065
73009	73028	73047	73066
73010	73029	73048	73067
73011	73030	73049	73068
73012	73031	73050	73069
73013	73032	73051	73070
73014	73033	73052	73071
73015	73034	73053	73072
73016	73035	73054	73073
73017	73036	73055	73074
73018	73037	73056	

Engines of this class are still being delivered.

4-6-0   Class 4MT

Introduced 1951. Designed at Brighton.
Weights : Loco.   69 tons 0 cwt.
          Tender 43 tons 3 cwt.
Pressure : 225 lb. Su.
Cyls. : (O) 18″ × 28″.
Driving Wheels : 5′ 8″. T.E. : 25,100 lb.
Walschaerts gear. P.V.

75000	75020	75040	75060
75001	75021	75041	75061
75002	75022	75042	75062
75003	75023	75043	75063
75004	75024	75044	75064
75005	75025	75045	75065
75006	75026	75046	75066
75007	75027	75047	75067
75008	75028	75048	75068
75009	75029	75049	75069
75010	75030	75050	75070
75011	75031	75051	75071
75012	75032	75052	75072
75013	75033	75053	75073
75014	75034	75054	75074
75015	75035	75055	75075
75016	75036	75056	75076
75017	75037	75057	75077
75018	75038	75058	75078
75019	75039	75059	75079

Engines of this class are still being delivered.

2-6-0   Class 4MT

Introduced 1953. Designed at Doncaster.
Weights : Loco.   59 tons 2 cwt.
          Tender 42 tons 3 cwt.
Pressure : 225 lb. Su.
Cyls. : (O) 17½″ × 26″.
Driving Wheels : 5′ 3″. T.E. : 24,170 lb.
Walschaerts gear. P.V.

76000	76007	76014	76021
76001	76008	76015	76022
76002	76009	76016	76023
76003	76010	76017	76024
76004	76011	76018	76025
76005	76012	76019	76026
76006	76013	76020	76027
76028	76033	76038	76043
76029	76034	76039	76044
76030	76035	76040	
76031	76036	76041	
76032	76037	76042	

Engines of this class are still being delivered.

2-6-0   Class 3MT

Introduced 1954.
Weights : Loco.   57 tons 10 cwt.
          Tender 42 tons 3 cwt.
Pressure : 200 lb. Su.
Cyls. : (O) 17½″ × 26″
Driving Wheels : 5′ 3″. T.E. : 21,490 lb.
Walschaerts gear. P.V.

77000	77005	77010	77015
77001	77006	77011	77016
77002	77007	77012	77017
77003	77008	77013	77018
77004	77009	77014	77019

Engines of this class are still being delivered.

2-6-0   Class 2MT

Introduced 1953. Designed at Derby.
Weights : Loco.   49 tons 5 cwt.
          Tender 36 tons 17 cwt.
Pressure : 200 lb. Su.
Cyls. : (O) 16½″ × 24″.
Driving Wheels : 5′ 0″. T.E. : 15,515 lb.
Walschaerts gear. P.V.

78000	78012	78024	78036
78001	78013	78025	78037
78002	78014	78026	78038
78003	78015	78027	78039
78004	78016	78028	78040
78005	78017	78029	78041
78006	78018	78030	78042
78007	78019	78031	78043
78008	78020	78032	78044
78009	78021	78033	
78010	78022	78034	
78011	78023	78035	

Engines of this class are still being delivered.

2-6-4T Class 4MT

Introduced 1951. Designed at Brighton.
Weight : 88 tons 10 cwt.
Pressure : 225 lb. Su.
Cyls. : (O) 18″ × 28″.
Driving Wheels :5′ 8″. T.E. : 25,100 lb.
Walschaerts gear. P.V.

80000	80029	80058	80087
80001	80030	80059	80088
80002	80031	80060	80089
80003	80032	80061	80090
80004	80033	80062	80091
80005	80034	80063	80092
80006	80035	80064	80093
80007	80036	80065	80094
80008	80037	80066	80095
80009	80038	80067	80096
80010	80039	80068	80097
80011	80040	80069	80098
80012	80041	80070	80099
80013	80042	80071	80100
80014	80043	80072	80101
80015	80044	80073	80102
80016	80045	80074	80103
80017	80046	80075	80104
80018	80047	80076	80105
80019	80048	80077	80106
80020	80049	80078	80107
80021	80050	80079	80108
80022	80051	80080	80109
80023	80052	80081	80110
80024	80053	80082	80111
80025	80054	80083	80112
80026	80055	80084	80113
80027	80056	80085	80114
80028	80057	80086	80115

Engines of this class are still being
delivered.

2-6-2T Class 3MT

Introduced 1952. Designed at Swindon.
Weight : 73 tons 10 cwt.
Pressure : 200 lb. Su.
Cyls. : (O) 17½″ × 26″.
Driving Wheels : 5′ 3″. T.E. : 21,490 lb.
Walschaerts gear. P.V.

82000	82002	82004	82006
82001	82003	82005	82007

82008	82018	82028	82038
82009	82019	82029	82039
82010	82020	82030	82040
82011	82021	82031	82041
82012	82022	82032	82042
82013	82023	82033	82043
82014	82024	82034	82044
82015	82025	82035	
82016	82026	82036	
82017	82027	82037	

Engines of this class are still being
delivered.

2-6-2T Class 2MT

Introduced 1953. Designed at Derby.
Weight : 63 tons 5 cwt.
Pressure : 200 lb. Su.
Cyls. : (O) 16½″ × 24″.
Driving Wheels : 5′ 0″. T.E. : 18,515 lb.
Walschaerts gear. P.V.

84000	84008	84016	84024
84001	84009	84017	84025
84002	84010	84018	84026
84003	84011	84019	84027
84004	84012	84020	84028
84005	84013	84021	84029
84006	84014	84022	
84007	84015	84023	

Engines of this class are still being
delivered.

2-8-0 8F Class WD

Ministry of Supply " Austerity " 2-8-0
locomotives purchased by British
Railways, 1948.
Introduced 1943. Riddles M.o.S. design.
Weights : Loco. 70 tons 5 cwt.
    Tender 55 tons 10 cwt.
Pressure : 225 lb. Cyls. : (O) 19″ × 28″.
Driving Wheels : 4′ 8½″. T.E. : 34,215 lb.
Walschaerts gear. P.V.

90000	90010	90020	90030
90001	90011	90021	90031
90002	90012	90022	90032
90003	90013	90023	90033
90004	90014	90024	90034
90005	90015	90025	90035
90006	90016	90026	90036
90007	90017	90027	90037
90008	90018	90028	90038
90009	90019	90029	90039

90040	90088	90136	90184	90232	90280	90328	90376
90041	90089	90137	90185	90233	90281	90329	90377
90042	90090	90138	90186	90234	90282	90330	90378
90043	90091	90139	90187	90235	90283	90331	90379
90044	90092	90140	90188	90236	90284	90332	90380
90045	90093	90141	90189	90237	90285	90333	90381
90046	90094	90142	90190	90238	90286	90334	90382
90047	90095	90143	90191	90239	90287	90335	90383
90048	90096	90144	90192	90240	90288	90336	90384
90049	90097	90145	90193	90241	90289	90337	90385
90050	90098	90146	90194	90242	90290	90338	90386
90051	90099	90147	90195	90243	90291	90339	90387
90052	90100	90148	90196	90244	90292	90340	90388
90053	90101	90149	90197	90245	90293	90341	90389
90054	90102	90150	90198	90246	90294	90342	90390
90055	90103	90151	90199	90247	90295	90343	90391
90056	90104	90152	90200	90248	90296	90344	90392
90057	90105	90153	90201	90249	90297	90345	90393
90058	90106	90154	90202	90250	90298	90346	90394
90059	90107	90155	90203	90251	90299	90347	90395
90060	90108	90156	90204	90252	90300	90348	90396
90061	90109	90157	90205	90253	90301	90349	90397
90062	90110	90158	90206	90254	90302	90350	90398
90063	90111	90159	90207	90255	90303	90351	90399
90064	90112	90160	90208	90256	90304	90352	90400
90065	90113	90161	90209	90257	90305	90353	90401
90066	90114	90162	90210	90258	90306	90354	90402
90067	90115	90163	90211	90259	90307	90355	90403
90068	90116	90164	90212	90260	90308	90356	90404
90069	90117	90165	90213	90261	90309	90357	90405
90070	90118	90166	90214	90262	90310	90358	90406
90071	90119	90167	90215	90263	90311	90359	90407
90072	90120	90168	90216	90264	90312	90360	90408
90073	90121	90169	90217	90265	90313	90361	90409
90074	90122	90170	90218	90266	90314	90362	90410
90075	90123	90171	90219	90267	90315	90363	90411
90076	90124	90172	90220	90268	90316	90364	90412
90077	90125	90173	90221	90269	90317	90365	90413
90078	90126	90174	90222	90270	90318	90366	90414
90079	90127	90175	90223	90271	90319	90367	90415
90080	90128	90176	90224	90272	90320	90368	90416
90081	90129	90177	90225	90273	90321	90369	90417
90082	90130	90178	90226	90274	90322	90370	90418
90083	90131	90179	90227	90275	90323	90371	90419
90084	90132	90180	90228	90276	90324	90372	90420
90085	90133	90181	90229	90277	90325	90373	90421
90086	90134	90182	90230	90278	90326	90374	90422
90087	90135	90183	90231	90279	90327	90375	90423

Class J71 0-6-0T No. 68279   [R. E. Vincent

Class J77 0-6-0T No. 68432   [A. B. Crompton

Class J83 0-6-0T No. 68474   [B. Yale

Above : Class J63 0-6-0T
No. 68207
[*H. C. Casserley*

Left : Class Y4 0-4-0T
No. 68127
[*H. C. Casserley*

Below : Class J88 0-6-0T
No. 68347 [*J. Robertson*

Above: Class J69/1 0-6-0T
No. 68623   [*P. J. Lynch*

Right : Class J68 0-6-0T
No. 68654
       [*R. H. G. Simpson*

Below: Class J67/1 0-6-0T
No. 68492 (running with
tender for working the
Lauder branch)
       [*C. L. Kerr*

Class N5 0-6-2T No. 69234   *[R. J. Buckley*

Class N1 0-6-2T No. 69430   *[H. C. Casserley*

Class N1 0-6-2T No. 69468 (with condensing gear ; since scrapped)   *[H. C. Casserley*

Class N2/2 0-6-2T No. 69490   [J. F. Aylard

Class N7/3 0-6-2T No. 69720   [J. Robertson

Class N7/5 0-6-2T No. 69663   [G. Wheeler

Class S1/1 0-8-4T No. 69902

[H. C. Casserley

Class L3 2-6-4T No. 69064

[H. C. Casserley

Class A5/1 4-6-2T No. 69811

[E. D. Bruton

70

Class A8 4-6-2T No. 69855   [J. Robertson

Class A8 4-6-2T No. 69832 (with D20-type boiler)   [P. Ransome-Wallis

Class T1 4-8-0T No. 69910   [A. B. Crompton

Class 7MT 4-6-2 No. 70009 *Alfred the Great*   [P. Ransome-Wallis

Class 6MT 4-6-2 No. 72009 *Clan Stewart*   [J. Robertson

Class 9F 2-10-0 No. 92002   [L. Elsey

90424	90472	90520	90568
90425	90473	90521	90569
90426	90474	90522	90570
90427	90475	90523	90571
90428	90476	90524	90572
90429	90477	90525	90573
90430	90478	90526	90574
90431	90479	90527	90575
90432	90480	90528	90576
90433	90481	90529	90577
90434	90482	90530	90578
90435	90483	90531	90579
90436	90484	90532	90580
90437	90485	90533	90581
90438	90486	90534	90582
90439	90487	90535	90583
90440	90488	90536	90584
90441	90489	90537	90585
90442	90490	90538	90586
90443	90491	90539	90587
90444	90492	90540	90588
90445	90493	90541	90589
90446	90494	90542	90590
90447	90495	90543	90591
90448	90496	90544	90592
90449	90497	90545	90593
90450	90498	90546	90594
90451	90499	90547	90595
90452	90500	90548	90596
90453	90501	90549	90597
90454	90502	90550	90598
90455	90503	90551	90599
90456	90504	90552	90600
90457	90505	90553	90601
90458	90506	90554	90602
90459	90507	90555	90603
90460	90508	90556	90604
90461	90509	90557	90605
90462	90510	90558	90606
90463	90511	90559	90607
90464	90512	90560	90608
90465	90513	90561	90609
90466	90514	90562	90610
90467	90515	90563	90611
90468	90516	90564	90612
90469	90517	90565	90613
90470	90518	90566	90614
90471	90519	90567	90615

90616	90646	90676	90706
90617	90647	90677	90707
90618	90648	90678	90708
90619	90649	90679	90709
90620	90650	90680	90710
90621	90651	90681	90711
90622	90652	90682	90712
90623	90653	90683	90713
90624	90654	90684	90714
90625	90655	90685	90715
90626	90656	90686	90716
90627	90657	90687	90717
90628	90658	90688	90718
90629	90659	90689	90719
90630	90660	90690	90720
90631	90661	90691	90721
90632	90662	90692	90722
90633	90663	90693	90723
90634	90664	90694	90724
90635	90665	90695	90725
90636	90666	90696	90726
90637	90667	90697	90727
90638	90668	90698	90728
90639	90669	90699	90729
90640	90670	90700	90730
90641	90671	90701	90731
90642	90672	90702	90732
90643	90673	90703	Vulcan
90644	90674	90704	
90645	90675	90705	

Total 733

2-10-0   8F   Class WD

Ministry of Supply " Austerity " 2-10-0
locomotives purchased by British
Railways, 1948.
Introduced 1943. Riddles M.o.S. design.
Weights : Loco.   78 tons 6 cwt.
                Tender 55 tons 10 cwt.
Pressure : 225 lb. Cyls.: (O) 19″ × 28″.
Driving Wheels : 4′ 8½″. T.E.: 34,215 lb.
Walschaerts gear. P.V.

90750	90757	90764	90770
90751	90758	90765	90771
90752	90759	90766	90772
90753	90760	90767	90773
90754	90761	90768	90774
90755	90762	90769	
90756	90763		**Total 25**

2-10-0   Class 9F

Introduced 1954. Designed at Crewe.
Weights : Loco.   86 tons 14 cwt.
           Tender 52 tons 10 cwt.
Pressure: 250 lb. Cyls.: (O) 20″ × 28″.
Driving Wheels : 5′ 0″. T.E.: 39,670 lb.
Walschaerts gear. P.V.

92000	92003	92006	92009
92001	92004	92007	92010
92002	92005	92008	92011

92012	92019	92026	92033
92013	92020	92027	92034
92014	92021	92028	92035
92015	92022	92029	92036
92016	92023	92030	92037
92017	92024	92031	92038
92018	92025	92032	92039

Engines of this class are still being delivered.

PULLMAN CARS ALLOCATED TO THE E. & N.E. REGIONS

K—Kitchen Car.   **B—Brake Car.**

ADRIAN (K)	CAR No. 66 (K)
AGATHA	,, ,, 67 (K)
BELINDA (K)	,, ,, 68 (K)
CYNTHIA (K)	,, ,, 69 (K)
EUNICE	,, ,, 70 (K)
EVADNE (K)	,, ,, 71 (K)
IOLANTHE (K)	,, ,, 72 (K)
IONE (K)	,, ,, 73
JOAN (K)	,, ,, 74
JUANA	,, ,, 75
LORAINE (K)	,, ,, 76
LUCILLE	,, ,, 77 (B)
LYDIA (K)	,, ,, 78 (B)
NILAR (K)	,, ,, 79 (B)
PHYLLIS (K)	,, ,, 80 (B)
SHEILA	,, ,, 81 (K)
THELMA (K)	,, ,, 82 (K)
URSULA	,, ,, 83
CAR No. 32 (K)	,, ,, 84
,, ,, 33 (K)	,, ,, 105 (B)
,, ,, 58 (K)	,, ,, 106 (K)
,, ,, 59 (HADRIAN BAR)	,, ,, 107 (K)
,, ,, 62 (B)	,, ,, 161 (B)
,, ,, 63 (B)	,, ,, 162 (B)
,, ,, 64	,, ,, 209 (B)
,, ,, 65 (B)	,, ,, 248 (B)

ELECTRIC UNIT NUMBERS

LIVERPOOL ST.—SHENFIELD 3-CAR ELECTRIC TRAIN UNITS

01	11	21	31	41	51	61	71	81	91
02	12	22	32	42	52	62	72	82	92
03	13	23	33	43	53	63	73	83	
04	14	24	34	44	54	64	74	84	
05	15	25	35	45	55	65	75	85	
06	16	26	36	46	56	66	76	86	
07	17	27	37	47	57	67	77	87	
08	18	28	38	48	58	68	78	88	
09	19	29	39	49	59	69	79	89	
10	20	30	40	50	60	70	80	90	

GRIMSBY—IMMINGHAM ELECTRIC TRAMS

1	7	13	17	21	25	29	32
4	8	14	18	22	26	30	33
5	11	15	19	23	27	31	34
6	12	16	20	24	28		

SOUTH TYNESIDE ELECTRIC MOTOR COACHES

E.29175E	E.29178E	E.29181E	E.29184E	E.29187E	E.29191E
E.29176E	E.29179E	E.29182E	E.29185E	E.29189E	E.29192E
E.29177E	E.29180E	E.29183E	E.29186E	E.29190E	

Motor Parcels Van E.29493E

NORTH TYNESIDE ELECTRIC TWIN-UNIT MOTOR COACHES

E.29101E	E.29113E	E.29124E	E.29135E	E.29147E	E.29158E
E.29102E	E.29114E	E.29125E	E.29136E	E.29148E	E.29159E
E.29103E	E.29115E	E.29126E	E.29137E	E.29149E	E.29160E
E.29104E	E.29116E	E.29127E	E.29138E	E.29150E	E.29161E
E.29105E	E.29117E	E.29128E	E.29139E	E.29151E	E.29162E
E.29106E	E.29118E	E.29129E	E.29140E	E.29152E	E.29163E
E.29107E	E.29119E	E.29130E	E.29141E	E.29153E	E.29164E
E.29108E	E.29120E	E.29131E	E.29142E	E.29154E	
E.29109E	E.29121E	E.29132E	E.29144E	E.29155E	
E.29110E	E.29122E	E.29133E	E.29145E	E.29156E	
E.29111E	E.29123E	E.29134E	E.29146E	E.29157E	

Motor Parcels Vans		Motor Coaches	
E.29467E	E.29468E	E.29165E	E.29166E

MANCHESTER — SHEFFIELD ELECTRIC MOTOR COACHES

E29401	E29403	E29405	E29407
E29402	E29404	E29406	E29408

ROUTE AVAILABILITY OF LOCOMOTIVES

Restrictions on the working of locomotives over the routes of the former L.N.E.R. are denoted by Route Availability numbers. In general a locomotive is not permitted to work over a line of lower R.A. number than itself. The scheme is as follows :

R.A.1 : J15, J63, J65, J71, Y1, Y3, Y8, Y10, Z4, DM1, Standard 2MT 2-6-2T.

R.A.2 : E4, J67/1, J70, J72, J77, Y9, Z5.

R.A.3 : B12/1, F4, F5, J3, J10, J21, J25, J36, J66, J67/2, J68, J69, J88, N9, N10, Standard 2MT 2-6-0.

R.A.4 : B12/3, D40, F6, G5, J1, J5, J17, J26, J55, J83, N4, N5/2, N8, N13, N14, V4, Standard 4MT 4-6-0, Standard 4MT 2-6-0, Standard 3MT 2-6-2T.

R.A.5 : A5, A8, B1, B2, B17, C12, C13, C14, D16, J2, J6, J11, J19, J20, J27, J52, J73, J94, K2, N1, N7, Standard 4MT 2-6-4T.

R.A.6 : C15, C16, D10, D11, D20, D30, D34, J35, J39, J50, K1, K4, N2, N15, O1, O2, O4, O7, Q6, V1, Y4.

R.A.7 : A7, B16/1, L1, L3, Q7, U1, V3, Standard 6MT 4-6-2, Standard 5MT 4-6-0, Standard 4MT 4-6-0.*

R.A.8 : B16/2, B16/3, D49, J37, J38, K3, K5, Q1, S1, T1, Standard 7MT 4-6-2, Standard 6MT 4-6-2.*

R.A.9 : A1, A2, A3, A4, V2, W1.

* With 5,000 gal. tender.

CLASSIFICATION OF L.N.E.R. LOCOMOTIVES

The L.N.E.R. locomotive classification scheme was based on that used on the former G.N.R. Each wheel arrangement was allotted a letter, and the classes of that arrangement were numbered in groups according to the pre-grouping ownership, in the order G.N., G.C., G.E., N.E., N.B., G.N.S. L.N.E.R. classes were at first usually added at the end of the list, but later standard locomotives have been given the lowest number. Many classes are sub-divided into " parts," denoted thus : " D16/3." This division is not entirely consistent, as some classes with comparatively wide variation, such as " A4," are not sub-divided, but others, such as " O4," have some divisions dependent only on details such as brakes and whether or not the tender has a water scoop. In these lists, sub-divisions are denoted by " parts " where these exist, but elsewhere it is to be assumed that any variations between the locomotives in the class are not covered by the classification (e.g. " A4 ").

Come on, fellows!!
It's time to join the NEW

Ian Allan Locospotters Club

I AN ALLAN LOCOSPOTTERS CLUB

IT'S THE SAME CLUB that more than 100,000 boys have joined during the last ten years—*but with a difference*! Flourishing branches in nearly all main centres are launching out on a scheme to help every ambitious Locospotter to store his mind with useful railway knowledge and fill his diary with memorable railway activities. The lucky chap who is in on this is called a Progressive Locospotter, and the day he earns the right to wear his " Top Link " badge is a proud one indeed.

This is an invitation—your chance to join up and join in. Before you fill up the application form (*on page 79*), however, you should read the Club Rule carefully, remembering that you must *promise* to obey the simple commonsense conditions of it from the moment you are accepted as a member. Then sign your promise, fill in the other details required and send the form with appropriate postal order and STAMPED ADDRESSED ENVELOPE (2½d. stamp affixed) to :

IAN ALLAN LOCOSPOTTERS CLUB (LSE),
Craven House, Hampton Court, East Molesey, Surrey.

THE CLUB RULE

Members of the Locospotters Club will not in any way interfere with railway working or material, nor be a nuisance or hindrance to railway staff, nor above all, trespass on railway property. No one will be admitted a member of the Club unless he solemnly agrees to keep this rule.

First published 1954
Reprinted 2008

ISBN (10) 0 7110 3330 7
ISBN (19) 978 0 7110 3330 6

© Ian Allan Publishing Ltd 1954 / 2008

Published by Ian Allan Publishing

an imprint of Ian Allan Publishing Ltd, Hersham, Surrey, KT12 4RG.

Printed by Ian Allan Printing Ltd, Hersham, Surrey, KT12 4RG.

Code: 0810/B2

This is a facsimilie reprint of an original edition first published in 1954,
and as such, all advertisements are no longer valid.

Visit the Ian Allan Publishing Website at
www.ianallanpublishing.com
Cover images reproduced courtesy of Colour-Rail